ANATOMY OF A PUBLIC POLICY

ANATOMY OF A PUBLIC POLICY

The Reform of Contemporary American Immigration Law

Michael C. LeMay

PRAEGER
Westport, Connecticut
London

Library of Congress Cataloging-in-Publication Data

LeMay, Michael C.
Anatomy of a public policy : the reform of contemporary American immigration law / Michael C. LeMay.
p. cm.
Includes bibliographical references and index.
ISBN 0-275-94902-8 (alk. paper)
1. United States—Emigration and immigration—Government policy.
2. Emigration and immigration law—United States. I. Title.
JV6493.L45 1994
325.73—dc20 94-6376

British Library Cataloguing in Publication Data is available.

Library of Congress Catalog Card Number: 94-6376
ISBN: 0-275-94902-8

First published in 1994

Praeger Publishers, 88 Post Road West, Westport, CT 06881
An imprint of Greenwood Publishing Group, Inc.

Printed in the United States of America

The paper used in this book complies with the Permanent Paper Standard issued by the National Information Standards Organization (Z39.48—1984).

10 9 8 7 6 5 4 3 2 1

This book is fondly dedicated to my brothers and sisters
Donald, Thomas, Joan, William, Joseph,
Marie, David, and Bernadette

Contents

Figures and Tables

FIGURES

TABLES

Acknowledgments

This book is based on several dozen oral interviews (see Appendix A), some 850 mailed questionnaires, as well as a thorough examination of the relevant documentary record (i.e., examination of various government reports, the *Congressional Record,* official studies by the GAO, DOL, and the like). The author was also given access to studies conducted by several other immigration scholar colleagues whose work also involved several hundred interviews and surveys. A special debt of acknowledgment is owed to Prof. Rosanna Perotti at Case Western Reserve University, and to the group of scholars involved in the Rand Corporation and Urban Institute research programs who analyzed the impact of the Immigration Reform and Control Act of 1986. Any book such as this one must also acknowledge the contributions of the many scholars who have preceded—as the rather extensive references at the end of this book demonstrate. Several people, moreover, deserve particular note for their special contributions.

Appendix A lists the many individuals who assisted the author in the numerous oral interviews conducted for Chapters 3, 4, and 5. The firsthand insights gleaned from those in the front-lines of IRCA's enactment, implementation, and evaluation were invaluable.

Several of my colleagues gave much of their time as well as many useful constructive criticisms by reading and commenting on all or parts of the draft of this manuscript. I acknowledge a special debt of gratitude to Anthony Affigne, John Bibby, William Diaz, Lawrence Fuchs, Virginia Gray, Marquerite Rivera Houza, Ira Kurzban, Gersham Nelson, Rosanna Perotti, Stephen Simpson, Lydio Tomasi, and George Vernez.

The process of preparing and mailing out over 850 questionnaires is a time-consuming and arduous task. I could not have managed it without the assistance of the following student workers: Tina Baker, Jennifer Barnhart, Lisa Bishop, Rebecca Byers, Kevin Campbell, Blair Harrison, Jennifer Lewis, Jeffrey McCauley, and Lynette Niland. Special thanks is owed to my primary student assistant, Corey Jones, who helped with a number of tasks during the preparation of this book, and to Mrs. Yvonne Gillespie, Departmental Secretary, who supervised the student helpers while preparing the questionnaire mailings.

Finally, I gratefully acknowledge the administration at Frostburg State University, which supported this research with a sabbatical leave and encouraged me throughout the process of writing this book: its then President Herb F. Rinehart; Dr. Daniel Pantaleo, then Vice President for Academic Affairs; Dr. Kenneth Stewart, then Dean of the School of Natural and Social Sciences; and Dr. Stephen Simpson, then my department chair.

At California State University, San Bernardino, I wish to thank the following for their assistance with several of the graphic figures: the contributions of Mr. Carey B. Van Loon, of the Audio-Visual Department; Mr. Christopher Farr, Graduate Assistant in the National Security Studies Program; and finally, for numerous clerical tasks, my secretary, Ms. Melody Powell.

Introduction

THE POLICY PROCESS

In recent years, the study of public policy has become an important focus within political science, emerging as a distinct subfield of the discipline. The focus on public policy helps to integrate virtually all the topics of general concern to the understanding of politics. This book analyzes a particular American policy area—immigration policy—to serve as a case study of the policy process. It may serve as a supplemental textbook for courses in public policy analysis and courses dealing with the legislative process and the politics of the U.S. Congress. It should also be of particular interest to general readers with a concern for immigration policy, as well as to the many government agencies (at the federal, state, and local levels), interest groups, community service agencies, and immigration lawyers who are directly involved in the implementation of immigration law.

This book employs a definition of public policy and an approach to the study of policy popularized by Professor James Anderson in his book, *Public Policy-Making,* wherein he defines public policy as "a purposive course of action followed by an actor or set of actors in dealing with a problem or matter of concern."[1]

His conceptual framework for the policy process goes on to distinguish six stages of activity: (1) problem formation, (2) agenda setting, (3) policy formulation, (4) adoption, (5) policy implementation, and (6) policy evaluation.[2]

In the first analytical stage of the policy process, a problem—seen as "a human need, deprivation, or dissatisfaction, self-identified or identified by others, for which relief is sought"—becomes a *public problem.*[3] This happens when a sufficiently large number of people become involved. Public problems are those having broad ranging impact, even including consequences for people not directly involved. A problem becomes public when enough people see it as one that government ought to handle. This leads directly to the second stage, the policy agenda.

The *policy agenda* concerns how problems get recognized by government. Literally thousands of needs and wants are felt by the public, and people respond by seeking government action. But only a small number of such problems are given serious attention by government policymakers. These few comprise "the public policy agenda."[4] The second analytical stage of the policy process, then, focuses our attention on why some problems achieve agenda status. The interaction of interest groups having sufficient power, status, or numbers may compel government to put a problem on its agenda. So too, political leadership is another important factor in agenda setting. Events, such as wars and depressions, may be viewed as "crises." Such events automatically attain agenda status.

The third stage, *policy formulation,* involves the development of pertinent and acceptable proposals for a course of government action to cope with the perceived problem. How the problem is viewed is critically important to the formulation of responses to that problem. Major sources for the formulation of policy proposals include the elected executive and the administrative branch, special commission, committees and advisory groups, legislators, and various interest groups.

The fourth stage, *policy adoption,* is seen as the building of a coalition to get formal government action approving some proposed course of action. Adoption strategies and the resulting policy formulation will differ depending on which and how many branches of government are involved in the adoption process.

Policy implementation, the fifth stage, is a critical one in the policy process. Once adoption has taken place, the action taken can be called a public policy. But the implementation, or administrative stage, is very important because without application the policy has no effect. During the application of policy, the implementation sometimes changes the very nature of the policy itself. Administrative agencies—public bureaucracies—are the primary implementors of public policy. But such implementation may also be shaped by the legislature, by elected executives, and by the courts. Implementation often affects policy content.[5]

Policy evaluation is the sixth stage of the process.[6] During this stage those who have made, implemented, or are being affected by the policy, or some combination of these, attempt to determine whether a policy has worked. Evaluation concerns appraising the content of policy and its effects—both intended and unanticipated. Evaluation often leads to additional policy formation, thus starting the policy cycle over again. Systematic evaluation of policy seeks to measure its impact and the extent to which the intended objectives of the policy are met. Such policy evaluation stresses the effects a policy has on the problem to which it is directed.

Each of these stages of the policy process will be dealt with in this analysis of U.S. immigration policy as exemplified by the Immigration Reform and Control Act of 1986 (IRCA) and the Immigration Act of 1990. Each of the following chapters is devoted to a stage of policy process. The study examines the process of how IRCA and the 1990 act came to be passed, when and how they were enacted, difficulties that developed in the manner in which Congress and the Immigration and Naturalization Service (INS) chose to implement IRCA, and an initial attempt at evaluating the impact of IRCA, assessing the degree to which it has been successful in achieving its stated goals. It highlights some unanticipated, as well as intended, consequences of the passage of these immigration reform laws.

This book also employs a model for analyzing public policy—the group theory model. This model begins with the proposition that the interaction among interest groups is the central fact of politics. Persons sharing common interests come together either formally or informally to demand action of some sort (positive or negative action) by government. Professor David Truman, one of the most important articulators of this view of politics, defines an interest group as "a shared attitude group that makes certain claims upon other groups in the society [and becomes a political group] if and when it makes a claim through or upon any of the institutions of government."[7]

In this view, individuals are important in politics only when they act as part of, or on behalf of, an organized interest group. The group serves as an essential link between the individual and government. Politics can thus be seen as the struggle among groups to influence government policy-making. In this framework, the essential task of the political system is to manage group conflict by (1) setting the rules of the game within which group conflict is played out, (2) arranging compromises and balancing interests, (3) enacting such compromises into some form of public policy, and (4) enforcing these compromises through law. This framework views public policy at any given time as the state of equilibrium reached in the group struggle. This state of equilibrium is established by the relative influence among the involved (usually competing) interest groups. Changes in the relative influence of any relevant interest group will tend to result in changes in public policy. Thus, policy changes move in the direction desired by groups gaining in power and away from those desired by groups whose influence is declining.[8]

Immigration policy is of particular interest to study the impact of interest groups because they clearly are so involved in process. As noted by one prominent immigration policy scholar:

> The interests of aliens are routinely represented by citizen groups, lobbies, and elected officials who empathize with or share the ethnicity of newly arrived groups. The U.S. Congressional Black Caucus, for example, has championed the cause of Haitian immigrants, just as Mexican-American elected officials and voters have championed the cause of Mexican immigrants. (Mark Miller, in Brubaker, 1989, 143)

THE IMPORTANCE OF IMMIGRATION POLICY ANALYSIS

One might well ask, why focus on immigration policy-making to illustrate or better understand the policy process? As argued elsewhere, there are several reasons why the study of immigration policy—and a case study of IRCA in particular—is especially pertinent for a grasp of the policy process.[9]

Immigration policy is a topic of substantive and timely interest. The United States is unique among the nations of the world in the degree to which it has absorbed immigrants. Since the country first began keeping count in 1820, more than 50 million people have migrated to the United States. As of the 1990 census, it is home to residents born in over 160 other nations. During the decade of the 1980s, an amazing two-thirds of all the world's immigration consisted of people entering the United States. The magnitude and the problems associated with such a vast influx have periodically, almost cyclically, made immigration policy a matter of great national concern and debate. The 1970s and 1980s were decades when immigration was of vexing concern in both the national media and in the halls of the U.S. Congress. It continues to be a topic of national interest today.

As another scholar of immigration notes so well:

> Every state must face the difficulty of regulating the entry of individuals into its natural territory. Likewise, the state must establish the conditions of residence for aliens, and the methods by which non-citizens can become citizens. Decisions such as these, concerning the control of a population within a given territory, are *not* simply technical, economic, or demographic choices; they are profoundly *political* choices that often must be made in moments of crisis, involving highly charged national debates. They literally can affect the lives of millions of people; and they can reveal in pristine form the innermost workings of the political system and the key philosophical assumptions upon which the system is based. What better way to study the relationship between the state, the individual, and society than to look at the way in which the state deals with foreigners, who are among the most vulnerable members of any (democratic) society, lacking many of the basic rights that are guaranteed to citizens.[10]

Another reason to focus on immigration policy is that it is an inherently interesting subject. How we cope with being a "nation of immigrants" is a subject rich in human interest. The great numbers and the variety of groups who have intermingled here—if not "melted" into one—compels our interest. How immigration policy affects, and in turn reflects, the composition of the influx of migration ought to be of significance to any student of public policy. As one scholar put it: "Although the [immigration reform] debate can be framed in the cool language of economics and demographics, immigration remains a highly emotional subject, with immigration policy a window into the national psyche" (Greenhouse, as cited in Tomasi, 1987, ix).

Moreover, immigration policy-making is an area of policy that affords a rich vein within which to mine insights into the policy process. Few policy areas, for instance, show such dramatic impact on society than does immigration policy. Shifts in policy open or close the door to entry in ways that immediately impact the lives of tens of thousands, even millions, of people thereby allowing them or their loved ones into this country or being excluded from such. And as we shall see more fully in the course of this book, the Immigration Reform and Control Act particularly affects all American citizens in a manner unique to American immigration policy in that it makes all employers agents of the INS and makes all people applying for a job—citizens and resident aliens alike—subject to its employer-sanctions provisions.

Changes in immigration law usually have specific effects on the economy and are often viewed as integral aspects of a nation-state's economic policy.

The study of immigration policy affords an excellent opportunity to gain insight into the complexity of regulatory policy. Anderson describes regulatory policy as one that involves the imposition of restrictions or limits on the behavior of individuals and groups.[11] Yet not all regulatory policy is as clear-cut as is immigration policy in the impact it often has upon the social, economic, and political environment. Seldom can the student of the policy process see a more extensive result from a change in policy than in the case of the gate-keeping policy of immigration. It is a particularly useful policy area in which to examine the impact of interest groups advocating or opposing changes in policy. As the gate-keeping function has profound implications for which groups are allowed in or denied entrance, it has significant social, economic, cultural, religious, and foreign-policy implications for the nation. Immigration policy clearly and dramatically reflects the pressures of interest groups either pushing for restrictions or the easing of such as the needs of those groups change over time or in response to a prior influx.

Another scholar of immigration policy recently noted well that:

> One of the most important lessons the Immigration Reform and Control Act can teach public policy observers is that the factions in public policy disputes often have complementary as well as conflicting interests. How and why factions discover and pursue these complementary interests in an effort to produce joint gains—that is, to what extent integrative bargaining occurs—explains how a great deal of public policy is made.[12]

The long and tortured history of IRCA's debate and eventual enactment sheds interesting light on the character and role of party leadership in Congress when that body is considering a significant piece of legislation that cuts across party lines. As will be seen, immigration policy clearly cuts across many lines or relevant Congressional voting blocs.

The posture taken by the leadership on immigration bills was complex, though not unusual for party leadership, and says much about the role of party leadership in the House.[13]

Finally, a study of IRCA offers considerable insight into the implementation of public policy. Attention to poiicy design is an effective method of linking the policy process with its eventual effects, and for specifying more rigorous explanations for policy outcomes.[14] To the extent that policy is a "blueprint" for purposive action,"[15] then the clear policy design of IRCA sheds light on the extent to which a disjuncture exists between a policy and its effects. The study of IRCA shows some key assumptions that underlie its approach regarding the nature of the illegal alien problem, its targets and their likely responses, costs and who should bear them, and the nature of the implementation context and how it might be shaped. The chapter on implementation offers preliminary evidence linking the assumptions of policymakers to local implementation of IRCA.

AN OVERVIEW OF THE BOOK

Chapter 1 concerns the stages of *problem formation and agenda setting*. These two distinct analytical stages are linked in this opening chapter because in the real world of practical politics they are integral and so intertwined that they are best discussed together. The chapter begins by detailing changes in the immigration law enacted in 1965 and shows how they affected the flow of migration to the United States. The 1970s witnessed a marked shift in the nature of the influx—both in its size and its composition. This, in turn, brought about a growing perception that the nation was being inundated with a renewed flood of immigrants, both legal and illegal, who were increasingly viewed as being less able or desirable to assimilate into the population. A growing sense of the problem emerged that we were facing a "crisis" in immigration, that we were indeed losing control of our borders.

Chapter 2 examines the stage of *policy formulation*. During the 1970s, a new approach to immigration policy was gradually shaped and proposed. Employer sanctions was put forth as a solution to the illegal alien problem—a method to "demagnetize" the pull of the U.S. economy drawing illegal aliens northward. Developments led to a second major aspect to that change, a counter-balancing proposal to legalize those undocumented aliens already here. Eventually these proposals emerged as variations and versions of what became known as the Simpson–Mazzoli bill.

Chapter 3 describes the *adoption stage*. It looks at how and why IRCA came to be passed in 1986 in the version of the law that was eventually accepted. It details the critical compromises that enabled the bill's enactment.

Chapter 4 concerns the stage of *policy implementation*. Examining the key provisions of IRCA, it looks at the difficulties encountered by the INS in implementing the law. The chapter discusses the complex intergovernmental aspects of the law and its somewhat innovative use of nongovernment agencies, called QDEs (Qualified Designated Entities), to assist in the legalization program.

Chapter 5 offers a first and admittedly tentative *evaluation* of IRCA. Using a "policy design" approach, it examines each of the law's major provisions and attempts to assess the degree to which they were successfully implemented. It notes improvements in the problem with which the law was designed to cope. It notes, as well, gaps and failures in the implementation process, showing where Congressional intent seems to have been frustrated. It highlights some apparent unanticipated consequences of IRCA as well.

Finally, Chapter 6 concludes with a brief discussion of where immigration policy is headed in the 1990s. It discusses passage of the Immigration Act of 1990, which changed "legal" immigration policy. It looks at some aspects of the perceived immigration policy that IRCA and the 1990 act either failed to address or unsuccessfully dealt with, thus requiring further action. It suggests where current immigration may lead in the future.

NOTES

1. James Anderson, *Public Policy-Making,* 2nd ed. (New York: Holt Rinehart and Winston, 1979), 3.

2. Ibid., and Anderson et al., *Public Policy and Politics in America,* 2nd ed. (Monterey, Calif.: Brooks/Cole, 1984), 5–10.

3. Anderson et al., 1984, *Public Policy and Politics,* 7.

4. Ibid.

5. Ibid., 8–9.

6. Ibid., 9–10.

7. David Truman, *The Governmental Process* (New York: Knopf, 1951), 15–17.

8. Thomas Dye, *Understanding Public Policy,* 6th ed. (Englewood Cliffs, N.J.: Prentice-Hall, 1987), 26–27.

9. Preface to Michael LeMay, *From Open Door to Dutch Door: An Analysis of U.S. Immigration Policy Since 1820* (New York: Praeger, 1987), xi–xii; and idem, *The Gatekeepers: Comparative Immigration Policy* (New York: Praeger, 1989), xi–xii.

10. James F. Hollifield, "Migrants into Citizens: The Politics of Immigration in France and the United States." Paper delivered at the 1989 Annual Meeting of the American Political Science Association, August 31–September 3, 1989, Atlanta, Ga.

11. Anderson, 1979, *Public Policy-Making,* 126–128.

12. Rosanna Perotti, "Beyond Logrolling: Integrative Bargaining in Congressional Policymaking." Paper delivered at the 1989 Annual Meeting of the American Political Science Association, August 31–September 3, 1989, Atlanta, Ga., p. 2.

13. Ronald Peters and Arturo Vega, "The Role of House Democratic Party Leaders on Non-Party Position Legislation with Partisan Consequences: The Immigration Bill." Paper delivered at the 1986 Meetings of the American Political Science Association, Washington, D.C., August 28–31, 1986.

14. Lorraine McDonnell and Paul Hill, "First Steps in Applying a Policy Design Framework: The Case of Immigration Reform." Paper delivered at the 1989 Annual Meeting of the American Political Science Association, September 2, 1989, Atlanta, Ga. See also A. Schneider and H. Ingram, "Behavioral Theories in Policy Designs." Paper delivered at the Annual Meeting of the Midwest Political Science Association, Chicago, Ill., April 1988.

15. P. W. Ingraham, "Towards a More Systematic Consideration of Policy Design," *Policy Studies Journal* 15(4; 1987): 610–628.

CHAPTER 1

Problem Formation and Agenda Setting: The Illegal Alien Influx and the Crisis of Border Control

CHANGES IN IMMIGRATION LAW, 1965

Immigration law has helped determine what sort of a nation we are and will determine what we become. In many ways, immigration shapes what happens to and in America. What sorts of jobs will open and to whom they will be open are impacted by immigration. States have reacted to the recent influx of Asian and Hispanic migrants by passing "English-only" laws, fearing the factionalization in society that could develop here as it has in Canada, or even the extremes of ethnic rivalry such as that racking Bosnia and other parts of the former Soviet bloc. Will the star players of some future Superbowl be Haitians, Mexicans, or some other ethnic group now flooding into the United States? The nature of our society—its culture, economics, and politics—is profoundly affected by the immigration process.

In recent years, various forces operating within the United States political system came to feel that the nation was losing control of its borders. It no longer seemed possible to say who could or who could not enter the United States to live and work. Such concern gave rise to a groundswell of public support for efforts to reform the nation's immigration laws. It led to a political movement designed to drastically alter the immigration policy of the United States culminating in several laws passed in the 1980s.

To fully understand the passage of the immigration reform laws of the 1980s, one must grasp the nature of the perceived problems with which these laws were intended to cope. And to fully grasp the nature of the immigration problem, one needs to go back to the last really significant revision of United States immigration law—the Immigration and Nationality Act of 1965. This law was more commonly known as the Kennedy immigration law. Prior to its passage, immigration flow into the United States was controlled by the highly restrictive policy of the national origins quota system passed during the 1920s and amended by the McCarran-Walter Act of 1952. Many of the migration patterns—especially those associated with the "illegal alien" influx—were established in the 1940s, particularly patterns set with the Bracero program. Established during World War II to bring in needed but temporary agricultural labor, the Bracero program annually allowed migrant labor from Mexico to enter the United States outside the confines of the quota system. The chain migration patterns forged during the Bracero program persist to this day.[1]

Although the McCarran-Walter Act was restrictionist in its reaffirmation of the quota system, in order to secure its passage two provisions were included that did involve opening new doors. The Act established very token quotas for those nations—previously excluded—that were defined as the "Asian-Pacific Triangle." It opened up, for the first time since the late 1880s and the 1920s, the possibility of some Asian influx (LeMay 1987, 104). Perhaps even more significant to our focus here, the McCarran-Walter Act passed only after the "Texas Proviso" was included. This provision exempted employers of illegal aliens from the harboring provisions of the law. It thereby legalized the hiring of illegal aliens. Under this proviso, which was essential to secure support for the bill from Southwestern growers, "No employer could be found to have violated federal law for hiring illegal aliens" (Glazer 1985, 52-53).

The election of President Kennedy in 1960 eased the way for a frontal assault on the quota system approach to immigration policy. The racially biased and highly restrictive immigration policy of the quota system had clearly become inadequate to cope with the immigration process of the 1960s. President Kennedy's election placed in the White House a chief executive who strongly desired a major revision in the approach to that policy (LeMay 1987, 109).

During Kennedy's first two years in office, however, foreign policy issues so dominated the agenda that little was done about his desire to amend immigration policy. Then the dramatic rise in agitation over civil rights, beginning in 1962, turned the focus of the Kennedy administration and of the nation inward. The Civil Rights movement marked a changing national attitude toward racism that undercut the highly restrictionist quota policy. The sort of bigotry prevailing in the 1950s that contributed to the lopsided majorities in favor of the quota system became increasingly less acceptable by the mid-1960s.

Ironically, black migration from the South to the Northeast and the Midwest was linked to reduced European immigration. It was only after the flow of Europeans to northern cities was so drastically reduced by the quota acts of the 1920s that a large number of job opportunities for blacks were opened. Blacks first began moving north in great numbers during World War I, and that flow increased following the restrictionist immigration laws of 1921, 1924, and 1929 that effectively curtailed European immigration to a trickle. Black migration north slowed during the Great Depression but picked up again during World War II when, along with women, blacks not in the military began meeting much of the labor demand from industry and the service sectors in the nation's northern urban centers. The very groups urging enactment of laws to restrict immigration during the 1920s so often and so blatantly on racial and ethnic grounds thus accelerated, albeit unintentionally, the migration of blacks to their states. Soon these new migrants were resented even more than the South/Central/Eastern Europeans who had preceded them.[2]

By the mid-1960s, however, the remaining labor supply in rural areas in the South dwindled or migrated to fill growing job opportunities in the expanding industrial centers in the South, such as Atlanta. This reduced pressures on blacks to migrate northward, and black migration from the South virtually ended during the 1960s. Indeed, during the early 1970s more blacks moved into the South than left the region, reversing a nearly century-long trend (Muller and Espanshade 1985, 12).

Furthermore, the success of the Kennedy administration's economic policy resulted in the end of the recessions that so plagued much of the Eisenhower period (roughly six of his eight years in office) and worked to reduce opposition to immigration reform. The healthy economy of the early through mid-1960s meant that even organized labor could espouse a more liberal immigration policy.

By the mid-1960s the traditional supporters of the national-origins quota system were disorganized and largely inactive. Sen. Edward Kennedy (D., Mass.) led the Senate forces advocating a change in the law. He met with leaders from the American Coalition, the American Legion, the Daughters of the American Revolution, and the National Association of Evangelicals. None of these groups raised significant opposition to eliminating the quota system (Chiswick 1982, 33).

In July 1963, President Kennedy sent his immigration reform proposal to Congress. Sen. Philip Hart (D., Mich.) and Rep. Emmanuel Celler (D., N.Y.) introduced companion bills. President Kennedy's assassination, coupled with some Congressional opposition, delayed passage of the bill.

But the President's assassination, viewed almost immediately as a "martyrdom," plus President Johnson's landslide victory in 1964, signaled an end to the quota system and its replacement by a preference system. President Johnson, as a former Senate Majority Leader, was one of the best "nose counters" in the business, and his landslide election victory swept into office a large number of liberal Democrats. Suddenly he had more noses to count than ever before. By 1964–1965, a significant number in Congress were climbing on the immigration-reform bandwagon. Literally dozens of bills were introduced to abolish the national-origins quota system (LeMay 1987, 111).

President Johnson's proposal (essentially the prior Kennedy bill) was submitted in the House by Representative Celler, then chairman of the House Judiciary Committee. It was introduced into the Senate on January 15 by Senator Hart, and co-sponsored by thirty-two others, including both Senators Edward and Robert Kennedy (D., N.Y.). This bill attempted to balance five major goals: (1) to preserve the family unit and reunite separated families; (2) to meet the labor need for some highly skilled aliens; (3) to help ease population problems created by emergencies, such as political upheavals, communist aggression, and natural disasters; (4) to better the understanding of people cross-nationally through exchange programs; and (5) to bar aliens from the United States who would likely represent problems of adjustment due to their physical or mental health, criminal history, dependency, or for national security reasons. Its major provisions are listed here:

1. It abolished the national origins quota system after a transition period to June of 1968.
2. It abolished the Asian Pacific Triangle provision.
3. It allowed the use of quota numbers unused in the previous year as a pool of additional numbers for each year of the transitional period, for preference applicants chargeable to over-subscribed quotas.
4. It revised previous preference categories into a new system of preferences strongly favoring (74 percent) relatives of citizens and permanent resident aliens.
5. It required that an alien coming to work in the United States and not entitled to a preference obtain certification from the Secretary of Labor that he or she would not displace nor adversely affect the wages and working conditions of workers in the same field in the United States.
6. It included refugees as one of the preference categories.
7. It set an annual ceiling of 170,000 on immigration of aliens in the preference and nonpreference classifications with a 20,000 limit for any single foreign state.
8. It established an "immediate relative" (previously called "nonquota") status for parents of adult U.S. citizens.
9. It increased the dependent area immigration (previously "subquota") to 1 percent of the 20,000 maximum allowable numbers available to the governing country, that is, from 100 to 200 annually.
10. It set the filing date of the petition to determine the chronological order of preference applicants.
11. It required that applicants be considered in the order of their preference class.
12. It created a Select Commission on Western Hemisphere Immigration to study the economic, political, and demographic factors affecting immigration.

13. It set a ceiling of 120,000 on immigration from the Western Hemisphere nations after July 1968.
14. It included all independent countries of the Western Hemisphere in "special immigrant" status (previously called "nonquota" system). (LeMay 1987, 112)

This bill changed the basic approach of immigration policy from the national-origins quota system to one of a preference system. The preference categories were:

1. **First preference:** unmarried sons and daughters of U.S. citizens;
2. **Second preference:** spouses and unmarried sons and daughters of permanent resident aliens;
3. **Third preference:** members of the professions and scientists and artists of exceptional ability;
4. **Fourth preference:** married sons and daughters of U.S. citizens;
5. **Fifth preference:** brothers and sisters of U.S. citizens;
6. **Sixth preference:** skilled and unskilled workers in short supply; and
7. **Seventh preference:** refugees. (ibid.)

A key compromise was extracted by Senators Everett Dirksen (R., Ill.) and Samuel Ervin (D., N.C.) that placed an overall ceiling of 120,000 for the Western Hemisphere. This was a compromise figure that replaced the prior unlimited immigration from the Western Hemisphere. It was based on the actual flow of immigration during the few years immediately preceding the act. That compromise enabled the measure to pass easily. The Senate approved it by a vote of 76 to 18; the House by a vote of 320 to 69. President Johnson signed the bill into law, in front of the Statue of Liberty, on October 3, 1965 (Immigration and Nationality Act of 1965, Pub. L. 89-236, 79 Stat. 911. See also Chiswick 1988, 37).

The 1965 law resulted in dramatic changes in the immigration flow—in both its size and its composition. During the decade following its passage, total immigration increased by 60 percent. Immigration from some countries registered really remarkable changes: Greek immigration rose by 162 percent; Portuguese by 382 percent; total Asian immigration rose by over 3,800 percent, with Korea by 1,328 percent, Pakistan by 1,600 percent, the Philippines by nearly 1,200 percent, Thailand by over 1,700 percent, and Vietnam by over 1,900 percent.

In stark contrast, European immigration declined by 38 percent overall. The countries that registered the largest negative changes were Austria, with a decline of over 76 percent, Ireland by over 77 percent, Norway by over 85 percent, and the United Kingdom by nearly 120 percent (LeMay 1987, 114).

The preference category for professionals was especially used by Asians.

Korean and Philippine health professionals entered in large numbers, later bringing in their families under Preference 2. By the end of the 1970s, over 70,000 medical doctors alone had immigrated. By that time, there were more Filipino physicians in the United States than native-born black doctors.[3]

The 1965 law was almost immediately outmoded, however, in provisions set aside for refugees. The law set what, at the time, seemed to be very generous amounts for an annual preference limit of refugees at 10,200 (6 percent of the total legal immigration from the Eastern Hemisphere ceiling of 170,000). Events in such places as Cuba, Vietnam, Cambodia, Laos, and Haiti soon outstripped the ability of that limit to cope with the demand for entrance into the United States based upon that seventh category.

THE DYNAMIC FLOW OF IMMIGRATION: THE CHANGING NATURE OF THE INFLUX DURING THE 1970s

Indeed, a combination of world economic developments, major political upheavals, and the unanticipated consequences of the 1965 immigration law all interacted with significant results to the flow of immigration into the United States during the 1970s (Muller and Espanshade 1985, 12).

The end of black migration from the South resulted in an increased demand for a new source of low-wage labor in the nation's urban centers. By the late 1960s, however, this demand was no longer concentrated in northern industrial cities. Indeed, the industrial Northeast and even the Midwest began, by the mid-1970s, an extended period of relative economic stagnation. Demand for labor was strongest in the South and West, the "Sun Belt states," led by Texas and California.

As two prominent immigration scholars have noted:

> The rural and nonmetropolitan sources of low-skilled, low-wage labor to complement an increasingly educated and skilled metropolitan population had to be replaced if a wage spiral was to be avoided. Changing social and economic conditions affected divorce rates, attitudes towards work, educational progress, and the growth of white-collar employment opportunities in low- and moderate-wage scales and clerical occupations. As a result, the share of all working women over the age of fifteen rose dramatically, from 39 percent in 1965 to 52 percent in the early 1980s; well over 10 million women came into the labor force in a sixteen-year period. (ibid., 13)

This substantial movement of women into the U.S. labor force, however, did not meet the demand for semi-skilled blue-collar and low-paying service jobs, especially those in the Southwest. During the 1960s, then, a number of factors influencing immigration converged: an increase in potential job opportunities in the United States, growing over-population in sender nations, increased political and economic instability in Mexico and Central America, lower travel costs, and timely revision in U.S. immigration law. These led to a swelling of the influx to the United States. The 3.3 million immigrants who entered during that decade resulted in the highest levels of immigration since the 1920s. The revised immigration law, moreover, "targeted" to a greater degree than previously such immigration to particular occupations where shortages existed: for example, to engineering and the professions. These workers had skills for which the domestic supply was considered insufficient. Sending nations began to complain of a "brain drain." This renewed flow in immigration has been called the "Fourth Wave" (ibid.).

Fourth-wave immigration began in the late 1960s and continues today. It is comprised of three primary groups: legal immigrants admitted as permanent residents, refugees, and the undocumented—more commonly referred to as illegal aliens. The timing of the new influx coincided with two major public policy events: (1) discontinuation of the Bracero program, and (2) the enactment of the 1965 immigration law.

Under the quota system, for roughly fifty years, immigrants entering the United States were overwhelmingly European. Today they come from Third World nations—largely Asian and Latin American. Of the 544,000 *legal* immigrants who entered the United States in 1984, to cite but one year as an example, more than 10 percent (57,000) were from Mexico, followed by the Philippines (42,000), and Vietnam (37,000). British immigration, by contrast, numbered only 14,000 and ranked ninth (LeMay, ed. 1989, 5).

The dramatic decline in European immigration and the especially sharp increase in that from the Western Hemisphere and Asia is graphically shown in Figure 1.1. It presents the origins of *legal* immigration to the United States by region of origin for the decades 1950 to 1980. Mexico, Cuba, China, Taiwan, Korea, and the Philippines emerge during this period as the principal sources of immigration to the United States.

The number of refugees seeking entrance to the United States also greatly expanded the influx and by the early 1970s clearly exceeded the amount set aside for them by the law's seventh preference category (6 percent). From 1960 to 1980, some 800,000 refugees came from Cuba alone. As the 1965 law defined refugees as those fleeing communism or from the Mideast, it did not even consider those fleeing right-wing dictatorships in the Western Hemisphere. But large numbers fled here from such countries as El Salvador and Haiti. Then, too, the collapse of the South Vietnamese government in 1975 created another large pool of refugees fleeing communism. From 1975 to 1979, over 200,000 Vietnamese came to the United States. Continued turmoil in Cambodia and Laos added still more.

When the boat people began to arrive in 1979, the Carter administration committed itself to allow in another 168,000 in 1980. In the spring of that year, yet another dramatic influx of Cubans arrived by boat. In all, from 1975 to 1980, some 500,000 refugees arrived from Southeast Asia alone. They were joined by an influx of Soviet Jews fleeing the Soviet Union which suddenly opened its emigration doors and contributed another 70,000 to the flow from 1969 to 1980. Such foreign policy pressures of the Cold War compelled the Congress to change the law further.

At first President Carter, through his Attorney General, responded to

Figure 1.1
Origins of U.S. Immigrants by Region, 1950–1980

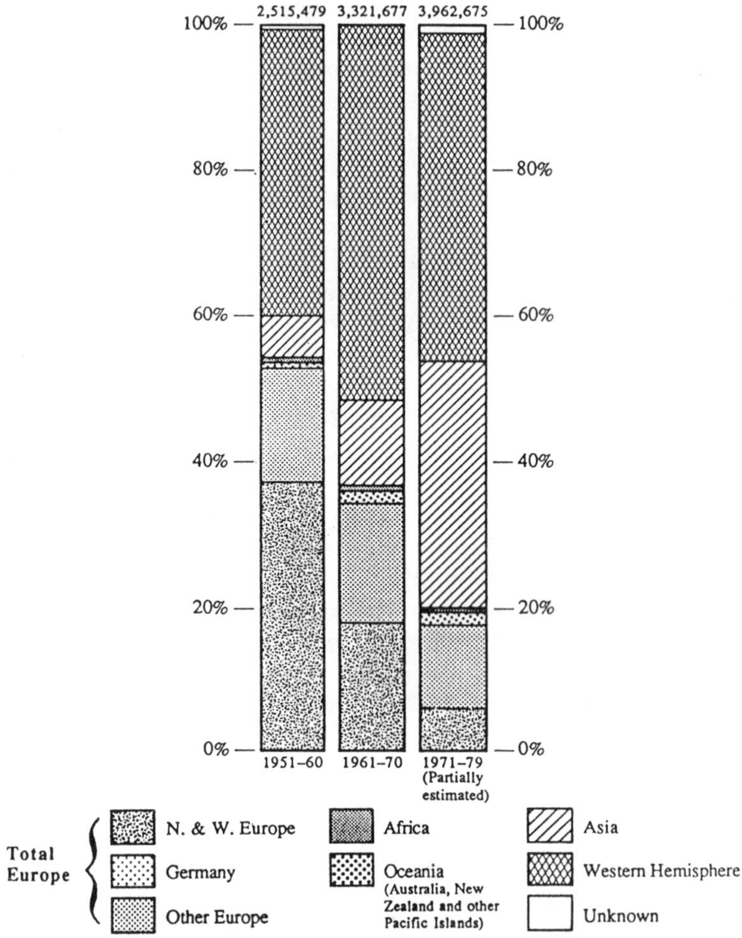

Source: Updated from LeMay 1987, 105. Adapted from data supplied by the Statistical Branch, U.S. Immigration and Naturalization Service, as cited in Leon F. Bouvier, "Immigration and Its Impact on U.S. Society," *Population Trends and Public Policy,* No. 2 (Washington, D.C.: Population Reference Bureau, Inc., 1981), 2.

these refugee pressures by using executive parole power to permit Cubans, Vietnamese, and others to enter in numbers far exceeding the refugee category limits. Congress joined in that effort by allocating funds to support the parolees and passed laws to adjust their status, such as the Indochinese Refugee Resettlement Program in 1975 (LeMay 1987, 115).

By the end of the decade, Congress, the President, and the various refugee relief agencies all realized that the limit on the refugee preference category was simply too low and too rigidly defined. Cuba and Vietnam alone had made permanent exiles of over 2.5 million people. Congress reacted by passing the Refugee Act of 1980. It amended the 1965 Act by redefining "refugee" as someone from anywhere in the world, not just communist countries or Middle Eastern nations. It expanded total immigration from 290,000 to 320,000. It strengthened the refugee procedures and gave the President greater power to deal with emergency events. It brought the U.S. legal definition closer to the prevailing one of international law. Since World War II, that has been set by the 1951 United Nations Convention Relating to the Status of Refugees and its 1967 Protocol, which extend the convention's provisions to current refugees. The U.N. Protocol defines a refugee as:

> Any person who, owing to a well-founded fear of being persecuted for reasons of race, religion, nationality, membership in a particular social group or political opinion, is outside of the country of his nationality and unable or, owing to such fear, is unwilling to avail himself of the protection of that country, or who, not having a nationality and being outside the country of his former habitual residence, is unable, or owing to such fear, is unwilling to return to it. (Ferris 1985, 2–3)

The 1980 law created the Office of the United States Coordinator to monitor, coordinate, and implement overall refugee policy, which is administered in one respect or another by the Immigration and Naturalization Service (INS), the Department of Justice, the Bureau of Refugee Programs at the Department of State, and the Office of Refugee Resettlement, Department of Health and Human Services (ibid., 109). The 1980 Refugee Act's change in definition of refugee increased at one time the number of people potentially eligible to enter from 3 million to nearly 15 million.[4] Although the question of refugee status is a complex one involving political, social, economic, and legal ramifications, the trends in political turmoil among Third World nations have led to what has been called "the global refugee crisis" (Kritz 1983, 157). The *1981 World Refugee Survey* put the number of refugees in the world at 12.5 million. Refugee movements in the 1980s have added to that number and are now estimated at 15 million, and such international movements of people are now higher than in any other period of recorded human history (Ferris 1985, 105).

During the 1980s the industrialized nations of the world became almost inured to the Third World refugee waves. But 1989 witnessed a movement of refugees not seen since the end World War II—hundreds of thousands of Europeans migrating from East to West: 100,000 Soviets, 250,000 East Germans, 300,000 Bulgarian Turks, 230,000 Poles, and 20,000 Romanians. This sudden outpouring of East Europeans heading West in part explains why the reduction of East/West tensions has not significantly relieved the world's refugee problem. And this movement may also shift the world's image of the refugee from the emaciated Ethiopian child seeking relief from famine in a dusty desert camp to today's refugee as one seeking better economic opportunity or political liberty rather than fleeing war or natural disaster. Even the nature of the "boat people" from Indochina is changing increasingly to fishermen and farmers who are less likely to be escaping political persecution and more likely to be searching for a better economic life. Many are now coming from northern Vietnam. As a result, the Asian nations receiving these new flows are challenging the "first-asylum" agreement. Yet despite the changes of the past few years in the refugee flows, most of the world's refugees are still fleeing their native lands for the simple reason of attempting to stay alive—like the 4 million refugees in Africa and the 5 million Afghans encamped in Pakistan and Iran.

The United States, like other industrialized nations, continues to grant asylum to refugees with whom it has historic ties. For example, from 1975 to 1980, the United States took in 677,000 refugees. These were mostly Soviet Jews (two-thirds of all Soviet emigrees head for the United States), the Indochinese, people from South and Central America, and the Caribbean region. That total exceeded by three times that of any other receiving country and was almost as many as all other major receiving nations combined (ibid., 106–107).

As one noted immigration scholar describes it: "Massive postwar migrations have posed a fundamental challenge to the nation-states of Europe and North America. They have compelled these countries to reinterpret their traditions, to reshape their institutions, to rethink the meaning of citizenship—to reinvent themselves, in short, as nation-states" (Brubaker 1989, 1). These data can be seen in Table 1.1.

During the 1970s, this enormous increase in the number of potential immigrants and refugees resulted in increased pressure on immigration policy. The world's growing economic and political interdependence, coupled with advances in transportation and communication, made the United States more accessible than ever before. These pressures, moreover, resulted from factors largely outside the control of the U.S. government and its policy, although it must be acknowledged that the United States, as did other industrialized nations, have also contributed both directly and indirectly to the problem. The world's economic interdependence and resulting political dependence has sometimes been imposed on Third World countries. The U.S. role in this regard is particularly relevant in Asia, Southeast Asia, Cuba, Haiti, Nicaragua, El Salvador, and Chile.

Thus, the worldwide population explosion, poverty, rising unemployment, and the political turmoil experienced by so much of the Third World have all added to the ethnic and religious tensions and natural disasters as powerful "push" factors driving the international migration to an unprecedented scale. And since the United States is unique among industrialized nations in that it has nearly 2,000 miles of border adjoining a Third World country, it has experienced the greatest immigration pressures.

Table 1.1
Refugees Accepted, by Country: 1975–1980

Country	Number	Country	Number
United States	677,000	Austria	4,300
China	265,000	New Zealand	4,100
Israel	105,700	Belgium	3,900
Malaysia	102,100	Argentina	2,800
Canada	84,100	Norway	2,700
France	72,000	Denmark	2,300
Australia	51,200	Romania	1,200
Germany [FRG]	32,100	Spain	1,100
United Kingdom	27,600	Italy	900
Tanzania	26,000	Chile	800
Hong Kong	9,400	Japan	800
Switzerland	7,500	Cuba	700
Sweden	7,300	Mexico	700
Netherlands	4,700		

Source: 1981 World Refugee Survey, ed. Michael J. Sherbinin. New York: U.S. Committee for Refugees, 1981; cited in Papademetriou and Miller 1984, 264.

Since the end of World War II, the United States assumed economic, military, and political leadership of the non-communist world. It placed containment as the centerpiece of its foreign policy. In trying to reverse communism and its influence, the United States portrayed itself, both at home and abroad, as the champion of freedom and human rights. It should not be surprising, therefore, that among many Third World peoples, the United States is viewed as the most desirable place for anyone to go. U.S. foreign policy, as was the case of its foes and its allies, directly and indirectly fomented or aggravated turmoil in Third World countries. Thus, the United States, by the very act of exercising its "free-world" leadership role, added to both push and pull factors for migration, especially in cases of unfavorable outcome to its military involvement.

These same forces have led to increased economic migration and occasional mass refugee flows that have been large enough and sufficiently concentrated in a few localities to raise considerable concern among the American public and Congress.

Figure 1.2 shows in graphic form the continued refugee influx into the United States through 1991. That flow is increasingly comprised of economic refugees fleeing Central American countries.

The plight and problems of the Haitian influx, for example, raised some perplexing issues. In U.S. policy, Haitian migrants were treated as "economic" refugees. They contrast sharply with the Vietnamese case. The Vietnamese were political allies for whom we felt a moral obligation. Thus, public opinion generally agreed with our assisting them. The Vietnamese refugees—especially the initial influx after the fall of Saigon—were largely well-educated, middle-class people. Two-thirds of them held white-collar jobs in Vietnam. Twenty-four percent were from professional, technical, and managerial occupational backgrounds. Only 5 percent were farmers and fishermen (Montero 1979, 23). The Vietnamese acculturated more rapidly than any previous Asian group, undoubtedly due in part to their middle-

Figure 1.2
Refugee and Asylee Admissions to Permanent Resident Status, FY 1946–1991

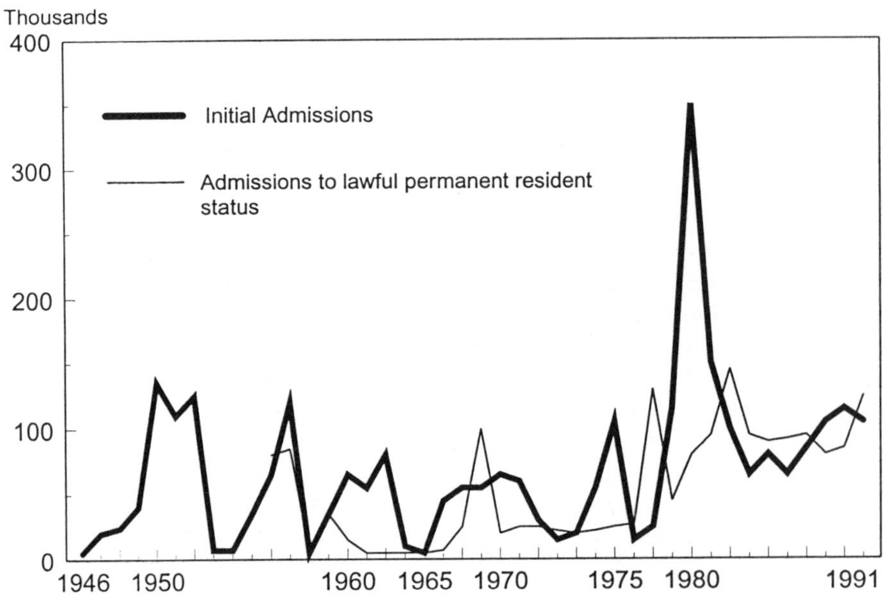

Source: Adapted from Immigration and Naturalization Service 1992, 75.

class status and to the assistance programs. The Haitian refugees, by contrast, were first treated as illegal immigrants. As "economic" refugees held to be fleeing dire economic conditions rather than political repression, they were not allowed in under the refugee category. They began arriving in large numbers in 1972. For years their legal status was clouded while the state department and the nation grappled with what to do with them.

As economic refugees they were not given the aid nor the public support given to such groups as the Cubans, Vietnamese, Hungarians, or Soviet Jews. They were overwhelmingly unskilled and illiterate. They were held in detention camps for years. Since being released from the camps (by court order), they have not been aided, as were other refugees, in finding jobs, housing, or otherwise acculturating to life in the United States. Their illiteracy, low job skills, and language problems have made them easily exploitable, often living in near slave-like conditions. They have been viewed as special threats to the labor market.

THE FLOOD OF ILLEGAL ALIENS

The decade of the 1970s was marked by the problems associated with the "economic refugees," such as the Haitian influx, and by an increase in the undocumented aliens, variously estimated from 3 to 6 million.[5] In 1984, the INS apprehended 1.3 million undocumented aliens (many of them more than once), and the agency estimated that two to three times as many slipped through. In 1978, the Select Commission estimated the total illegal immigration population in the country at between 3.5 and 6 million. A National Academy of Sciences study released in 1985, however, disagreed sharply with the INS figures. It put the total at between 2 and 4 million. These included everyone from people deliberately overstaying their visas to the Haitian boat people who washed ashore in Florida. But by everyone's standards, the majority of illegal immigrants were Hispanics, about two-thirds of whom were Mexicans driven by poverty and unemployment across the highly porous 2,000 miles of the Mexican/U.S. border (LeMay, ed. 1989, 6).

The dramatic increase in the apprehension rate at U.S. borders by the INS's Border Patrol is detailed in Figure 1.3. It graphically shows the build-up in the illegal alien influx that contributed to the political pressures for passage of IRCA, the law designed to stem the flow of illegal aliens to the United States by "demagnetizing" the draw of the U.S. labor market.

The illegal influx from Mexico reflected in part an unanticipated consequence of a prior policy shift—the ending of the Bracero program in 1964. That program had allowed U.S. employers to import workers from Mexico on a temporary basis. It began during World War II as a measure to cope with the labor shortage in agriculture created when millions of workers left the farms for the high-wage jobs of the war production in the industrial plants of our metropolitan areas. The expanding U.S. economy after the

Figure 1.3
INS Apprehensions at U.S. Borders, 1960–1988

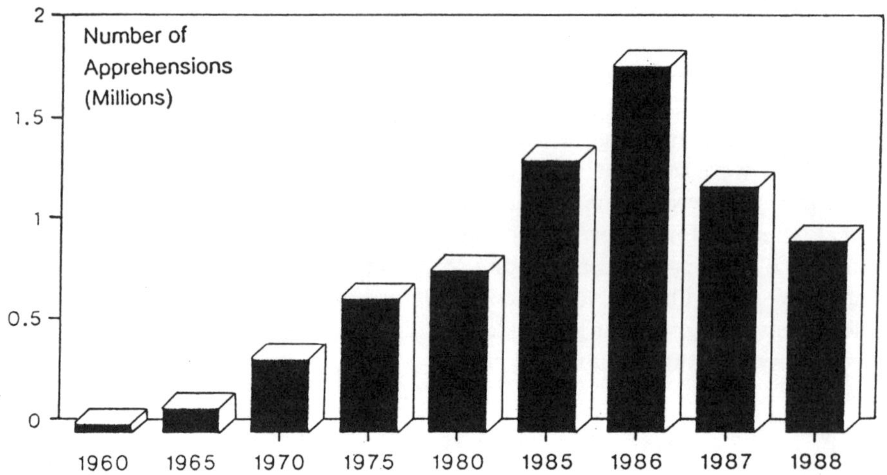

Source: Adapted from graph and data in GAO, *Immigration Reform: Status of Implementing Employer Sanctions after One Year* (Washington, D.C.: U.S. Government Printing Office, 1987a), 8; with 1987 data added from U.S. Department of Justice, *INS Reporter* (Washington, D.C.: U.S. Government Printing Office, 1988), 21; and updated to 1988 by INS data cited in "Border Attacks Worry INS Agents," *Washington Post,* 16 October 1988: A18.

war continued the need for, and even the expansion of, the Bracero program. It peaked in the mid-1960s. Organized labor and various patriotic and other restrictionist groups argued that the program was getting out of hand. Their agitation resulted in the program's termination in 1964. Its controlled entry of temporary farm workers was thus replaced by the flow of illegal aliens, particularly from Mexico. These were essentially the same workers who supplied the Bracero program (Muller and Espanshade 1985, 13).

The volume of *legal* immigration to the nation rose dramatically during the 1970s, to nearly 4.5 million. That was the highest level since the 1910–1920 period and the fourth highest level for any decade in the nation's history. The 1980 census data, however, enumerated 5.6 million foreign-born persons who had entered during the 1970s—representing the total legal and illegal entrants who had arrived during that decade. This figure does not count those foreign-born who came then but were *not counted* by the census. Although no firm data are available for these uncounted, estimates of 1 million or more are likely. Thus, net immigration totaled 6.6 million for the

1970s, which *exceeded* the net *legal* immigration here for the decade beginning 1910 which had totaled only 4.3 million. The net immigration for that period is estimated at 5.4 million. Thus, it is likely that net flow into the country during the 1970 and 1980 decades was at the highest level for any period in this century (ibid., 14).

These fourth-wave immigrants are typically young, some 60 percent being between the prime working years of 16 to 44. Among the undocumented aliens, that proportion is even higher, estimated at two-thirds of the total. Less than one-half the native population falls into that age range.

These new immigrants are overwhelmingly Asian and Latino: 34 percent are from Asia, 34 percent from Central and South America, and 10 percent from the Caribbean. Only 16 percent are from Europe. The remaining 6 percent are from Canada, other continents, or "unspecified nations." Prior to 1960, 69 percent of immigrants came from Europe (ibid., 15).

There are a number of other characteristics of this fourth wave worthy of note. Their educational level, with the exception of those from Mexico, far exceeds the educational level of earlier immigrants and even of the native population. A high percentage have college degrees. They are highly urbanized. Nearly 90 percent of them have settled in metropolitan areas. Indeed, about 40 percent of those counted in the 1980 census reside in just two metropolitan areas—Los Angeles and New York. They are highly concentrated in six states—California, Florida, Texas, Illinois, New York, and Arizona (LeMay, ed. 1989, 8).

Hispanic-American population is now estimated at over 20 million. This catch-all phrase designates all people of Spanish-speaking backgrounds. A 1990 Census Bureau report shows them as follows (in percent): Mexicans, 63; Puerto Ricans, 12; Cubans, 5; Central and South Americans, 12; and all other Spanish-speaking, 8. A study released by the Population Reference Bureau estimates that the Hispanic population will reach 47 million by the year 2020, displacing blacks as the nation's largest minority group. The Hispanic growth rate since 1980, the Census Bureau reported, has been 39 percent, with half the growth attributable to immigration and the rest to births. The Central and South American group has grown the fastest since 1980, increasing by two-thirds, while the Mexican and other groups increased by nearly one-third each. In 1980 the Hispanic population was about 14.5 million, or 6.5 percent of the total population. The Hispanic growth rate for the decade was five times as fast as that of the rest of the country. The 20.1 million figure puts Hispanics at 8.2 percent of the population ("Hispanic Population of U.S. Growing Fastest," *Washington Post,* 12 October 1989, A3).

Fourth-wave immigrants are more diverse than earlier arrivals. There are sharp cultural and social differences among them. Central and South Americans include middle-class refugees escaping political conflict, as well as rural residents fleeing turmoil and seeking economic improvement. Professionals from Argentina have little in common with laborers from Colombia. The Caribbean basin includes Spanish-speaking Cubans, English-speaking Jamaicans, and some islanders speaking French. The tens of thousands of Indochinese refugees range from primitive Hmong mountain people from Laos to sophisticated urban dwellers from Saigon; and Sikhs from India or Buddhists from Korea, to entrepreneurs from Hong Kong (Muller and Espanshade 1985, 15).

Mexican immigrants, who comprise 63 percent of Hispanic immigrants, are similar in several ways to blacks who moved from the rural South in the 1930s, 1940s, and 1950s. They come from rural areas and small towns, having left because of dire poverty. They have little formal education, few job skills, and no capital. Men frequently come first, sending for their families only after they are established. Like blacks, their darker skin marks them for severe discrimination. Mexicans are more often sojourners than many of the earlier immigrant waves. That is, because they reside geographically close to their native areas, they often return to their place of origin. Thus, strong family and other social and cultural ties remain. Unlike blacks, however, Mexicans come from a very structured society—almost feudal—with strong cultural and national identities. They speak Spanish and are thus distinguished not only by color but by language. Because Mexicans are almost all Catholics, their religion is inextricably intertwined with their culture (ibid., 17). Thus, while earlier wave immigrants were typically eager to become U.S. citizens, having come here expecting to remain permanently and having usually cut ties to their former countries, Mexican immigrants, especially the undocumented, consider the border a nuisance rather than a barrier. Many frequently move back and forth, retaining strong Mexican ties and slow naturalization.

Although both push and pull factors have always been involved in the immigration process, push factors seem to have become more important in recent years. As noted, immigration reached a twentieth-century high during the 1970–1980 decade. This was the first time that a peak has been reached precisely when the U.S. economy was wracked by "stagflation" and unemployment was growing rapidly. Worldwide population growth had certainly contributed as a dominant push factor. As noted in the *Final Report* of the U.S. President's Select Commission on Immigration and Refugee Policy (SCIRP):

> One of the greatest pressures for international migration is and will be world population growth. Projections of this growth show more than a 50 percent increase from 1975 to the year 2,000, from 4 billion to 6.35 billion. It has been estimated that 92 percent of this growth will take place in countries whose resources are least able to accommodate the needs of new population. . . . World economic and political instability would be threatened by the sudden, large-scale population moves which could result from widespread political or economic chaos in developing nations. (1981a, 19–20)

Population pressures in South and Central America, Asia, Africa, and the Caribbean have been accelerating. Decreasing costs in transportation have cut the cost of entering the United States, legally or illegally. These rising push factors, to the extent that they differ from factors inducing previous waves of immigration, may have a more significant long-term impact than any other factor.[6]

THE CRISIS OF BORDER CONTROL

What resulted from these changes in the nation's flow of immigration during the 1970s was a growing sense of crisis. There was widespread dissatisfaction registered in the mass media, general public opinion polls, and within the government over the adequacy of our immigration laws to meet this new challenge. Among U.S. citizens, there was a growing sense that immigration policy seemed to be out of control. We seemed, as a nation, to have lost control of our borders (U.S. President's SCIRP 1981a, 10; see also Bean and Sullivan 1985, 67–73).

The increased size of the new wave and its changing composition, coupled with the massive scale of the illegal flow, raised a number of interrelated questions. These questions posed challenges to the nation's policymakers. Could the United States control its borders? What about increased problems of morale, corruption, and incompetence within the INS? Could the United States maintain civil rights and liberties while searching out and controlling the undocumented alien influx? Was bilingualism successful or did it contribute toward separatism? What was the economic impact of the new "flood" of immigrants? (LeMay, ed. 1989, 8–10).

As seeming millions of illegal immigrants were here and were being added to by an estimated annual influx of tens of thousands more, a sense that we had literally lost control of our borders emerged and created a sense of frustration about the problem.

Even for those who entered legally, the INS seemed unable to keep track of them and ensure that they obeyed the terms of their visas. The nation was greatly embarrassed by the inefficiency of the INS record-keeping brought to light during the Iranian hostage crisis. President Carter and the nation were shocked to learn that the INS did not know how many Iranian students were living here, let alone how many were doing so illegally. Many of the Iranians who the INS was able to identify as being subject to deportation simply failed to attend deportation hearings or to leave when told to do so. Visa overstayers were estimated to be several hundreds of thousands annually (ibid., 8–9).

Problems of corruption flowed naturally from the tremendous pressures for immigration coupled with restrictions on legal immigration and the inefficiency of the INS. Such corruption was held to be extensive in the INS, the state department's visa-related operations, and even among some immigration lawyers (Crewdson 1983; Morris 1985).

The underfunding of the INS compelled it to engage in more secondary enforcement activities to locate illegal aliens: stopping traffic at checkpoints; watching air, bus, and train terminal passengers; checking ranches and other areas of employment that had traditionally high levels of illegal aliens with warrantless searches; and following up on specific leaks. These types of activities by the INS, however, posed particular problems regarding the civil rights of individuals; and numerous instances occurred where such rights were abused.

Another problem generated by the heavy immigration influx, especially by the Mexican "undocumented" aliens, was the fear that the immigrants were increasingly unable or unwilling to assimilate. A central aspect of that concern was the growing program of bilingualism. The federal Bilingual Education Act of 1968 engendered programs involving nearly 1.5 million students who were enrolled in U.S. schools in federal, state, and local programs.

By far, the most controversial problem, however, was the one that stirred the greatest debate—the economic impact of immigration, especially the illegal influx. Numerous scholars and interest groups aligned on both sides of that hotly debated issue.[7] One 1982–1983 study found illegal aliens contributed more revenue to the state than it spent on them. Another study concluded that undocumented aliens contributed less than the $2,900 it cost per year to educate a public school student (cited in LeMay, ed. 1989, 10).

Some of the confusion in the results of these contradictory studies undoubtedly lies in the different methodologies and economic assumptions employed in the various analytical studies. The picture that emerged from the actual jobs held by undocumented aliens uncovered during INS sweep operations substantiated that their impact was at the lower level of jobs, concentrated in what many would consider "undesirable" jobs. Such sweeps, however, were too skewed a sample to reliably measure the total job displacement picture.

Economists argued back and forth as to whether or not, or to what degree if so, illegal aliens "drove down wages and working conditions." Some economists argued that they filled an "economical wage" niche. Their jobs paid wages low enough to allow the employer to make a profit. Faced with the loss of such cheap labor, these economists argued, the employer would replace them with machines, move their operations overseas or across the border, or simply go out of business. For example, when the Bracero program ended in California, only the lettuce and citrus growers raised their wages in an attempt to attract domestic workers. The tomato growers began using mechanical harvesters, the asparagus growers moved to Mexico, and marginal growers in all crops simply closed down and sold their farms.

Economist Walter Fogel, however, countered that the flow of illegal aliens exacerbated the job and income problems of blacks, legal residents of Hispanic origin, and other secondary job-market workers by reducing the number of such jobs available to them, depressing wages for those jobs they did hold, and generally undercutting working conditions as well (cited in Papademetriou and Miller 1984, 88).

The sense that such immigration-related problems, and especially the flood of the "illegal alien influx," had reached a "crisis" stage forced the problem onto the national agenda. Congress felt compelled, as it periodically did, to confront anew the need to revise immigration laws. The nature of how those immigration problems were perceived, moreover, meant that the approach taken to "reform" immigration laws would involve a radically new approach to immigration policy. The method of "employer sanctions" was soon viewed as an approach that might "demagnetize" the pull of the U.S. economy that thus drew so many illegal aliens north across our borders. The next chapter discusses the development of specific legislative proposals to deal with these perceived public policy problems.

NOTES

1. Numerous studies and scholars make the point and establish the importance of the early Mexican immigration patterns to the United States setting up the chain-migration patterns that persist after the end of the Bracero program which influence today's illegal immigration flows. See, for example, Bustamente 1981; Chiswick 1988; Cockroft 1986; Conover 1987; Kiser and Kiser 1979; and Kirstein 1977.

2. Muller and Espanshade 1985, 11–12; LeMay 1987, 73–102; and Stanley Lieberson, *A Piece of the Pie* (Berkeley, Calif.: University of California Press, 1980).

3. Cited in Chiswick 1982, 41. See also, Rosemary Stevens, *The Alien Doctors* (New York: Wiley, 1978); and Mamot 1974.

4. See A. Leibowitz, "The Refugee Act of 1980: Problems and Congressional Concerns," *Annals of the American Academy of Political and Social Science* (1983), 167; Ferris 1985, 108; and "Europe's Migrants Swell Refugee Wave," *Washington Post,* 6 October 1989, A41, A48.

5. See, for example, McClellan 1981; Crewdson 1983; Cross and Sandos 1981; Glazer 1985; and Bean, King, and Passel 1985, 13–16.

6. Muller and Espanshade 1985, 17; Cheng and Nitz 1989, 12; *Governing,* 1989 and 1992.

7. For a detailed discussion of the economic impact issue, see Muller and Espanshade 1985, Chapters 4–6; U.S. President's SCIRP 1981a, 38–41; Kritz 1983, 191–285; Chiswick 1982, 251–358; Cornelius and Montoya 1983; and North 1978, 1980. Additional viewpoints and elaborations on the labor impact are provided by Bonacich 1976, 34–41; Piore 1979; and Cheng and Nitz 1989.

CHAPTER 2

Policy Formulation: Development of the Immigration Reform Proposals

BEGINNINGS OF THE EMPLOYER-SANCTIONS APPROACH

Most often, public policy changes in an incremental fashion, with slight changes being enacted during a given Congressional session or within a few years of time. Occasionally, as was the case with IRCA, public policy is marked by a rather dramatic shift from the previous state of policy. When a significant public policy shift occurs, it comes about only after long, difficult legislative manuevering over the issue. Such was the case with the Immigration Reform and Control Act of 1986. This chapter details the rather long and tortured history of the various bills and proposals that led up to the enactment of IRCA.

By the early 1970s, organized labor moved to deal with its perceived threat from the illegal alien influx. The rising unemployment, especially in the lower wage level jobs, helped labor leaders to convince Rep. Peter Rodino (D., N.J.) that the undocumented aliens were taking jobs that rightfully belonged to U.S. citizens. Organized labor's support (primarily the AFL-CIO and the International Ladies Garment Workers Union), along with that of the NAACP (which also saw illegal immigration as threatening the jobs of poor urban blacks), moved Rodino to propose an employer's sanctions amendment to the Immigration and Nationality Act, essentially eliminating the "Texas Proviso" of the 1952 law (Perotti 1989b, 83–84).

Both the House and the Senate Judiciary subcommittees held hearings on the matter. The Nixon administration openly supported the employer-sanctions approach. In September of 1972, the House of Representatives passed the bill making it illegal to *knowingly hire* illegal aliens. In the Senate, however, the Judiciary subcommittee was chaired by Sen. James Eastland (D., Miss.). Senator Eastland was a friend of the growers who opposed that approach (principally the National Council of Agricultural Employers and the American Farm Bureau Federation at that time). He failed to hold hearings on the House-passed bill and the measure died quietly in committee. In 1973, Rodino again succeeded in getting a bill using the employer-sanctions approach approved in the House. This time Senator Eastland even more openly opposed the legislation and blocked the bill by refusing to release it from the committee.[1]

In 1974–1975, Sen. Edward Kennedy (D., Mass.), and in 1975 Rep. Rodino and Rep. Joshua Eilberg (D., Pa.) persisted in following a somewhat different strategy, for the first time linking the employer-sanctions idea with limited legalization and antidiscrimination provisions (ibid., 88). Also in 1975, the Ford administration began an inquiry into solutions to the immigration problem. At the same time, both the Senate and the House Judiciary subcommittees held hearings on employer sanctions. Rodino and subcommittee chairman Eilberg linked the employer-sanctions approach to that of legalization and antidiscrimination provisions in order to gain the support—or at least somewhat neutralize the opposition—from Hispanic and human rights groups. This ploy, however, alerted the Hispanics to the potentially dire effects that employer sanctions might have on the Latino community. Hispanics supported the new provisions but opposed employer sanctions. Although the bill passed the Judiciary Committee by a vote of 25 to 5, Rodino, Eilberg, and committee supporters of the bill, sensing that they lacked sufficient support for the bill in the full House, decided not to ask the Rules Committee to clear the bill for floor consideration.[2]

In 1975, the Senate also undertook consideration of immigration reform proposals. Senator Eastland, then full chairman of the Senate Judiciary Committee and of its Subcommittee on Immigration and Naturalization, had his staffers work on an employer-sanctions bill. But Senator Eastland made it clear that he would take no action on any immigration reform bill that did not have a foreign workers' program, making the approach acceptable to growers by replacing illegal workers with temporary workers by expanding an existing program—the H-2 temporary workers program.

Eastland ultimately decided not to release the bill from the committee. That, plus a steadily declining unemployment rate, strong opposition to the bills in both the House and the Senate from employers, ethnic and religious groups, and organized labor, and Rodino and Eilberg's failure to move their bill to a House floor vote, all combined to keep the employer-sanctions bills from being considered in 1975. Once again the idea died in committee.[3]

Congress, however, did enact some revisions in the 1965 law. In 1976, the House Judiciary Committee reported on the effect of ending the Good Neighbor open-door policy of unlimited immigration from the Western Hemisphere that was a critical compromise enabling passage of the 1965 preference system law: a steadily increasing backlog of legal immigration applicants from Latin America, with prospective immigrants waiting in excess of two years for a visa. The House Judiciary Committee noted:

> When repealing the national origins quota system, the 89th Congress did not provide an adequate mechanism for implementing the Western Hemisphere ceiling. . . . The result, completely unforeseen and unintended, has been considerable hardship for intending immigrants from this hemisphere who until 1968 [the date the 1965 provision for a ceiling on Western Hemisphere immigration took effect] enjoyed the privilege of unrestricted immigration. (U.S. President's SCIRP 1981b, 209)

In 1976, Congress passed a new law to make regulations controlling immigration the same for both hemispheres,thereby applying to Western Hemisphere nations the same 20,000-per-country limit and the preference system that was in effect for Eastern Hemisphere nations (LeMay 1987, 115).

The only controversial provision of the 1976 act was its application of the 20,000-per-country limit to Mexico. Mexican immigration had exceeded that limit every year since the 1965 law was passed. Considerable support was evident for the idea that special provisions should be permitted for contiguous countries (i.e., Canada and Mexico) because of our shared borders. Both President Ford, when signing the 1976 bill into law, and President Carter, in 1977, endorsed the idea of special provisions for bordering nations. Congress, however, failed to act on the idea.

The 1976 law maintained the last two vestiges of the geographic origins approach to immigration: separate annual ceilings of 170,000 for the Eastern and 120,000 for the Western Hemisphere and the special ceiling (of a mere 600 visas per year) assigned to colonies and dependencies (e.g., Hong Kong).

In 1976, the Ford administration established a cabinet-level committee to study immigration policy options. Although it failed to develop a specific bill, the Domestic Policy Council did develop recommendations for the President, including support for employer sanctions, limited amnesty, reexamination of the adequacy of the H-2 program, and increased funding for the INS and the Department of State. This signaled executive-branch support for the employer-sanctions approach. Such support continued, in 1977, when the incoming Carter administration became involved. President Carter's new Secretary of Labor, Ray Marshall, was a University of Texas economist long interested in the issue. He tied his acceptance of the appointment to a commitment to work on illegal immigration. The Carter administration was split, however, on details of the approach. Secretary Marshall and Attorney General Griffin Bell advocated a limited amnesty and a work eligibility card. INS Commissioner Leonel J. Castillo and White House aides, by contrast, led a campaign for a liberal amnesty and deplored the civil liberties implications of such a card (Perotti 1989b, 94–95).

In 1978, Congress reacted to immigration problems resulting from the geographic limitation provisions by combining ceilings for both hemispheres into a worldwide total of 290,000, with the same seven-category preference system and per-country limits applied to both. Sen. Edward Kennedy, one of the law's sponsors, cited the benefits from the 1978 legislation:

> In the long term, this reform makes more flexible the provisions of the preference system, and in the short run it has the likely effect of allowing the use of more non-preference visas next year for the backlog in the Western Hemisphere and the use of more conditional entry visas for the Indochinese refugees—a need that is extraordinarily urgent in Southeast Asia today. All this will not involve, however, any increase in the total annual immigration authorized under the law.[4]

Concern about the Indochina refugee question was an important consideration enabling passage of the 1978 act that set a worldwide ceiling. It also reflected the continuing concern of Congress to tinker with immigration revisions and the need to more fully grapple with the growing refugee problem. At the time of Senator Kennedy's remarks, it was apparent that the Western Hemisphere seventh-preference limit, which was applicable only to Cuba as that hemisphere's only communist country, was problematic in that Cubans were not permitted to leave in sizable numbers. Its limits were going unused, while the demand for entrance from the Eastern Hemisphere (after the fall of Saigon) was great. The worldwide ceiling would thus permit the visas to go where the refugee need was the greatest, without regard to hemisphere of origin.

The 1978 law, however, barely touched the full range of issues raised by the U.S. refugee policy. Mass-refugee movements generated new problems pointing to the inadequacy of using conditional entry provisions when dealing with large-scale emergencies. Although when these provisions were enacted (in 1952), Congress intended that they would be measures through which most refugees would be admitted; the parole provision of the 1952 act was actually the major authority for the entrance of large groups of refugees.[5]

Under the parole authority, the Attorney General is given the discretion to parole any alien into the nation temporarily, under such conditions as the Attorney General may prescribe, in emergencies or for reasons deemed to be strictly in the public interest. As we have seen in Chapter 1, that parole authority was used between 1962 and 1979 to allow over 690,000 Cubans to enter. In 1975, two parole programs were adopted to aid in the resettlement of Indochinese refugees, and still more between 1976 and 1979. In June of 1979, President Carter announced that the number of Indochinese paroled in would be set at 14,000 per month. During that same period, Soviet refugees totaling 35,000 for the year were also paroled in, as were slightly more than 1,000 Chilean and Lebanese refugees (U.S. President's SCIRP 1981b, 213–214).

Reliance on the emergency parole authority, however, became increasingly inappropriate to what were recurring situations. Attorney General Bell noted some of the major problems of relying on the parole authority to deal with refugee crises. In effect, the Attorney General had more power than Congress did in determining limits on the entry of refugees into the country. Such use of parole authority also prevented the United States from giving clear signs to other nations as to the willingness and ability of the United States to respond to worldwide refugee needs. In essence, individual refugees were "hostage to a system that necessitates that their plight build to tragic proportions so as to establish the imperative to act" (ibid.).

These concerns led to the enactment of the Refugee Act of 1980. As mentioned earlier, this law broadened the definition of refugee by removing the geographic and ideological limits of the earlier (1952 and 1965) laws. The act further established a limit of 50,000 for normal refugee admissions, through 1982, and strengthened procedures by which the President, in consultation with Congress, could increase this number annually in response to unforeseen circumstances. It also provided for a special conditional entry status with adjustment to permanent resident alien status after one year in the country. Finally, the act established the ongoing responsibility of the federal government in assisting in the resettlement of refugees accepted under the act, including provisions for up to 100 percent reimbursement to states for cash and medical assistance provided to refugees during their first 36 months in the United States and even for grants to voluntary agencies for some of their costs incurred in resettlement. As we shall see more fully, these provisions served as a precedent for aspects of the approach used by IRCA.

But these measures failed to move immigration reform in the direction of employer sanctions. Congressman Rodino grew frustrated that despite cabinet-level commissions in both the Ford and Carter administrations recommending packages similar to Rodino's—with the essential ingredients of employer sanctions, legalization, and stronger enforcement measures—nothing could pass the Senate because of Senator Eastland's intransigence.

The late 1970s, then, saw the nation wracked by severe inflation and high unemployment—dubbed "stagflation." The highly publicized influx of huge waves of refugees, plus the continued increases in illegal immigration, heightened the public's awareness of the "crisis" in immigration policy. Media hype reflected the public sentiment in estimating the annual illegal alien flow at a rate of 2 million, with a total of at least 10 million already in the country (e.g., *New York Times,* 16 January 1980). It seemed that the country was, indeed, losing control of its borders, and that the near-record level of unemployment was a result of the illegal aliens taking jobs away from American citizens. There developed a pervasive sense of fear that Hispanic separatism, akin to the French Quebec problem in Canada, might develop in the

United States. Others feared the changes in American culture resulting from the illegal alien (i.e., Hispanic) influx and from the Asian (i.e., refugee) flow (Peters and Vega 1986, 8). For example, the rapid influx of Asians into California's Monterey Park prompted bumper stickers that reflected such sentiment, reading: "Will the Last American to Leave Monterey Park Please Bring the Flag" (*Time,* 8 July 1985).

President Carter's administration responded to these pressures by reintroducing Rodino's employer-sanctions bill and adding legalization provisions to it. This proposal again failed to reach the floor of the House, once again stymied by both pro-immigration and restrictionist interests, especially the intransigence of Senator Eastland (*National Journal,* 7 March 1981, 390; Peters and Vega 1986, 8; Perotti 1989b, 95).

As a result, in 1978, President Carter and Congress, prompted by Representative Eilberg and Senator Kennedy, and by academics and others pressing for comprehensive revisions in the law, created the Select Commission on Immigration and Refugee Policy (SCIRP), authorizing it to study the entire issue of immigration.

While Representative Eilberg had little difficulty in getting the Select Commission blueprint approved in the House (he attached it to another immigration reform bill), Senator Kennedy had to use a parliamentary trick to avoid its being trampled again by Senator Eastland, who, though about to retire, could still have killed the proposal. Senator Kennedy, the incoming Judiciary Chairman, saw the SCIRP proposal as a way to carve out for himself a pivotal role in any sanctions legislation (Perotti 1989b, 96).

Set up in 1979, SCIRP submitted its final report in 1981. We next turn our attention to the critical role played by SCIRP in leading to the eventual enactment of IRCA.

THE IMPACT OF SCIRP: LEGITIMIZATION OF THE DUALITY OF EMPLOYER SANCTIONS AND LEGALIZATION

The Select Commission on Immigration and Refugee Policy opened in May 1979. It was comprised of members of Congress, the executive branch, and the public. Congress was represented as follows: from the Senate, by Charles Mathias (D., Md.), Alan Simpson (R., Wyo.), Edward Kennedy (D., Mass.), and Dennis DeConcini (D., Ariz.); and from the House by Peter Rodino (D., N.J.), Elizabeth Holtzman (D., N.Y.), Robert McClory (R., Ill.), and Hamilton Fish (R., N.Y.). The executive branch was represented by the Secretary of State, Cyrus Vance; the Attorney General, Benjamin Civiletti; the Secretary of Labor, Ray Marshall; and the Secretary of Health, Education, and Welfare, Patricia Harris. Members of the public included Joaquin Otero of the Brotherhood of Railway and Airline Clerks, Judge Cruz Reynoso of the California Court of Appeals, Rose Ochi of the Office of the Mayor of Los Angeles, and Reubin Askew, the former Governor of Florida, who was designated its chairman.

By the time the commission was seriously under way in October 1979, however, President Carter appointed Askew to another job and named the Reverend Theodore Hesburgh, then President of Notre Dame University and former chairman of the Civil Rights Commission, as the new SCIRP chairman. Selected as the staff director of the commission was Dr. Lawrence Fuchs, a distinguished professor at Brandeis University and an acknowledged ethnic and immigration scholar.

The commission began its really serious work in October 1979, in the highly charged political atmosphere of a presidential election, the Mariel boatlift from Cuba, and a resulting dramatic liberalization of refugee admissions. SCIRP's members drafted an initial formula for an agreement on the illegal alien issue, submitting their final report in January 1981, along with a staff report and nine appendixes dealing with major areas of SCIRP's work, and an additional appendix that constituted a full rewriting of the Immigration and Nationality Act by the legal research staff of the commission (U.S. President's SCIRP 1981a; see also Perotti 1989a, 6).

The final report of SCIRP ran over 450 pages, and was supplemented by a staff report in excess of 900 pages. The recommendations, briefly summarized here, covered the full spectrum of "problem" concerns developed around the immigration policy debates of the 1970s.

SCIRP recommended "closing the back door" to undocumented immigration while opening slightly the front door to accommodate more legal immigration. It stressed the need to define our immigration goals more clearly. It recommended the need to provide a more effective structure to implement the goals by setting forth procedures that would lead to fair and efficient adjudication and administration of U.S. immigration laws. SCIRP maintained that immigration unquestionably served humanitarian needs and that continued immigration was, indeed, in the national interest. While it stated that immigration entailed many benefits to U.S. society, the commission also recognized the nation's limited ability to absorb large numbers effectively. SCIRP held that "it is not the time for large-scale expansion in legal immigration, for resident aliens or temporary workers, because the first order of priority is in bringing undocumented or illegal immigration under control, while setting up a rational system of legal immigration," and recommended a "modest increase in legal immigration sufficient to expedite the clearance of backlogs," mainly to reunify families. It recommended that numerically restricted immigration be increased from 270,000 to 350,000 (U.S. President's SCIRP 1981a).

The commission argued that illegal immigration could also be reduced by strengthening and increasing the "family reunification" preference category, by putting immigrants whose entry would reunite families on a separate track from other immigrants, and by putting spouses and minor children of lawful permanent resident aliens under a separate numerically limited category without country ceilings, thereby helping to assure the reunification of families on a first-come, first-served basis within a fixed worldwide ceiling. It further advocated the creation of a separate category for nonfamily immigrants—an independent category—to provide immigration opportunities to those people who came from countries where immigration to the United States had not been recent or from countries that had no immigration base here. SCIRP called for upgrading the system for administering immigration laws and stressed the need to streamline deportation procedures and the importance of English-language acquisition. By a narrow margin, SCIRP recommended a system of employee eligibility with a reliable identifier between legal and illegal workers.

Its clear stress, however, was recommending the enforcement of existing immigration laws via the imposition of employer sanctions, increased law enforcement, an amnesty program, and a restructuring of legal immigration. While each of these ideas had been formulated before, the importance of the work of the commission was in the way that it linked all these proposals together. The impact of SCIRP was to *legitimize the duality* of the employer sanctions and the legalization approach. Its approach was very comprehensive. The final report of SCIRP said, in essence, that you cannot have one without the other. Legalization would allow the INS to concentrate its resources on border apprehension where such efforts were more efficient, rather than to disperse them trying to track down and deport the illegal aliens already here. Employer sanctions would serve to "demagnetize" the pull of the economy drawing a continued influx of undocumented aliens to the United States. The commission set the agenda for all subsequent discussions of and proposals to reform immigration law. Its prestige gave weight to proposals and ideas that before had been stymied in the Congressional committee.

Perhaps its most important contribution was the shared information it gave to the disputants—information as to alternative solutions and about the other parties' positions. It spotlighted the joint benefits to be gained through immigration reform by showing liberals that they could achieve more open immigration if the restrictionists were allowed their desire to exclude undocumented workers. Perhaps equally important, it demonstrated a new structure to the issue. The power to influence the issue was seen to be more balanced between the labor and the agricultural factions, particularly with the retirement of Senator Eastland. In the words of Professor Perotti:

> Whereas, prior to the Select Commission, the labor/restrictionist faction worried it would not get its bill passed, now growers worried. In a clear two party dispute, the balance of power made each side nervous that, given just a little more power, the other side might win a distributive victory. This uncertainty led to the opening of negiotiations. (Perotti 1989b, 102)

The commission's inclusion of so many issues among its recommendations, moreover, provided enhanced possibilities for many more trades and compensations.

Its clear stress on the problem of undocumented immigration as "the most pressing problem" shaped and limited the focus of debate over immigration policy reform for the next half decade. It issued a clear message: "Most U.S. citizens believe that the half-open door of undocumented/illegal migration should be closed" (U.S. President's SCIRP 1981a, 35).

Finally, it was from the commission's Congressional membership that many of the primary movers of Congressional leadership on the IRCA proposals emerged. Its research was seminal for the work of Simpson and Mazzoli's staffs. Its procedures illustrated the methods by which the conflict might be resolved (Perotti 1989b, 104).

THE SIMPSON-MAZZOLI-RODINO PROPOSALS

The Reagan administration responded to the findings of SCIRP by establishing a Task Force on Immigration and Refugee Policy on March 6, 1981. The task force was chaired by Attorney General William French Smith and presented recommendations to the President at three meetings in July 1981. The major points of the immigration proposals of the Reagan administration are summarized here:

1. *Amnesty.* Aliens living in the United States illegally since January 1, 1980 would be permitted to remain, being made eligible for resident-alien status after being here ten years, and would also be free to seek U.S. citizenship (estimated number, 5 million).
2. *Guest Workers.* A program allowing 50,000 Mexicans annually to come to work temporarily, gradually increasing in numbers over several years until up to hundreds-of-thousands annually.
3. *Employer Sanctions.* Employers with more than four employees who "knowingly hire" illegal aliens would be subject to fines for up to $1,000 per violation.
4. *Boat People.* Boats carrying Haitians would be intercepted. Detention camps would be established to hold as many as 6,000 people pending hearings on their deportation.
5. *Enforcement.* Increase the budget of the INS by 50 percent and add 1,500 officers to the Border Patrol to enhance enforcement of immigration and labor laws.
6. *Immigration Limits.* Allow 610,000 new immigrants to the United States annually, with a special preference to persons from Canada and Mexico. (LeMay 1987, 138, from "U.S. Immigration and Refugee Policy," Department of State, 30 July 1981, and critiques of the plan in "Reagan's Plan for Illegal Aliens," *U.S. News and World Report,* 3 August 1981, 42–43)

The task force's boldest proposals were for allowing the Coast Guard to intercept boats carrying Haitians to the United States so they could be returned to Haiti or to some other country, and for a counterfeit-resistant Social Security card, although the latter idea was dropped from its final report.

By the fall of 1981, both the House and Senate Judiciary subcommittees on immigration had completed their hearings. Their chairmen, Sen. Alan Simpson (R., Wyo.) and Rep. Romano Mazzoli (D., Ky.) translated the SCIRP recommendations into legislative proposals they considered to contain the essential provisions to serve as incentives for the competing groups to cooperate. They quickly emerged as the principal actors behind the immigration reform issue. On March 17, 1982, identical Simpson–Mazzoli bills were introduced to their respective chambers (S-2222 and HR-5872). These bills incorporated many provisions of the earlier S-1765 and HR-4832, as well as aspects of the Reagan proposal. Their bill, unlike the Reagan proposal, included the SCIRP recommendation for a national identity card, and had a modified (from the Reagan bill) scheme for employer sanctions and amnesty (LeMay 1987, 141; Cornelius and Montoya 1983, 318–319).

During the original debates on the bill, several amendments were offered. Sen. Walter Huddleston (D., Ky.) proposed one that would have included refugees within the overall total for immigrants; and Sen. Dale Bumpers (D., Ark.) submitted one that would have set the limit for refugees at 75,000, but permitted no increase over that limit without express Congressional approval. Senator Simpson argued against both amendments, stressing the danger of emasculating the refugee program if it were forced to compete with regular immigration. The Huddleston amendment failed by a vote of 35 to 63 (*Congressional Record,* 12 August 1982, S-10361). The Bumpers amendment, seen by many as fatally flawed by being too inflexible, failed by a vote of 41 to 45 (*Congressional Record,* 13 August 1982). Restrictionist Senators like John East (R., N.C.) and Jesse Helms (R., N.C.) tried unsuccessfully to scuttle the amnesty program. Their motion was defeated 17 to 82 (*Congressional Record,* 12 August 1982, S-10337). Grower advocates, led by Sen. Samuel Hayakawa (D., Calif.), likewise were unsuccessful (by a vote of 78 to 21) with an amendment to create a one million worker or guest-worker program (*Congressional Record,* 13 August 1982, S-10461).

The initial Simpson–Mazzoli bill departed from several of the SCIRP recommendations. It did not even consider the crown-colony ceilings recommendation. The commission's recommendations to increase total legal immigration ceilings from 270,000 to 350,000 and to provide another 100,000 visas per year for the next five years to clear up backlogs in various preference categories were likewise never given serious consideration in the Congressional hearings. The Simpson–Mazzoli bill followed more closely, however, the recommendations of SCIRP with respect to due process, H-2 certification; the exemption of spouses, minor children, and parents of U.S. citizens from the numerical restrictions; and its general emphasis on family reunification. Both versions (House and Senate) of the bill agreed with the SCIRP's assertion of the need to keep the front door open, at least at present levels, to retain special admission of refugees separate from that of immigrants, and to provide for a substantial amnesty program for those illegal aliens already here (LeMay 1987, 139).

The Simpson–Mazzoli bill also set up new procedures for asylum adjudication, a problem stressed in the commission's findings. It established an asylum adjudication officer specifically trained in international law and prohibited any existing INS officer from holding the new position. The bill specified a U.S. Immigration Board, similar to the existing Parole Board, that would hear appeals. Its members would be Presidential appointees and were to be independent of the Attorney General. No judicial appeal from the decisions of these independent administrative tribunals would be permitted. While Congress was seeking a fair process, it was clearly a more curtailed one. The state department was specifically excluded from any role in the process.

These adjudication procedures were objected to by both the Reagan administration and by asylum advocates. The administration's approach advocated greater control over the process by placing it under the Attorney General and by involving the state department. This approach was generally followed by the Senate's version of the bill as it progressed through the Senate to passage. By contrast, the asylum advocates wanted to have judicial review placed over a truly independent administrative structure. The House Judiciary Committee adopted this latter approach (ibid., 140).

The Congressional subcommittees of both chambers held their own hearings on the Simpson–Mazzoli bills, reporting them out by mid-May. Senator Simpson worked closely with Sen. Strom Thurmond (R., S.C.) to bring the measure before the full Senate Judiciary Committee. After slightly amending the bill, the Senate Judiciary Committee approved it on May 27, and reported the bill out on June 9. The measure reached the Senate floor late in the summer and was easily passed, by a vote of 81 to 19, on August 17 (*Conressional Record,* 17 August 1982; see also Perotti 1989b, 157).

Meanwhile, the Simpson–Mazzoli bill had not fared so well in the House. Chairman Rodino, apparently having become impatient at the failure of the Senate to move on previous House bills in the 1970s to reform immigration law, announced that the House Judiciary Committee would not hold a markup session on the bill until the Senate passed its version of it. Rodino was also apparently upset that Mazzoli had not sought out his support on a proposal that he had been working on for nearly a decade. He deleted the section restricting the immigration of brothers and sisters of U.S. citizens and capping legal immigration. And Rep. Don Edwards (D., Calif.), at the urgings of state and local governments, proposed an amendment assuring 100 percent reimbursement to state and local governments for the costs of legalization (see Peters and Vega 1986, 9; Perotti 1989b, 157–158).

Representatives Mazzoli and Hamilton Fish (R., N.Y.) introduced a clean version of HR-5872 as HR-6514 and with the Senate's passage of S-2222, the House Judiciary Committee took up HR-6514 for mark-up in mid-September 1982. The full Judiciary Committee approved the Mazzoli version of the bill.

The Simpson–Mazzoli bill compromised on the earlier Reagan administration proposal by excluding a provision for a guest-worker program. Instead, it expanded and strengthened a version of the H-2 program with which it was deemed easier for employers to import temporary workers from Mexico. It incorporated administrative rules that the Department of Labor used in the H-2 program during the years following the end of the Bracero program. In committee, however, congressmen sympathetic to employer interests succeeded in incorporating changes designed to open up the flow of legal temporary workers through the H-2 channel should other provisions of the proposed law effectively cut off the supply of undocumented (and thus cheap) workers. As previously mentioned, the Senate rejected an amendment that would have set up a large-scale guest-worker program. It also rejected one by Senator Kennedy that would have retained the H-2 as it was (LeMay 1987, 141).

The bill that ultimately passed the Senate contained several provisions that would have affected the number and type of H-2 workers entering the United States for temporary employment, enabling an expanded temporary worker program. The Senate version would also have greatly restricted the role of the Department of Labor (DOL) in the certification process. The Simpson–Mazzoli bill as originally submitted would have converted the DOL certification from the advisory status to a mandatory one. By eliminating this aspect, the Senate version allowed for the possibility that the INS, an agency less sensitive to domestic labor conditions, could ignore or overrule the DOL recommendations (ibid.; Cornelius and Montoya 1983, 133).

Senator Kennedy offered several amendments which would have deleted those provisions from the bill that were of most concern to Hispanic Americans: easing family reunification and doing away with the H-2 temporary worker expansion provision. Groups like the Mexican American Defense League (MALDEF), the Spanish International Network (SIN), and the national Spanish-language network, lobbied strongly against the Simpson–Mazzoli bill. SIN blasted it as the "most blatantly anti-Hispanic bill ever." It called upon the Hispanic community to make its views known in Congress by writing or contacting Senator Kennedy's office about the issue. More than 8,000 letters and mailgrams from outraged Hispanics were delivered to Kennedy's office in less than a week, in addition to a nearly constant barrage of telephone calls to the Senator's office and to sympathetic Hispanic Caucus members' offices (oral interviews; see also Crewdson 1983, 323).

Because of overlapping jurisdiction, House Speaker Thomas P. O'Neill (D., Mass.) referred the bill sequentially to four other committees: Education and Labor, Agriculture, Ways and Means, and Energy and Commerce. Each considered the bill and it finally reached the Rules Committee in early December, during the "lame duck" session of the 97th Congress. After more hearings, the Rules Committee sent the measure to the floor with an open rule.

By the time the Simpson–Mazzoli bill reached floor action in the House (in mid-December), over 300 amendments had been filed showing the strong opposition the bill faced in the House. Its most vocal opponents were Hispanics, who feared that the employer-sanction approach would only exacerbate the already extensive job discrimination they faced. Strong opposition was also voiced by the Chamber of Commerce and by organized labor. Hispanic organizations (principally the National Congress of Hispanic–American Citizens, MALDEF, SIN, and the National Council of La Raza) worked with the Hispanic Congressional Caucus. Members of the caucus prepared more than 100 amendments on the employer-sanctions provision alone. They also strongly lobbied Speaker O'Neill. As a result, the bill received only lukewarm support from the House Democratic leadership. Speaker O'Neill worried that the measure would increase divisions within the party among Hispanics, liberals, and moderates. He also feared that people with dark skin would face even greater employment discrimination if the employer-sanctions approach were enacted. As a result, the Speaker announced that he had scheduled the bill for floor action only out of courtesy to the White House and the Republican House leadership (Peters and Vega 1986, 10; *Congressional Record,* 18 December 1982, H-10319). After three days of emotional, even bitter late evening debates, no action was taken on the bill, and it died as the 97th Congress adjourned (Perotti 1989b, 158–159).

The heated debate on the bill cost the leadership somewhat. Frustrations among the bill's supporters were evident, especially during the final hours of debate on the bill. Several rose to express their frustration with the amount of time they were allotted to raise questions about the measure. Representative Mazzoli, during the first evening of the debate on the bill, addressing the fact that the measure was taken up so late in the session and in that evening, said:

> I think that the gentleman was aware that the gentleman from Kentucky—in fact all of us—urged the leadership of the House, and we have for the last two weeks, to get our bill up. We have done almost everything from begging to shining shoes to get it up. (*Congressional Record,* 16 December 1982, H-10069, as cited in Peters and Vega 1986, 10)

Rep. E. Clay Shaw (R., Fla.), on the final day of the debates, assailed the leadership for how it scheduled debate:

> I think it shows and exemplifies the shabby way in which the leadership has treated this particular bill that should have been debated for hours on end. The committee

has been through its work for a long time. I quite agree that 1:30 in the morning is not the time to talk about something like this. The members should be listening to the arguments and thoroughly debating it. . . . The members have not been given the opportunity to do so. I am not the correct party nor of the correct seniority to make schedules around here. However, I would suggest that this does not happen again with such an important piece of legislation. (*Congressional Record,* 18 December 1982, H-10336, as cited in Peters and Vega 1986, 10)

In 1983, with the 98th Congress, Simpson and Mazzoli renewed their efforts at immigration reform by reintroducing versions of their bills identical to those passed in the Senate or by the House Judiciary Committee in 1982. Once again, proponents and opponents organized their respective sides of the issue. Agricultural interests, headed by the Farm Labor Alliance and advocated by Hamilton Fish, developed a proposal, the "transition program," designed to slowly adjust to a foreign workers program.[6] Rep. Edward Roybal (D., Calif.), a leader of the Congressional Hispanic Caucus, proposed an alternative bill that focused on tougher enforcement of existing labor laws and minimum wage laws to clamp down on the hiring aspects of immigration, as a substitute for the employer-sanctions approach.

By spring, both the House and Senate Judiciary subcommittees on immigration had approved their respective versions of the legislation. Chairman Rodino, however, once again waited for the Senate to complete full action on the Simpson version of the bill before holding mark-up sessions on the Mazzoli version. In the Senate, the Judiciary Committee reported the bill out over Senator Kennedy's objections. Senator Helms again unsuccessfully tried to delete the amnesty provision. Senator Bradley (D., N.J.) likewise failed to get a 100 percent reimbursement provision for state and local governments (Perotti 1989b, 159). The Senate passed its version by late April. Rodino scheduled the House version in the first week in May. The full Senate approved the Simpson version by mid-May.

The Senate-approved version, moreover, did make some important concessions to growers; with the tacit approval of Senators Simpson and Kennedy, Senators De Concini (D., Ariz.) and Pete Wilson (R., Calif.) worked out a three-year transition program for agriculture. A provision ending warrantless searches in open farm fields was adopted, over Simpson's objections, by a vote of 63 to 33. Senators Simpson and Kennedy worked out a compromise regarding liberal opposition to the asylum adjudication provision. It established a full judicial review of deportation, exclusion, and asylum cases in the Federal Court of Appeals (ibid., 160).

In the House, the Mazzoli bill once again moved sequentially through referrals to Education and Labor, Agriculture, Ways and Means, and Energy and Commerce. Representatives Mazzoli and Rodino, with the backing of the Reagan administration and the House Republican leadership, pressed for quick floor action. With the 1984 elections in the wings, they felt the timing of the bill's consideration by the full House was critical for its passage. Rep. Claude Pepper (D., Fla.), Chairman of the Rules Committee, agreed and tried but failed to achieve a compromise rule for the measure's floor consideration among the four committees that had sequential jurisdiction over the bill. Pepper abandoned the idea of a compromise when it became clear the differences were too great to be resolved short of a floor debate and votes on the issue (Peters and Vega 1986, 11).

The various issue factions again used the opportunities afforded by the various committee referrals through which the bill progressed. In the Judiciary Committee, for example, Rep. Tom Kindness (R., Ohio), moved an amendment backed by the U.S. Chamber of Commerce, that made it voluntary for employers to verify the employment status of their workers. In the Agriculture Committee, Western growers pushed for a separate 300,000-person temporary workers program, proposed through the Panetta–Morrison amendment. And in the Education and Labor and Judiciary committees, a coalition of Hispanic, civil liberties, and religious groups, through an alternative bill sponsored by Representative Roybal, sought to replace employer sanctions with stiffer wage and hour laws and worked on an array of amendments to liberalize the legalization program and include antidiscrimination provisions (Perotti 1989b, 160).

Speaker of the House O'Neill pulled the bill from the House floor consideration in October, again fearing splits in his party over the measure. Once again, the Hispanic Caucus, with Representative Roybal leading the opposition, convinced the Speaker of the political repercussions that might ensue if the bill were passed before the upcoming election. Roybal feared that the Reagan administration would veto the Simpson–Mazzoli bill, if it passed, in order to curry favor with the Hispanic vote. The press unleashed a barrage of criticism of the Speaker for placing short-term political partisanship over the national interest of immigration reform.[7]

The Reagan administration denied its intention to veto the bill, however, and called for the Speaker to allow floor consideration of the bill. Six weeks later, the Speaker announced he would let the measure come to the floor in the following session.

Thus, in April, the House Rules Committee held hearings on the bill and reported it out with a modified open rule, allowing 69 amendments to be considered. The Rules Committee categorized these amendments into the specific sections of the bill and allotted each specific times, threatening to impose a new rule if the measure was being used to filibuster. Consideration of the bill was delayed until after the June 5 California primary, and on June 11 the House finally took up the measure. It debated the bill intensely for seven days, finally passing the bill on June 20 by a slim five-vote margin of 216 to 211.

Although most of the amendments were defeated, they showed how close the division was over the measure. Conservatives generally opposed the legalization program. Liberals opposed the employer-sanctions approach. Heavy opposition to the measure came from the Texas and California delegations. Even majority leader Jim Wright (D., Tex.), who for years had been relatively cool on the bill, offered and had accepted an amendment concerning the amnesty provisions of the measure. It provided for a two-year period of legal residence for immigrants, after which they could apply to become permanent residents, but to qualify they had to be employable, to try to learn English, and to enroll any children they had in school. The Wright amendment, passed by a vote of 247 to 170, also elicited grave concern among Hispanic groups.

The House version of the bill, responding to pressure from growers of perishable crops (i.e., the Farm Labor Alliance), allowed for a vastly expanded temporary worker program reminiscent of the Bracero program. This was known as the Panetta–Morrison program. Its House sponsor, Rep. Leon Panetta (D., Calif.), argued that the imported workers program would not allow their exploitation because of its provision that their wage and working conditions could not "adversely affect" those of domestic workers and because those temporary workers, once here, were free to leave the growers who brought them in. Critics argued, however, that as the growers were able to import workers by name, they could quickly "blacklist" from future jobs anyone considered to be a troublemaker.

Such critics also noted that although the amendment contained requirements for active recruitment of domestic workers to prevent displacement, growers had routinely been able to evade such requirements under the much smaller current H-2 program, and would be able to continue to do so under the new law. The vastly larger size of the new program, moreover, which was estimated by the Agriculture Committee to include as many as half a million workers annually, would greatly increase the already difficult job of enforcing those labor standards that applied to the guest workers (LeMay 1987, 141).

Finally, the House version was amended by an overwhelming vote to include Rep. Barney Frank's (D., Mass.) strong antidiscrimination provision that created a special counsel in the Department of Justice to handle charges of employment discrimination based on alienage (Perotti 1989b, 163).

Hispanics succeeded in influencing the bill despite their failure to delete the employer-sanctions provision. They improved the legalization program, when, with the help of Rodino and Rep. Bill Richardson (D., N.M.), they got the cut off date advanced to January 1, 1982, by a vote of 247 to 170. Restrictionists showed their influence with the Wright amendment, and with a narrowly failed effort by Rep. Bill McCollum (R., Fla.) to kill the legalization program by a vote of 233 to 195. The business faction, which opposed the bill, lost on the floor. The Kindness amendment for a voluntary verification process was replaced by a provision to set up a telephone verification system enabling employers to validate the Social Security numbers of people applying for jobs. Rep. Sam Hall, Jr. (D., Tex.), an ardent restrictionist close to the Federation for American Immigration Reform, proposed the system. It passed by a vote of 242 to 155 (ibid., 164–165).

> The final vote on the bill in 1984 was like a suspense novel, as its fate teetered back and forth during the final 15-minute roll call. "No" votes outnumbered the "yes" until just a few seconds before the end, when the tally tied at 210 and Congressional arm-twisting on the floor obtained the few more votes that led to victory. Both Democrats and Republicans were divided in their support (Democrats 138 to 125 and Republicans 91 to 73). (ibid., 165)

With passage—though in different versions—by both chambers of Congress, the only procedural obstacle to enactment of the measure was the House-Senate Conference Committee. These deliberations would take place within the heated political context of the Presidential race. Actions at the 1984 Presidential nominating conventions did not auger well for the conference committee's work. At the Democratic convention, Hispanic delegates threatened to boycott the first ballot, and in response to that pressure, nominees Walter Mondale and Geraldine Ferraro publicly opposed the immigration reform bill. At the Republican convention, the administration's position was less clear. Vice Presidential nominee George Bush, in a speech to the National Council of La Raza, said that the President would not tolerate a bill that discriminated against Hispanics. Senator Simpson also announced that President Reagan, in a telephone conversation of July 29, had said that he would sign a conference committee version of the bill as long as it contained a Senate restriction on reimbursement to the states for legalization costs. Yet later, Attorney General William French Smith raised public objections to the Frank antidiscrimination provision (Perotti 1989a, 7).

The close vote margin of the 1984 vote encouraged the opposition factions to attempt first to block the creation of the conference committee, and when that failed, to work at deadlocking the conference committee when it did meet. As Professor Perotti describes it:

> Strange bedfellows emerged, as opponents of the bill embarked on a campaign of guerrilla tactics. The Chamber of Commerce, Hispanic groups, the ACLU, and the construction workers union—acting in coalition—sent an unprecedented telegram to all members of Congress urging the defeat of the bill. The coalition even worked with restrictionist opponents of legalization in letter-writing, phone calling and news-planting campaigns to kill the bill. (Perotti 1989b, 166)

Speaker O'Neill, in deference to Judiciary Chairman Rodino, delayed in naming the conferees. The conference committee finally met (twelve weeks after the vote) between September 13 and October 4, 1984. The conference moved quickly to resolve differences in the amnesty and employer-sanctions provisions. A near impasse over the House's antidiscrimination provision threatened breakdown of the conference committee's work in late September. This near impasse was resolved, however, through the efforts of Representative Frank, sponsor of the House provision and member of Mazzoli's judiciary subcommittee. But the conferees failed to reach a compromise over the $1-billion ceiling for reimbursing the states' expenses in implementing the legalization program of the measure. Despite last-ditch efforts by Mazzoli, Simpson, and Frank, the conference committee was unable to resolve the issue, and the 98th Congress adjourned with the conference committee dissolved and the measure once again lost (Peters and Vega 1986, 12; Perotti 1989a, 7; LeMay 1987, 142).

Although the conference committee's failure to achieve a compromise in 1984 delayed passage of the bill, it nonetheless laid an important base for the future. The compromises achieved on the Frank antidiscrimination provision became part of that base. Moreover, the principal players had by then become resigned to the fact that some type of guest-worker program would have to be included in order to secure passage of an immigration reform law. A new player, Rep. Charles Schumer (D., N.Y.) began discussions among immigration subcommittee members to try to bridge the gap between farm labor advocates and growers over a guest-worker provision. During six days of intense "shuttle diplomacy," working closely with Simpson, Mazzoli, and Frank, he announced a compromise on October 5. Workers would be able to file charges of employment discrimination with the special counsel only if they alleged a knowing and intentional discriminatory act or a pattern or practice of discrimination. And such charges would be valid only if the worker signed a statement that he intended to become a citizen. Schumer also tried, but failed, to secure a compromise on the hotly debated cap on federal support for state and local government costs incurred through the legalization program. His compromise failed by a 15 to 13 vote.

While the bill finally "failed" in conference committee over the state and local funding issue, the key negative votes on that compromise were members of the California delegation who opposed the compromise for the temporary workers program devised by Panetta, Morrison, and Simpson. They apparently had responded to pressures by growers and California Gov. George Deukmejian to block any bill not containing an adequate guest-worker program (Perotti 1989b, 168–169).

In May 1985, Senator Simpson introduced a new version of his bill, this time without the cosponsorship of Representative Mazzoli, who declined to sponsor the bill without the support of the Democratic House leadership and from the black and Hispanic Congressional Caucuses, who strenuously opposed it.

Simpson's 1985 version had some details changed from earlier bills, although the centerpiece remained the imposition of employer sanctions—

including fines up to $10,000 per violation—against employers who knowingly hired illegal immigrants, and the eventual amnesty of those illegal aliens who had arrived prior to January 1, 1980 and had been living in the United States continuously since then. It still required no responsibility of employers to authenticate the documents shown by potential employees. His new bill again called for the development of a "tamper-proof" Social Security card, and stiffer penalties (up to two years in prison) for ID counterfeiters and traffickers. His 1985 version weakened the "amnesty" provision: In the 1984 bill, amnesty was to start automatically ninety days after the bill's enactment into law, but the 1985 proposal had the legalization program only take effect after a Presidential commission had certified that the new law had resulted in a "substantial" reduction in illegal immigration, estimating that such an effect would take place within a year's time. His 1985 version of the bill placed a $1.8-billion limit on federal reimbursement to states for services extended to those undocumented aliens who were processed through the program. Congressional critics maintained that figure was far too low. Senator Simpson's stated goal for the new bill was to produce a compromise that would finally pass Congress (*Time,* 8 July 1985; "Simpson Tackles Immigration Reform Again," *Minneapolis Star and Tribune,* 24 June 1985, A10).

Such a compromise was not yet forthcoming. Senator Kennedy introduced an amendment that granted amnesty at the same time as employer sanctions would take effect. It failed by a vote of 26 to 65. Similarly, Sen. Pete Wilson (D., Calif.) offered an amendment that would give growers of perishable crops a large, mobile, temporary work force of foreign workers to pick fruit and vegetables. That measure was first voted down 48 to 50 ("Immigration Legislation Voted Down," *Cumberland Times/News,* 14 September 1985, A1). Senator Wilson sponsored a new amendment to allow 350,000 guest workers into the country annually. Its passage, by a narrow margin, sealed the fate of the farm worker issue; any House bill was going to have to include a guest-worker program as the Senate had added its approval to the 1984 Panetta–Morrison program. The only question that remained was precisely what such a program would look like because none of the principal leaders in immigration reform—Simpson, Rodino, and Mazzoli—wanted such a program. The bill passed in the Senate on September 19, 1985, by a vote of 69 to 30, a slightly narrower margin than that in 1983 (76 to 18), and even more narrow than the 1982 vote (80 to 9) (Perotti 1989a, 7–8).

Meanwhile, in the House, Congressman Rodino introduced a bill cosponsored by Rep. Romano Mazzoli in July 1985, which was very similar to the compromise version that died in the final days of the 1984 conference committee. The Rodino–Mazzoli measure provided civil and criminal penalties for employers who knowingly hired illegal aliens and amnesty for undocumented aliens who had arrived before 1982. To discourage discrimination against Hispanics, it also created an Office of Special Counsel in the Justice

Department that was empowered to investigate and prosecute civil rights violators. Like the Simpson measure in the Senate, the Rodino–Mazzoli bill also strengthened the enforcement of immigration laws by increasing funding for the INS (LeMay 1987, 143).

As in previous years, the Hispanic groups and the American Civil Liberties Union opposed both the House and Senate versions of the measure. Working through the Hispanic Congressional Caucus and the Black Congressional Caucus, they opposed the employer-sanctions approach, arguing that it would inevitably increase discrimination against all Hispanics. They also opposed the guest-worker program, arguing such workers had historically been highly exploited.

By contrast, growers insisted on a guest-worker program, and generally opposed both versions of the bill as being too small on this issue. The House Judiciary Committee insisted that the amnesty provision had to be tied to any employer-sanctions provision. The White House strongly backed the Senate version, as it granted amnesty only after a presidential commission had been established and only when such employer sanctions were shown to have succeeded in reducing the number of illegal aliens entering the country. In 1985, the Senate Judiciary Committee rejected all attempts by the Senate Democrats to make the Senate version more like the House version.[8]

After the conference committee was unable to agree upon a compromise version of the bill, it seemed to be an issue on which the proposed bill was "a corpse going to the morgue." How the "corpse" was resurrected with the final key compromises to get the bill adopted and signed into law is the subject of the next chapter.

NOTES

1. Miller 1985. See also Peters and Vega 1986; Perotti 1989a; and Perotti 1989b, 78–95.

2. See Perotti 1989a, 5; Peters and Vega 1986, 7; and Miller 1985, 53–54.

3. Perotti 1989b, 90–91. See also *Congressional Quarterly Weekly Report,* 20 March 1976, 637.

4. U.S. President's SCIRP 1981b, 211.

5. Ibid., 214–215; Library of Congress, Congressional Research Service, *Review of the U.S. Refugee Resettlement Programs and Policies* (Washington, D.C.: U.S. Government Printing Office, July 1979), 42.

6. Oral interview with Congressional staff member. See also the discussion in Peters and Vega 1986, 11.

7. Peters and Vega 1986, 11. See also *Time,* 17 October 1983, 19; *New York Times,* 5 October 1983, A26, and 9 October 1983, Sec. 4, p. 19; *Christian Science Monitor,* 5 December 1983, 3–4; *Los Angeles Times,* 7 October 1983, Sec. 2, p. 7; and *Washington Post,* 13 October 1983, A23; and Perotti 1989b, 161.

8. See "Try to Stem the Illegal Tide," *Time,* 8 July 1985, Special Edition; "Immigration Legislation Voted Down," *Cumberland Times/News,* 14 September 1985,

A1; "Immigration Issue Heats Up Again," *Washington Post,* 28 July 1985, 8; "Illegal Immigration," *Cumberland Evening Times,* 22 July 1985, 8; "Simpson Tackles Immigration Reform Again," *Minneapolis Star and Tribune,* 24 June 1985, A10; and "Immigration Reform Elusive Goal," *Minneapolis Star and Tribune,* 24 June 1985, A10.

CHAPTER 3

Policy Adoption: The Passing of IRCA, 1986

CRITICAL COMPROMISES TO THE ENACTMENT OF IRCA IN 1986

When the conference committee failed to achieve a compromise version of the bill in 1984, it seemed to be an issue on which the bill was, indeed, a "corpse going to the morgue."[1] Senator Simpson reintroduced his bill, which the Senate passed for a third time in September 1985. The House once again left the bill open to tinkering by submitting its version of the bill to six committees to sequentially deal with the measure. In 1985, the Judiciary Committee again seemed to be deadlocked over the farm worker provision and did not finish its drafting of the measure until the end of June, and only then did the five other committees work on it throughout the summer. Late in September 1986, when the House rejected a rule for considering the bill HR-3810, immigration reform was again called a dead issue (*New York Times,* 13 October 1986, A16). A small group of legislators long committed to passage of immigration reform, however, refused to let it die. This chapter will hopefully explain how the bill came to be enacted.

It details first the final key compromises enabling passage in October 1986. It presents a summary of IRCA's key provisions that reflect those compromises. It examines the various voting blocs on the bill, hopefully clarifying why a seemingly "dead" issue was actually and finally passed in October 1986. It offers an interpretation of Congressional decision making, an "integrative bargaining model," that provides insight as to why such a compromise version finally passed. It closes with a section that discusses what the law indicates was the *policy strategy and intent* of Congress in enacting IRCA. That section will preview the basis for problems involved in the implementation of IRCA, the subject of the next chapter.

The September 1986 deadlock over the farm workers provision was broken by a compromise crafted by several members of the Judiciary Committee. Led by Rep. Charles Schumer (D., N.Y.), they put the pieces back together again.

Representative Schumer met with Representative Rodino, the committee chair, and Hamilton Fish, its ranking Republican. Schumer and Representatives Howard Berman (D., Calif.) and Panetta arranged the key compromise for the temporary farm worker provision. Extensive discussions with Representatives Dan Lungren (R., Calif.), the ranking Republican, and Romano Mazzoli, the chairman of the Judiciary, Immigration, Refugees and International Law Subcommittee, resulted in further fine tuning of the bill's provisions. After the House members agreed on the package of provisions, including numerous points designed to protect the rights of the temporary workers, they secured Senator Simpson's approval as well.

After a decade and a half of dealing with proposals to reform immigration policy, Congress was finally in a better mood and position to act than in any previous year. As the Mexican economy deteriorated late in 1985 and early 1986, and the peso plunged in value, the INS caught a record number of illegal aliens attempting to cross the border. Their apprehensions rose by 31 percent during the fiscal year—to a record high 1.8 million (see Figure 1.3). The growing conservative mood of the country seemed to convince liberal opponents of the bill that continued resistance would only lead to more restrictive legislation in 1987.

A key shift came when the Hispanic Caucus split on the bill, with five of its members supporting the bill and six opposing it. That split also enabled the Black Congressional Caucus to split on the bill: ten for and eight against. Table 3.1 details these key split votes.

Representative Schumer's negotiated compromise on the temporary farm workers provision also split the opposition to the bill among growers. His compromise served to meet the demands among Western fruit and vegetable growers for foreign workers, while allowing for sufficient protection of the workers against likely exploitation so as to win over enough of the Hispanic, liberal, or union votes in Congress for enactment. Representative Schumer described the new bill as slightly "left-of-center," in contrast to the "right-of-center" version killed by the House Democrats in 1984, when they opposed it by a margin of 138 to 125. In October 1986, Democrats supported it by a vote of 168 to 61. The House passed the new compromise version on October 10, 1986, by a vote of 230 for to 166 against, with 36 not voting (*Congressional Record—House,* Roll Call #457, H9800–9801). As Table 3.2 shows, though split, there was a statistically significant level of association between party affiliation and the IRCA vote. The Democrats more often supported IRCA for its amnesty provision whereas the Republicans very nearly split their vote. Those who favored it did so for its employer-sanctions approach.

This successful passage of the bill by the House of Representatives once again necessitated a conference committee to make adjustments between the

Table 3.1
House Roll Call Vote, October 10, 1986

Hispanic Caucus Members

Yes Vote	No Vote
Bustamente, D., Tex.	de la Garza, D., Tex.
Coelho, D., Calif.	Edwards, D., Calif.
Ortiz, D., Tex.	Garcia, D., N.Y.
Richardson, D., N.M.	Gonzalez, D., Tex.
Torres, D., Calif.	Martinez, D., Calif.
	Roybal, D., Calif.

Black Caucus Members

Clay, D., Mo.	Crockett, D., Mich.
Collins, D., Ill.	Dellums, D., Calif.
Dixon, D., Calif.	Dymally, D., Calif.
Ford, D., Tenn.	Hawkins, D., Calif.
Gray, D., Pa.	Hayes, D., Ill.
Mitchell, D., Md.	Leland, D., Tex.
Owens, D., N.Y.	Savage, D., Ill.
Rangel, D., N.Y.	Towns, D., N.Y.
Stokes, D., Ohio	Wheat, D., Mo.

Not Voting: Conyers, D., Mich., Fauntroy, D., D.C.

IRCA Vote by Black/Hispanic Caucuses, with affiliates

Caucus	Vote for IRCA	V. IRCA	Totals
Black	15 (43%)	14 (45%)	29
Hispanic	20 (57%)	17 (55%)	37
Totals	35 (100%)	31 (100%)	66

Chi Square = .005; .95 level of significance

Table 3.2
IRCA Vote, Total Congress, by Party Affiliation

Party	For IRCA	Against IRCA	NV	Totals
Democrats	196 (65%)	88 (45%)	17 (50%)	301
Republicans	105 (35%)	109 (55%)	17 (50%)	231
Totals	301 (100%)	197 (100%)	34 (100%)	532

Chi Square = 20.32; .001 level of significance

two differing versions. Six issues remained in significant conflict. They are summarized here:

1. The House version terminated employer penalties automatically after six and one-half years. The Senate version, and the Reagan administration, vigorously opposed that provision.
2. The House version contained an amendment, sponsored by Rep. Joseph Moakley (D., Mass.) that granted temporary legal status to Salvadorans and Nicaraguans who were here illegally while the Senate version, and the White House and State Department, strongly objected to the Moakley provision.
3. The House version had a provision, the Frank Amendment, that barred an employer from discriminating in hiring on the basis of citizenship and created a special counsel's office in the Justice Department to investigate such alleged discrimination. This provision was also opposed by both the Senate and the administration.
4. The two versions differed in the dates for starting the "legalization" program. The House version set the eligibility date at January 1, 1982. The Senate version granted amnesty to those aliens here prior to January 1, 1980.
5. The two versions differed in how the federal government would reimburse states for costs associated with the complex amnesty program. The House version provided for 100 percent federal reimbursement. The Senate version provided for $3 billion over six years after enactment.
6. The House version included a provision sponsored by Rep. Howard Berman (D., Calif.) that provided free legal services to farm workers entering the country under the H-2 temporary workers program. (LeMay 1987, 145)

Unlike the 1984 conference committee that deadlocked over differences between the two houses' versions of the bill, the 1986 conference committee agreed on a series of compromises to settle those six issues and were able to report back to their respective houses a conference report on a unified bill that was to become the Immigration Reform and Control Act of 1986.

The House members agreed to the Senate version without an automatic end to employer sanctions. In exchange for that compromise, the Senate members agreed to a three-year annual review of the program by the General Accounting Office at which time the program could be terminated by a joint resolution if the Comptroller General determined that the employer-sanctions program had resulted in widespread discrimination. The House also agreed to give up the Moakley provision on Salvadorans and Nicaraguans in return for a pledge by the administration not to deport any Salvadorans to areas stricken by an October earthquake. In addition, Chairman Rodino promised to consider a bill on the subject early in the 100th Congress, and Senator Simpson promised he would not prevent Senate consideration of such a bill if it passed the House. The Senate agreed to accept the Frank antidiscrimination provision and accepted a slightly modified form of the free legal representation for H-2 workers. Such legal work could only apply to job-related problems such as wages, hours, and working conditions.

The "state refunding" issue that was ostensibly the issue over which the 1984 conference committee deadlocked was resolved by another key compromise: It set up a $1-billion-per-year mandated appropriation for the next four years, with the unspent money in one year being available in the following year. Any unused money at the end of fiscal year 1990 could be carried over through fiscal year 1994 (making it essentially a seven-year program budgeted at $4 billion). This compromise version further provided that the amount of government payments for Social Security supplements and Medicaid be deducted from the $1-billion annual appropriation. Finally, the Senate accepted the House's version of the beginning date for the amnesty program, that of January 1, 1982 (ibid., 146).

In urging his colleagues to vote for the conference committee bill, its primary House sponsor, Representative Mazzoli, stated:

> Ladies and gentlemen of the House, your conferees kept faith with you and the votes you cast on this bill. It has generous legalization. You sent us to conference to keep it, and we kept it. It has tough antidiscrimination provisions. You sent us to conference to keep it, and we kept it. It has legal services for H-2 workers. You sent us to conference to keep it, and we kept it. It has universal application of employer sanctions. You sent us to conference to keep it, and we kept it. (*Congressional Record—House,* 15 October 1986, H-10586)

The bill's tangled history helped make these compromises possible in 1986. More will be detailed later about how and why Congressional voting blocs split, but clearly the increased concern with the immigration problem reached such an apparent crisis proportion by late 1986 that nearly everyone involved desperately wanted some sort of bill to pass. Previous fights meant there was less need for continued political posturing this time around. There was no longer an immediately looming Presidential election to complicate such compromise moves by the legislators representing the interests of the various factions. The conferees "didn't want to do this again" (*Congressional Quarterly Weekly Report,* 18 October 1986, 2596). In the words of Representative Mazzoli, who urged its passage, "It's not a perfect bill, but it's the least imperfect bill we will ever have before us" (*Washington Post,* 16 October 1986, A5; LeMay 1987, 146).

The House passed the measure by 238 to 173 on October 15, 1986. The Senate approved it 63 to 24 on October 17, 1986 (see roll call votes in Appendix B). The President signed it into law on November 6, 1986. The following is a summary of the law:

Employer Sanctions

- Made it unlawful for anyone to knowingly hire, recruit, or refer for a fee any alien not authorized to work in the United States.

- Required employers to verify all newly hired people by examining various documents.
- Permitted the President to implement a more secure verification system upon notice and approval of Congress.
- Established civil and criminal penalties for hiring illegal aliens after a six-month education period. During the subsequent 12-month period, a violator would be given a warning citation for the first offense.
- Established fines after the citation period ranging from not less than $250 for first offense to not more than $10,000 per illegal alien for the third offense.
- Authorized criminal penalties of up to six months' imprisonment and/or a $3,000 fine for a "pattern of practice" of knowingly hiring an illegal alien.
- Required employers, recruiters, and those who refer for employment to keep records, and set civil fines from $100 to $1,000 for failure to do so.
- Terminated sanctions after three years if the Comptroller General determined that sanctions resulted in discrimination in employment or had unduly burdened employers, and Congress enacted a joint resolution adopting that determination. Expedited procedures for Congress to consider a joint resolution terminating sanctions.

Antidiscrimination Measures

- Created an Office of Special Counsel in the Justice Department to investigate and prosecute discrimination from unlawful immigration-related employment practices.
- Barred employers from discriminating against legal residents simply because they were not full-fledged citizens.
- Authorized an administrative law judge to order a violator to hire the aggrieved person, to award limited back pay, and to pay a penalty of $1,000 for each individual discriminated against.
- Terminated the antidiscrimination provisions if the employer sanctions are lifted.

Increased Enforcement and Service

- Provided a two-year authorization for the INS providing an additional $422 million in FY 1987 and $419 million in FY 1988. It also authorized $12 million in FY 1987 and $15 million in FY 1988 for the Executive Office of Immigration Review to carry out added duties for the INS imposed by the bill.
- Beefed up penalties for smuggliing aliens into the country.
- Authorized a contingency fund of $35 million for use in immigration emergencies such as the 1980 boat-lift from Cuba.

Legalization

- Provided temporary resident status for aliens who resided continuously in the United States since before January 1, 1982, and who cannot be excluded for reasons specified in the immigration law.
- Allowed these temporary residents to become permanent residents after 18 months if they can show minimal understanding of English and history and government of the United States or are pursuing a course of instruction to gain such knowledge.

- Provided permanent resident status for specified Cuban and Haitian refugees who entered the country before January 1, 1982.
- Appropriated $1 billion in each of four fiscal years after enactment to reimburse states for public assistance, health and education costs resulting from legalizing aliens. Unspent money from one year would carry over to the next year.
- Reimbursed states for costs of incarceration of certain aliens.

H-2 Workers

- Revised and expanded the existing temporary foreign workers program.
- Required the labor secretary to decide on the requests for labor no later than 20 days in advance of an employer's need.
- Provided an expedited procedure for getting workers if the labor secretary determined that available U.S. workers were found by the employer not to be qualified.

Special Seasonal Agricultural Workers

- Provided temporary resident status for up to 350,000 aliens who could prove that they lived in the country for a least three years and who could prove they had worked at least 90 days in American agriculture in each of those three years. They could adjust to permanent resident status after an additional year or within three years of enactment, whichever was later.
- Provided for "replenishment" farm labor to replace those who left agriculture and allowed these new workers to enter the United States as temporary residents. They would have to work at least 90 days in agriculture for three years, after which they could apply for permanent resident status. They would be barred from receiving most public aid.

Miscellaneous

- Increased the legal immigration ceilings from colonies from 600 to 5,000. This provision is designed to help immigrants from Hong Kong.
- Authorized the Attorney General and the Secretary of State to establish a three-year pilot program for up to eight countries allowing tourists from these countries to enter the United States without first obtaining a visa.
- Required the expeditious deportation of convicted illegal aliens and required the government to list facilities available to incarcerate those aliens who were going to be deported.

Reports

- Required the President to submit several reports to Congress, including three studies on legal immigration, the program for granting visas. Among the other reports: one on the factors that cause illegal immigration, two on the legalization program, and two on employer sanctions.
- Required the administration to submit reports on the H-2 program every two years. (Abstracted from the *Congressional Quarterly Weekly Report,* 18 October 1986, 2597–2598)

SPLIT CONGRESSIONAL VOTING BLOCS

The House vote on October 15 saw the Black and Hispanic Caucus members split once again as they had on October 10 (Table 3.1). Indeed, these final key compromises split the votes of various blocs in Congress over this highly controversial issue. As mentioned above, the immigration issue cut across several such blocs upon which the voting hinged. With respect to *political party affiliation,* after the conference committee compromises, House Democrats split 162 for to 80 against, with 11 not voting; the Republicans split 76 for to 93 against, with 10 not voting (for details, see Appendix B). In the Senate, the party split was 34 Democrats for passage to 8 against, with 6 not voting. Senate Republicans split their votes 29 in favor to 16 against, with 7 abstaining.

When one looks at the Black Congressional Caucus in its broadest terms (i.e., including those who list themselves as "associate" members), it split 15 for to 14 against. The Hispanic Caucus, including those who describe themselves as "associate" members, split 20 for to 17 against.

The Hispanic Caucus members who continued to oppose the bill did so convinced that although the bill had some commendable provisions—such as the legalization program, the Frank antidiscrimination provisions, and the much-needed increase in resources for the INS—the linchpin of the bill remained the employer-sanctions provision that they held to be a totally failed concept proven ineffective whenever and wherever tried, both in the United States and abroad. They also strongly opposed the Seasonal Agricultural Workers (SAW) provision, which they characterized as economic exploitation that reinvents indentured servitude. All felt that, despite the Frank antidiscrimination amendment, the law would still lead to more discrimination, particularly against Hispanics (see, for example, their respective comments in the *Congressional Record—House,* 15 October 1986, by Representatives Edwards, at H-10587; Gonzalez, at H-10589; Roybal, at H-10589–19590; Garcia, at H-10591; and Martinez, at H-10594–10595).[2]

The members of the Hispanic Caucus who left their previous position of opposition and voted for the bill did so reluctantly, but feeling this bill was the best compromise obtainable. As stated by Rep. Albert Bustamante, "I will support this imperfect bill because I am committed to do something about immigration policy" (*Congressional Record—House,* 15 October 1986, H-10596). These representatives felt pressures from their own districts—even from Hispanics there—to do something about the flow of illegal aliens that had a continued negative impact on migrant workers who were here legally. They also felt the continued influx was contributing to a tremendous amount of anti-Hispanic sentiment in the country, and that IRCA was the bill attainable to respond to that pressure. They were more hopeful than their colleagues who continued to oppose the bill that the Frank antidiscrimination provision would work well enough to live with the law. They felt it dealt enough with the various concerns raised by civil rights groups and by the Hispanic Caucus members. They felt that it was essential that the millions of illegal aliens already here be dealt with and therefore the legalization program was needed to ensure that it be an orderly process.

They felt that the increased enhancement of the Border Patrol would enable it to concentrate more fully on border enforcement, which they favored. Finally, they accepted the State Legalization Impact Assistance Grant (SLIAG) compromise as an adequate provision to ensure the appropriation of money to refund state and local governments for the costs incurred by the amnesty program (staff interviews; see also Tomasi 1989, 1–5; Vega 1985, 9).

Can we account for why some Hispanic Caucus members voted for IRCA, while others continued to oppose it? Two characteristics associated with the individual representative and two others associated with their respective districts do associate with the way they voted on IRCA to a statistically significant degree. The degree of the individual Congressman's "liberalism," as shown in Table 3.3, associates with their IRCA vote. Whether or not the representative had been recently elected or had served for many years is also associated with the IRCA vote. The liberalism index is comprised of scores on six indicators: the member's ADA score, ACLU score, COPE score, and *National Journal* liberalism scores on economic issues, social issues, and foreign policy issues. Hispanic Caucus members who scored above an 80 as their average for the six scores opposed IRCA. Those who scored less than 80 on those six indicators tended to vote for IRCA. Hispanic Caucus mem-

Table 3.3
Congressional Hispanic Caucus Votes on IRCA, by Liberalism and Tenure

	Above 80	Less than 80	Total
Hispanic Caucus Member Voted for IRCA	1 (17%)	4 (80%)	5
Hispanic Caucus Member Voted against IRCA	5 (83%)	1 (20%)	6
Total	6 (100%)	5 (100%)	11

	Elected 1978 or Before	Elected After 1978	
Voted for IRCA	1 (17%)	4 (80%)	5
Voted against IRCA	5 (83%)	1 (20%)	6
Total	6 (100%)	5 (100%)	11

Chi Square = 4.27; df = 1; .05 level of significance

bers who were elected prior to 1978 opposed IRCA; those elected after 1978 supported it. These data are presented in Table 3.3.

Likewise, Hispanic Caucus members from districts which voted for President Reagan voted for IRCA; those from districts which had voted for Mondale for President tended to oppose IRCA. And Hispanic Caucus members elected from districts with less than 60 percent minority populations (total of Hispanic, Black, Asian, and American Indian) tended to support IRCA, while those from districts with more than 60 percent minority populations all opposed IRCA. These data are shown in Table 3.4. (For the full data on these factors, see Appendix C.)

Another potentially relevant caucus, the Border Caucus, reflected a similar split: 9 for to 6 against. Likewise, the issue split the leadership in Congress as well. When one defines the leadership as those identified as Majority and Minority Leaders, Whips, Whips-at-Large, and Whips/Zone, the split was less even, but still a sizable one at 67 for to 26 against.

Even state delegations were rather dramatically split over the issue. There were six key states (i.e., those with the largest number of illegal aliens) which

Table 3.4
Hispanic Caucus Members Vote on IRCA, by District Characteristics

	District Voted For Reagan	For Mondale	Total
Voted for IRCA	5 (71%)	0 (0%)	5
Voted against IRCA	2 (29%)	4 (100%)	6
Total	7 (100%)	4 (100%)	11

	District 60% or More Minority	District Less than 60% Minority	Total
Voted for IRCA	0 (0%)	5 (71%)	5
Voted against IRCA	4 (100%)	2 (29%)	6
Total	4 (100%)	7 (100%)	11

Chi Square = 5.25; df = 1; .05 level of significance

would be affected by the legalization program: Arizona, California, Florida, Illinois, New York, and Texas. As we shall see more fully, collectively, these states accounted for roughly 90 percent of the legalizing aliens. The following details how those key state delegations split their votes on the passage of IRCA:

Arizona (5 votes total): 1 vote for, 3 against, 1 not voting. 1 Democrat for, 3 Republicans against, 1 Republican not voting.

California (45 votes total): 31 votes for, 13 against, 1 not voting. Democrats totaled 27, with 18 for, 9 against. Republicans had 18 votes, 13 for, 4 against, 1 not voting.

Florida (18 votes total): 13 for, 5 against. Democrats had 12 votes in all, 11 for and 1 against. Republicans had 6 votes, split 2 for and 4 against.

Illinois (22 votes total): 11 votes for, 9 against, with 2 not voting. Democrats had 13 in all, split 9 in favor and 4 against; and Republicans had 9 who voted, 2 in favor, 5 against, with 2 not voting.

New York (34 votes total): 19 votes for, 13 against, with 2 not voting. Democrats split their 19 vote total as 12 in favor, 5 opposed, with 2 not voting. Republicans split their 15 total as 7 in favor and 8 opposed.

Texas (27 votes total): 6 voted for the law, 20 opposed it, and 1 did not vote. Democrats split their 17 votes as 6 in favor, 10 opposed, with 1 not voting. The 10 Republicans all opposed the law.

EXPLAINING ENACTMENT: CONFLICTUAL VERSUS INTEGRATIVE BARGAINING

When Senator Simpson left the conference committee to announce the successful results of its work, he stated, "Everyone of us gave up something as painful as hell . . . but we stayed at the table" (cited in Perotti 1989b, 2). And indeed, those deliberations represented the culmination of the bill's long and tangled history of negotiations during which the various Congressional labor activists and those others favoring restictions had compromised their crusade for tight restrictions, settling finally for a legalization program for illegal aliens and for a program for foreign farm workers. In turn, Hispanic legislators, who had bitterly opposed the restrictionist employer-sanctions approach, agreed in the end to accept that approach in exchange for a generous amnesty program and stronger antidiscrimination provisions. Then too, the Western growers dropped their opposition to sanctions in order to get a seasonal worker program. These key compromises—legalization, antidiscrimination provisions, and the SAW program—had all been developed with the input of the legislators seated around that conference table in October 1986. Understanding why these key compromises had been made can be usefully aided by a perspective of the public policy conflict resolution process known as "cooperative resolution."[3]

Most often the resolution of conflict in the policy process is viewed and described as *competition.* In this traditional perspective of the policy process, the various opposing factions are seen as having conflicting interests. The major actors (lobbyists for opposing faction groups, their legislative supporters, vested bureaucratic actors, and the like) are viewed as acting interdependently, but seeking to maximize their relative gains. They become involved in competitive bargaining and in intrafaction bargaining in what is essentially seen as a zero-sum game where one faction's gains or losses are directly related to the losses or gains of another competing faction. Groups are viewed as competing over the fixed payoffs in a dispute (Perotti 1989b, 10). Policy is described as the result of the coalition of sides for or against specific policy proposals. In this view, according to traditional group theorists, "Public policy at any given point is the equilibrium reached in the group struggle" (see Dye 1992, 27). Graphically, this view of policy conflict is seen as shown in Figure 3.1.

But conflict in the public policy process can also be resolved through cooperation, that is, by constructive or mutually beneficial resolution rather than by a win-loss solution or simply splitting the differences between opposing factions. Such resolution to conflict may be achieved when two conditions are met enabling the factions to cooperate in public policy conflict:

Figure 3.1
A Traditional Group Conflict View of Policy as Equilibrium

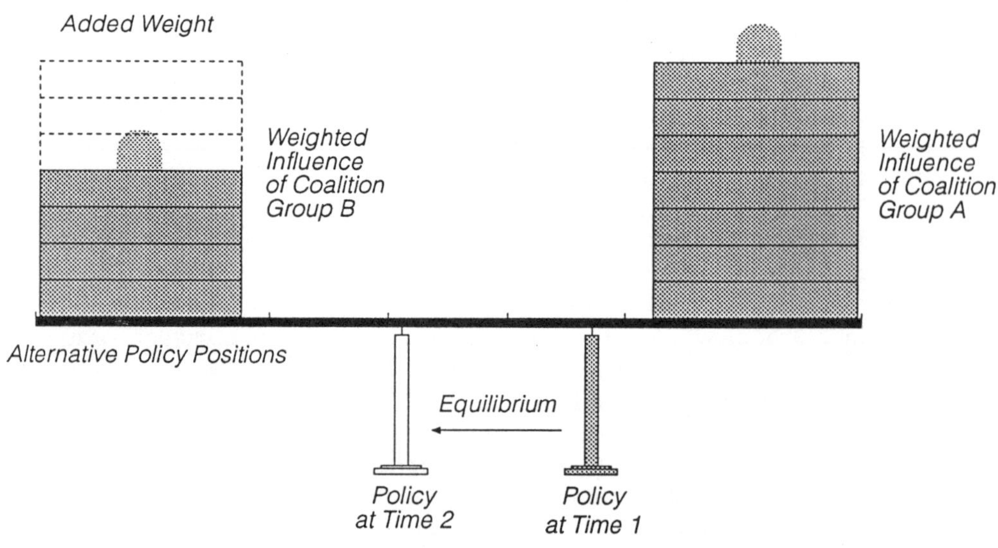

Source: Adapted from Thomas Dye, *Understanding Public Policy,* 7th ed. (Englewood Cliffs, N.J.: Prentice Hall, 1992), p. 27.

(1) the factions engaged in the policy debate must be interdependent, that is, where each faction can affect the prospects for policy change; and (2) the factions must be involved in mixed-motive, or nonzero-sum conflict, that is, they must have both complementary and conflicting interests (Quirk 1989, 905–906).

For instance, if the opposing factions in a dispute differ in the importance they attach to the various issues in the dispute, they can achieve joint gains by exchanging concessions accordingly. IRCA exemplifies such a case. The combination of the employer-sanctions provision, the amnesty provision, and the seasonal agricultural workers provision allowed an exchange among business, labor, and Hispanic and ethnic groups comprising the factions involved in the immigration policy issue (ibid., 906).

Instead of viewing policy as the equilibrium point achieving a simple balance between opposing groups, as in Figure 3.1, we might see policy as the resulting vector of change in the direction of an ongoing policy that is the *sum* of the contributions or influences of the involved policy factions. Imagine a change in policy at any given time as a billiard ball being struck simultaneously as it rolls along by several other balls. It will move in a direction that is the sum of the forces of all the balls that hit it. Figure 3.2 labels the various interest-group balls as those groups involved in the factions that achieved the changes in immigration policy resulting in IRCA.

Unless acted upon, a policy will continue to follow the path of previous policy. In this case, a policy change (IRCA) moves in the direction of the sum of all the forces cooperatively or sequentially striking it, as shown in Figure 3.2. The new policy is more restrictionist than prior policy, but it moves less so in that direction (the vector representing IRCA) than would have been the case had the policy conflict been won by the restrictionist side. The force of the legalization side kept the vector closer to a more open immigration policy.

The competitive perspective sees policy as involving disputes in which the actors either have no complementary interests or are unwilling or unable to act upon them. They follow a strategy that Quirk labels "conflictual strategy." Each side in the dispute seeks distributive gains or avoidance of distributive loss through defeat of the opposing side. Each faction uses competitive tactics, such as making high demands, withholding information about its positions, manipulating other negotiators' perceptions of their preferences, and the like. The final outcome of such a policy process is often a stalemate, a win-loss situation, or a compromise along only one dimension. In the latter case, one faction is able to impose its policy preferences on the other side.

When several factions are involved, some win and some lose on the issue. This type of policy conflict is exemplified by such policy concerns as the abortion debate or the debate over the Equal Rights Amendment. The very nature of such an issue, or the inability of the competing groups to see any common ground, leads them to forego negotiation and compromise and in-

Figure 3.2
A Cooperative Resolution View of Policy Conflict: The IRCA Case

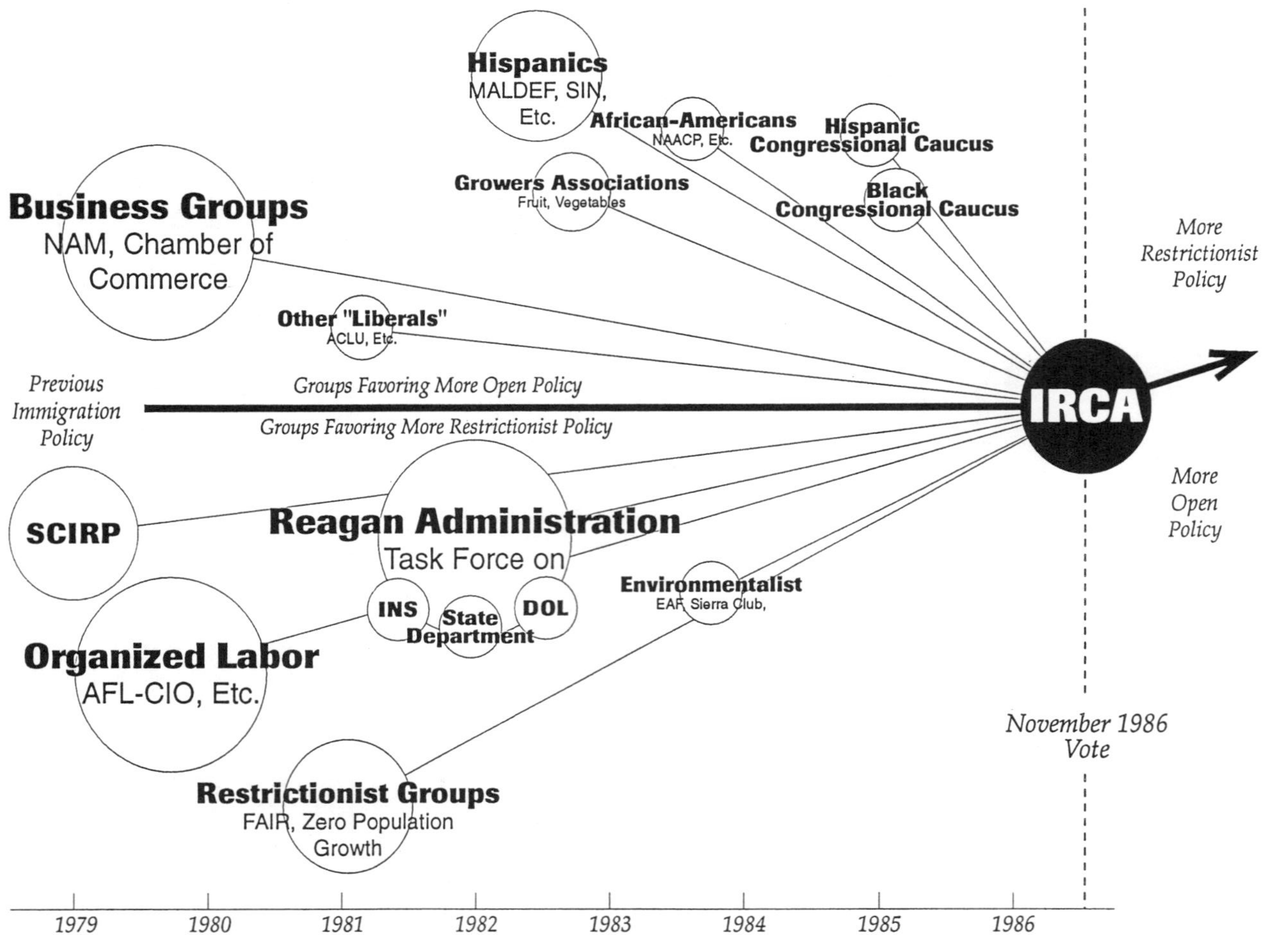

spires them to adopt and pursue a confrontational approach. Resolution of such conflict, if it is achieved at all, typically comes about by forging a minimum winning coalition, or a competitive coalition, and taking a vote in the hopes of having a majority (Perotti 1989b, 394–395).

The alternative policy view proposed here, and one that more accurately depicts what happened in the IRCA case, entails cooperation. This occurs in public policy disputes when the sides have complementary interests and adopt a strategy seeking joint gains or the avoidance of joint losses. They employ tactics that involve increasing joint gains. Involved parties exchange information about their respective interests. Mediators use integrative methods to find common ground. As long as the other faction reciprocates, involved factions moderate demands and consider significant concessions (ibid., 395).

The final outcome of this process, if the actors are able to stay at the negotiating table long enough to achieve one, is one of a set of integrative solutions. They are resolved through face-to-face deliberations and discussions that attempt to forge a consensus. Thus, the solution achieved means more than a win-loss one arrived at through a majoritarian winner-take-all principle, although there are typically distributive aspects to any solution. Resolving policy conflict through cooperation means developing acceptable proposals that *improve* the situation of both or all major factions vis-à-vis competing. Thus, such resolution is more than simply molding a winning coalition necessitated by the legislative decision-making process. Rather, it is a coalition of factions wherein all the factions perceive they have won a little yet lost less in a dispute. Such was the case in reaching the enactment of IRCA (ibid., 396).

It is among the types of cases that one might call—in Quirk's words—negotiable disputes. The basic conditions for cooperation existed in this dispute. There were complementary interests, although initially they were not readily apparent to the involved factions. Clearly, the factions were interdependent. Early on in the dispute it became clear that labor's desire for employer sanctions had significant implications for growers, and of course, the growers' need for a cheap and flexible labor force had significant implications for labor. As the conflict developed, other interdependent factions emerged. The need of Hispanic and black minority groups for protection against discrimination had a significant impact on the restrictionists' desire to limit the number of aliens in the United States. The underlying conditions to the dispute meant there was the possibility that it could be resolved cooperatively.

During the 1970s, the various factions used competitive tactics. They began moving toward cooperation in the very late 1970s and early 1980s with the work of the Select Commission on Immigration and Refugee Policy (SCIRP). As they moved quite tentatively toward negotiation, each of the involved groups saw some opportunity for joint gain. The adding of the legalization program, an increase in the H-2 program, and antidiscrimination measures were included as tentative steps toward a comprehensive agreement on immigration reform.

Another reason for staying at the negotiating table was that the consequences of not doing so seemed more costly than did those of participating in an agreement. Proponents of immigration reform knew they could not win alone. Some of the opponents joined them because they feared an eventual loss that would be even worse. After the SCIRP report, it seemed to many that some Congressional enactment of employer santions would emerge. Not being a part of the process meant accepting a distributive loss once the other parties had reached an agreement.

Once the various factions decided to negotiate, they bickered over the details of an agreement. During the mid-1980s, they sought to define a formula acceptable to all, then detailed refinements to the basic formula. They used integrative tactics to shed light on common interests to achieve the formula and to refine its details. Key actors served as mediators who acted as the crucial force maintaining a cooperative posture among the involved groups (e.g., Fuchs and the SCIRP; Senator Simpson; and Representatives Mazzoli, Rodino, Frank, Schumer, Panetta, Morrison, Wilson, and others [see Perotti 1989b, 397–399]). They forged key integrative agreements:

1. **Compensation.** The amnesty and antidiscrimination provisions shared the characteristic of being nonspecific compensation. Both of these provisions entailed joint gains, as both offered Hispanics some benefit in return for accepting the hardship of employer sanctions. Labor and the environmentalists, meanwhile, had little to lose by granting these compensating provisions. Though they helped promote an integrative solution, the danger of compensation is that the solution will not yield the highest joint gains, because such proposals are normally suggested by the compensator rather than the compensated.
2. **Logrolling.** The various temporary worker provisions offered over the tangled history of the bill's progression through Congress exemplified logrolling solutions. Demanded specifically by the growers' faction, these provisions would have lowered the gains of both the advocates of restrictionism (labor and the environmentalists, both of whom opposed bringing in foreign farm workers), and the growers themselves (who thus would have to accept some regulation with that program instead of the open labor market they enjoyed and were accustomed to from the undocumented alien influx).

   Logrolling occurs when the various factions make particularly coherent or specific demands. It wasn't until the Western growers had split from the East and developed clear ideas about how many workers they needed and during what seasons, for example, that they were able to put forth specific logrolling solutions. Also, they had to be less dependent than other groups among the bargaining opponents, the advocates of sanctions. They had to be well organized around these specific demands, in short, by demonstrating their "veto power" role. Only in this way were they able to craft a specific logrolling solution.

3. **Bridging.** The final type of integrative agreement was a bridging solution—exemplified in the IRCA case by such proposals and provisions as the SCIRP recommendations, the Hawkins (and later the Frank) antidiscrimination amendments, and the SAW program. All three of these "solutions" were crafted over a long period of integrative bargaining involving numerous "mediators." All three reoriented the positions of the parties in ways that addressed their core interests. The antidiscrimination amendment saw the underlying interests of labor and Hispanics and restrictionists. The antidiscrimination amendment was a trade—a new procedure (a special prosecutor to investigate charges of illegal hiring) replaced the old proposal that simply mandated criminal penalties for illegal hiring. It also included a new procedure for discrimination grievances (the special prosecutor for alien age discrimination) in place of the older proposal that simply focused on national origin discrimination.

The SCIRP report recommendations also exemplified a new trade—a loosening of legal immigration in exchange for tightening of the law to cope with illegal immigration. This was intended to address the interests of restrictionists and of liberals in a new way: Restrictionists got employer sanctions and liberals were offered greater opportunities for legal immigration. The SAW provision bridged the interests of growers and farm workers by offering them a new position to address their underlying interests. A farm worker legalization program replaced an earlier proposal for a guest-worker program. Some of the SCIRP recommendations were accepted. The Hawkins amendment was not; the SAW was after much effort on the part of Representative Schumer and other negotiators.

Thus, the IRCA case illustrates that when a public policy dispute exhibits the essential preconditions for cooperation—interdependence and mixed-motive conflict—then many potential solutions are possible to resolve the underlying interests of the involved factions. In the IRCA policy dispute, three of the four main provisions of the act—the legalization program, the antidiscrimination provision, and the SAW program—had not been anticipated prior to their being discussed and developed with Congressional staff in the mid-1970s.

Studies of Congressional decision making have stressed the importance of one approach to policy resolution—that of logrolling. Even then, logrolling is perceived only as an aspect of the competitive coalition-building process. However, legislative policy making, as we have seen in this IRCA case, may be usefully viewed as a forum for exchanging information necessary to devise a variety of solutions. These are achieved when the leadership of each faction—serving as negotiators and mediators—moderate their demands and accept an agreement. Such a process took place during the IRCA legislative struggle over more than a decade.

Major segments of each of the involved factions—labor, business, the growers, black and Hispanic groups—made the deliberate choice to negotiate. Labor showed its tacit acceptance of an amnesty program by the mid-

1970s, thus indicating it was prepared to negotiate. Labor continued to make alliances among the opponents of employer sanctions, even accepting the SAW program, through to the passage of IRCA in 1986. By 1983, business negotiated with the House subcommittee on voluntary verification. Growers negotiated by 1982 when they worked with Senator Simpson to devise alterations to the H-2 program.

By 1983, Hispanic groups decided to negotiate when they began working on an alternative bill. It signaled their assessment that if they could not stop some sort of sanctions law from passing, at least they could moderate IRCA's negative impact upon them. Major portions of all but business finally decided to seek benefits that would otherwise have been unattainable had they continued their opposition to a particular portion of IRCA's complex package. Labor gave up opportunities for severe restriction and accepted legalization and the SAW program. Growers gave up their opposition to sanctions and their desire for a large-scale guest-worker program in order to get an agricultural legalization program (SAW).

Hispanics ultimately split in their opposition to sanctions in return for the legalization and antidiscrimination provisions. Each faction gained at least something by making a key concession—an alternative to losing in a purely distributive outcome. Each faction finally compromised because it feared the result of losing in a distributive outcome, believing that a distributive resolution was imminent. Labor allied itself with Hispanics fearing they would have the power, as they had been successfully showing on the House floor since 1982, to scuttle sanctions. Growers also negotiated with Hispanics in the end out of a fear that Hispanics and farm workers, through the leadership of Representative Rodino, would kill any bill that contained a guest-worker program. Hispanics, in turn, negotiated with growers fearing that the latter had enough votes to pass some sort of guest-worker program over the objections of Senator Simpson and Representative Rodino. They also feared that restrictionists would be successful in killing off the legalization program, which they were only seven votes shy of doing so in 1985.

Growers—by means of the Panetta, Morrison, and Wilson amendments—had shown their ability to achieve a distributive victory in Congress. All the factions were convinced that the next bill would be more punitive to each should they fail to compromise.

Issue factions in public policy disputes consist of public officials, interest group spokespersons, and mass membership of the relevant groups. Congressional members of the factions have to maintain their own reputations and working relationships in Congress that go beyond any single issue which they are currently debating. This often compels them toward moderation. Interest group leaders, moreover, in order to retain their credibility with legislators, often take a more moderate stance than their mass membership. Because factions are thus divided, moderate segments can often emerge within them seeking consensus on a policy. The key activists from each segment of the factions involved often reconsider their interests as a result of the negotiating process itself.

Labor leaders, for example, grew more accommodative, first agreeing to the amnesty program and then to the antidiscrimination amendment, and finally even to the SAW program. The concessions labor made involved aspects it considered less threatening to the immediate workplace interests of labor's mass membership. Indeed, as the negotiations proceeded, labor leaders even saw some potential gains to be made, for instance, from enlistment of newly legalized aliens. The International Ladies Garment Workers Union (ILGWU) had already been enlisting some undocumented workers. Labor leaders also saw another interest in these negotiating processes—that Hispanics were a valuable political ally worth making some concessions for. Then too, getting the support of the mass membership for this moderation in their stance did not seem too difficult, as immigration was simply not a big enough issue with the rank and file.

Hispanic leaders began to moderate for the same reasons that labor leaders did—realizing that changes in the bill could address their interests and because they were working in a coalition. Hispanics became divided as a result of some leaders' moderation. The moderation stemmed in part from changes in the faction leadership. New Hispanic members elected to the House in 1983 and 1985 realized that if legalization were defeated they might lose a potentially great voting bloc (the Hispanic-origin illegal aliens residing in their districts who might eventually be able to vote after being legalized and becoming naturalized citizens). These members, along with liberal Democrats who sided with them, came to believe that given the national mood, the 1986 session might be the last one in which a legalization provision might be tolerated.

In prior years, the Hispanic leaders' best alternative to negotiation had been the status quo or a delay in the hopes of crafting an even more pleasing bill. By 1986, this had changed as the restrictionists had appeared ready to kill the whole concept of legalization.

Among the Hispanic leadership, which had been rigidly opposed to IRCA, Rep. Esteban Torres (D., Calif.) ended his rigid opposition and began working behind the scenes as a lobbyist for the National Hispanic Leadership Conference and played a secret role, trying to get an agreement among Hispanics, labor, and growers that set the stage for the SAW negotiations. So, too, Charles Kamasaki, of the National Council of La Raza, was given approval by his board to "make deals"; that is, to bargain with the House immigration subcommittee. Even American Civil Liberties Union (ACLU) lobbyist Wade Henderson, a critical actor in shaping the antidiscrimination amendment, continued to negotiate for a better bill even when he knew such a bill would still contain sanctions that his organization formally opposed.

Working in coalition encouraged this moderation within the Hispanic and liberal factions. It helped coalition leaders see other interests at stake in the immigration reform debate. Hispanic and civil liberties groups forged a powerful alliance with labor and the American Jewish Committee, both advocates of employer sanctions. Accommodating those groups became indispensable for getting their support on the liberal legalization program that the Hispanic and civil liberties groups had struggled for so long to put together. Thus, the negotiators at the center of the dispute began to see it as in their interests to accept sanctions and make some concessions from their original positions.

Despite some of their formal opposition following passage of the bill, all of the moderate faction members – for example, Representative Torres and the moderate Hispanic legislators, plus La Raza and the League of United Latin American Citizens (LULAC), felt that IRCA was the best deal available (Perotti 1989b, 411). The availability of moderate actors marginalized the more rigid ones who refused to recognize new interests or positions. Both the immigration subcommittee staffs and the members of the liberal faction realized that Congressmen Garcia and Roybal, and that MALDEF, for instance, were no longer key players. Their position did not seem to be supported by public opinion or by the judgment of other negotiators.

The business faction also divided as a core group of decision makers to moderate as well. Large businesses, such as those represented by the National Association of Manufacturers (NAM) and the Business Roundtable, ultimately accepted the agreement. They began to see new interests as they moderated their stance during the latter periods of negotiation. They wanted to remain on good terms with Senator Simpson and the supporters of immigration reform. They began to see the bill as a means of gaining more information on their own personnel, taking them "off the hook" for asking applicants about their citizenship status. Smaller businesses, represented by the National Federation of Independent Business and the U.S. Chamber of Commerce, continued to oppose the final bill (ibid., 412).

Even among restrictionists some moderates emerged, splitting the faction. The Federation for American Immigration Reform (FAIR) split from the nativist groups and from restrictionist legislators. Congressmen William McCollum (R., Fla.) and Carlos Moorhead (R., Calif.), for example, who had advocated abandoning legalization and capping the total number of legal immigrants, withdrew their support from the House bill. The moderate faction leadership concluded that getting some sort of immigration control was more important than the posture being taken by McCollum and Moorhead. This faction's most significant concession was accepting the SAW program after only minor changes. FAIR felt the bill would be doomed without such concessions. Although the board split on supporting a bill containing such a program, FAIR continued its support because then-Executive Director Roger Conner felt the need to remain consistent (ibid., 413).

This chapter closes its discussion of the passage of IRCA with an overview of its legislative strategy.[4] In the next chapter, this perspective will help focus subsequent examination of the problems encountered when implementing IRCA, and, in Chapter 5, will orient the discussion of the evaluation of IRCA.

CONGRESSIONAL POLICY STRATEGIES AND INTENT

IRCA is not just a new approach to immigration policy—though it clearly does do that. IRCA represents a law that embodies immigration policy, but also employment, agricultural labor, civil rights, welfare, and federal reimbursement policies. Obviously, a law that is as complex as is IRCA involves a complicated legislative strategy. Insofar as policy design is a "blueprint for purposeful action" (Schneider and Ingraham 1988, 4), then discerning the implied theory or legislative intent of the policymakers helps us when analyzing policy to focus on the relationship among the problem definition, policy enactment, implementation, and policy results or impacts on the environment.

In passing IRCA, Congress modified existing immigration policy by expanding the targets of immigration policy. It did so by including illegal aliens. But it also did so by creating conditions that would make it problematic for undocumented aliens already in the country to remain, and for those still in sending nations to be less ready to come. That is IRCA's *primary* legislative purpose. But IRCA seeks to achieve its primary purpose by focusing upon a variety of intermediate targets—individual employers, the INS, local educational and social service agencies, and community-based organizations—so that they would respond to the law in ways that would encourage the individual alien, the ultimate policy target, to behave in ways consistent with the law's basic assumptions.

IRCA also relies on various policy instruments, from its strong mandate that regulates employers' hiring practices, to inducements in the form of the amnesty program to encourage undocumented aliens already here to change their status, and to financial grants to states and localities that serve this population.

Furthermore, IRCA is an exceedingly large program. It covers all U.S. employers. It processed over 3 million legalizing aliens in its regular and SAW legalization programs. SLIAGs exceed those allocated for the first few years of recently enacted federal welfare programs.

Finally, IRCA is both time-bound and contingent legislation. The amnesty programs were set up for a one-time grant of amnesty, all phases of which were to have been completed by September 1990. Also, SLIAGs were allocated for a fixed four-year period. The employer-sanctions provisions were contingent. They would be automatically terminated after three years by a joint Congressional resolution if the GAO were to find that they had caused a widespread pattern of discrimination. In short, IRCA is a large-scale and complex law that could nominally be ended after only a relatively short implementation phase.

Congressional supporters of IRCA made certain assumptions. IRCA defines the problem it was designed to deal with as having five major aspects. First, the problem was primarily one of economic factors *pulling* immigrants to the United States rather than political or economic conditions in the sending country that acted to *push* citizens out. IRCA sought to "demagnetize" the pull of the U.S. labor market.

A second aspect of the problem was derived from a sort of legal formalism that sought to ensure that U.S. laws were consistent with each other and that practice generally reflected the intent of such laws. The mediator most responsible for defining the problem in this manner was Sen. Alan Simpson. His concern for legal formalism led him to focus on the internal inconsistency of U.S. immigration law that made it illegal for undocumented aliens to work but not for employers to hire them.

As Richard Day, chief counsel for the Subcommittee on Immigration and Refugee Affairs of the Senate Judiciary Committee noted, speaking of immigration policy before the passage of IRCA and clearly articulating this perspective:

> The current policy is irrational, it does not make sense, and as Senator Simpson says, only in America would you have laws that say it's illegal for you to enter this country and take employment, but not illegal for the employer to hire and use you. . . . Further, U.S. immigration laws are widely, commonly, and frequently, without any sort of penalty, violated, and this widespread flouting of a significant body of federal law undoubtedly encourages the flouting of other laws. (in Tomasi 1987, 13–14)

For some proponents of IRCA, such as Congressmen Mazzoli and Rodino, IRCA was a sort of "jobs bill" that protected the employment of native-born and legal American workers from illegal ones.

IRCA's proponents also saw limits on continuing to rely solely on traditional border and interior enforcement aimed at apprehending and deporting illegal aliens. They concluded that such current efforts were ineffective and that significant improvement required increases in enforcement personnel and unwanted intrusions into local communities.

Finally, as with most U.S. immigration law, a nativist sentiment also shaped the manner in which policymakers defined the problem they were addressing.

Thus, the multifaceted perception of the "immigration problem" led policymakers to a corresponding set of strategies that relied mostly on employer sanctions and legalization. Because the problem was viewed as one of pull rather than push factors, IRCA was aimed at changing the economic conditions for illegal aliens already in the United States and for dissuading others who might be intending to come. Sanctions were selected as the major vehicle for weakening the pull of the U.S. labor market. The rationale and chain of causality implicit to the employer-sanctions approach was described as follows:

> Employment is the magnet that attracts aliens here illegally or, in the case on nonimmigrants, leads them to accept employment in violation of their status. Employers will be deterred by the penalties in this legislation from hiring unauthorized aliens and this, in turn, will deter aliens from entering illegally or violating their status in search of employment. (U.S. House of Representatives, Committee on the Judiciary 1986, as cited in McDonnell and Hill 1989, 11)

Employer sanctions was further viewed as a way to correct the legal inconsistency then embodied in the Texas Proviso (which made it *legal* to hire illegal aliens), provide an alternative to limits on traditional border and interior enforcement, and, to a lesser degree, provide more jobs for legal workers.

Legalization was seen as a humanitarian provision. It was also viewed as a strategy to reduce the enforcement burden faced by the INS. By legalizing millions of undocumented aliens, the INS could target more of its efforts on interdicting the flow of new illegal aliens rather than diluting their efforts by seeking out those already here. The capture of illegal aliens already in the United States was seen as a more costly and difficult apprehension task, and also one more likely to involve infringement of the civil rights and liberties of American citizens. Amnesty would also make the enforcement of employer sanctions easier. Also, the educational requirements that were included in the legalization program were seen as addressing the final problem of Americans' perceived unwillingness or inability to accept people with different cultural values and customs.

Implicit in these policy instruments were a set of choices as to who the targets of the revised immigration policy should be, and a set of assumptions about how such targets would respond to the mandates or the inducements of IRCA. As we shall see more fully in the next two chapters, if the policymakers err in their understanding of either the targets' incentives or their capacity to behave in a manner consistent with the policy's intent, then implementation problems will result and the policy will be far less likely to produce its intended effects or may even produce totally unintended results.

Thus, while illegal aliens were the ultimate target of the employment-sanctions approach, IRCA *assumed a causal chain* that went from the INS and its enforcement strategy to individual employers and finally to the undocumented worker. Congress made three basic assumptions as to the INS enforcement strategy: (1) that INS inspection to check employer compliance with IRCA was to cover all classes and sizes of firms; (2) that although the inspections were to be broad-based, the INS was to focus its efforts on those firms that had traditionally employed illegal aliens—the most egregious violators; and (3) that the INS was to concentrate on violators who knowingly hired undocumented workers rather than on "paper-work" violators who failed to complete an I-9 form or to verify employment documents.

Congressional sponsors made two assumptions about employer compliance: (1) that most would do so voluntarily, and (2) that those who thought the antidiscrimination provision unnecessary felt that companies would check the documents of all new hires and that they would not refuse to hire qualified job applicants who were legally entitled to work; while those who pressed for the antidiscrimination amendment assumed that some companies would engage in discriminatory behavior, but that the Office of Special Counsel mechanism, the formal oversight by the GAO, and informal monitoring by various civil liberties and ethnic welfare groups would be sufficient to ensure that such behavior would be identified and remedied.

IRCA assumes that a broad-based inspection program by the INS, together with targeted enforcement, would result in widespread employer compliance. Over time, such compliance would lead to illegal aliens experiencing difficulty in finding jobs, and thus to their eventual departure, and for those thinking about coming, to their deciding not to do so. Even IRCA's proponents, however, were careful to say that they did not expect immediate results from IRCA in discouraging the illegal influx. They realized that without some sort of secure and universal work authorization document to monitor the process, the use of phony documents was possible, thereby enabling illegals to continue to find jobs. Proponents expected that in time, however, it would become harder for the undocumented to secure employment.

The targets of the legalization program were primarily those undocumented aliens illegally residing in the United States prior to January 1, 1982. The INS was an intermediate target charged with administering the program. QDE (qualified designated entity) organizations were also intermediate targets designated to accept legalization applications. Other intermediate targets were the public and private community-based and educational agencies that were to provide assistance to the aliens in meeting the language and civic requirements of IRCA. Congress made three assumptions about the INS role in the legalization program: (1) it would administer the program in a liberal manner; (2) it would conduct sufficient outreach to inform those eligible about the program's opportunities and requirements; and (3) it would have the capacity to complete the program within the designated timeframe.

Although Congress designated the INS as the major agency to administer the amnesty program, it assumed other intermediaries might be needed—hence the inclusions of organizations that functioned as qualified designated entities. These organizations were religious groups such as the Catholic Charities and Episcopal Church groups who had established traditions and programs of working with the undocumented-alien target group, and community-based agencies such as SER-Jobs for Progress and the Polish Welfare Association. The program's ultimate target was the individual immigrant who could meet the 1982 residency test.

IRCA's assumed chain of causality for the legalization program was from the INS and QDEs who were to administer it to the eligible aliens, who would presumably apply for legalization, on to the employers who would now have a larger labor pool from which to hire and who would thus be more likely to comply with employer sanctions, back to the INS, which could therefore devote more of its resources to enforcing employer sanctions and apprehending new illegal arrivals, and finally on to the undocumented alien who would be convinced to leave, or not to come in the first place (McDonnell and Hill 1989, 13–17).

The proponents of IRCA also made certain basic assumptions about its costs and who would bear those costs. Policy initiators make decisions about how much they wish to spend and then estimate how much targets are willing to bear. The implementation process tests the validity of that cost calculus.

The employer-sanctions program of IRCA entails the enforcement costs involved in monitoring for compliance and imposing sanctions on those who do not comply. Mandates impose two types of costs on policy targets, compliance or avoidance costs. Compliance costs are those the individual company incurs when it obeys the law. Avoidance costs rise from attempts to circumvent the mandated policy, those incurred while bargaining with enforcement agencies about the terms of compliance, or those resulting from using political influence and litigation to change mandates. Targets calculate whether to comply based on estimates of the likelihood of enforcement times the severity of sanctions. If such costs are seen to be greater than the benefits gained from noncompliance (minus any avoidance costs), then targets are likely to comply.

In IRCA's case, compliance costs for employers range from minor bookkeeping ones to fairly major ones of seeking an alternative labor pool, paying higher wages and benefits, or changing the location or mode of production (e.g., mechanizing some of the labor associated with production). Avoidance costs include such things as appealing a fine or lobbying to have the law or INS regulations modified.

Legalization also has costs. These include costs of administering it, and opportunity costs incurred when the performance of the services required by a new policy forces the reallocation of agency attention and staff resources away from its more traditional functions.

Policymakers can manipulate both cost levels and who bears them. They can decide to spend very little on monitoring, for example, in the hopes that a few well-publicized cases will induce targets to conclude that the costs of sanctions are high enough to justify compliance. Or to the contrary, policymakers may set compliance standards so low that few targets would have difficulty in meeting them. In the case of inducements, policymakers may decide to minimize the costs to the government by awarding a nonmonetary benefit, such as legalized status, but shift the costs of producing it to the targets.

In IRCA's case, both proponents and opponents assumed that the law would impose only minimal costs on employers. Compliance costs were reduced in three ways. First, IRCA established an "educational period" of six months during which time the INS would inform U.S. companies of their new obligations under IRCA. During this phase no penalties would be imposed. For one year following that phase, warning citations rather than fines would be issued for first offenses. In short, compliance was phased in over eighteen months, giving immigrant-dependent businesses an extended period within which they could find alternative sources of legal workers.

Second, a "grandfather" clause in IRCA exempted companies from being fined for continuing to employ undocumented workers who had been hired prior to the IRCA enactment. While the INS could still deport any such undocumented aliens, their employers could not be held liable for civil fines or criminal penalties.

Third, IRCA set up a system of "affirmative defense" for employers. As long as employers could show that they had checked employment documents and were keeping the necessary records (e.g., I-9 forms), they were assumed to have made a good faith effort at compliance with IRCA. Businesses would not be required to become police, aggressively checking for fraudulent documents. Thus, the cost of compliance for most companies was assumed to be minimal.

By *assuming widespread voluntary compliance,* Congress further assumed that the costs of enforcement could be minimized and that no new mechanism would need to be established even though IRCA would cover more than 7 million employers. IRCA set a 26 percent increase for the INS budget, most of which was to cover its additional responsibilities under IRCA (e.g., implementing the legalization program and an increased role in drug interdiction). INS inspections of employment documents were to be supplemented by the U.S. Department of Labor (DOL), as part of its regular wage-and-hour compliance inspections. In short, IRCA assumed that less than 1 percent of the nation's companies would be inspected in any given year. Congress assumed that enforcement costs could be kept small precisely because most employers would view compliance costs as low, and for those that did not so view it, the strategic targeting of the most egregious violators would result in a credible threat.

The costs of legalization were primarily to be borne by the applicants themselves. The provisions for language and civic classes were funded by the SLIAG program. The short timeframe and anticipated volume of applicants, however, meant that the INS would incur start-up costs in staffing a new program and some opportunity costs in that the legalization effort might deflect some staff time and resources away from such traditional service activities as enforcement, naturalization exams, and visa processing (McDonnell and Hill 1989, 17–20).

When new national policies are implemented, they are done so within a pre-existing context. Such a context includes the institutional culture and capacity of the organizations charged with implementation; other policies that may work to reinforce, negate, or weaken the intended effects of the new policy; and the demographic, economic, and political characteristics of the different local environments within which the national policy must be implemented. Some elements of the implementing context, such as the tightness of local labor markets, might be critically important for the success of a policy such as IRCA, but are nonetheless largely beyond Congressional influence over whether such factors tend to reinforce or weaken IRCA's ability to change employer or immigrant behaviors. Other elements in the implementing context, however, can be shaped by Congressional actions.

Factors long identified by policy research as significant are the goals and capacity of the implementing agencies. In IRCA's case, Congress made the decision to use the INS as the primary implementor. Yet it seems to have done so with little deliberation. There was virtually no consideration of alternatives to the INS as the primary implementor of both employer sanctions and legalization, and there was little discussion about the capacity of the INS to do so, other than the need for more resources (ibid., 21).

The INS had long been a proponent of the employer-sanctions approach, of course, and such a new program was still consistent with its organizational mission. Yet the INS had a notorious reputation for inefficiency, even by one journalistic account being called the "worst-managed, least effective federal agency in Washington" (Crewdson 1983, 114). More scholarly accounts attributed the blame more broadly, including Congressional neglect and lack of funding, but likewise were highly critical of the INS's ability to meet its service and enforcement missions (Morris 1985, especially 144–145; LeMay 1987, 125–132).

While Congress addressed some problems of the INS's capacity with IRCA—more funding, a more effective enforcement mechanism, greater Congressional and public visibility—it also assumed that an agency that had traditionally dealt almost exclusively with enforcement and apprehension could philosophically adjust to legalization. It also assumed that an agency that had traditionally dealt almost exclusively with individual aliens could now expand its target of enforcement to include large corporations that were more publicly visible and had the resources to question INS authority and regulations in ways simply not available to most illegal aliens. Congress also assumed that an agency notorious for its long backlog of processing naturalization applications could somehow manage a substantial legalization program with complicated phases, all of which had to be completed within forty months.

Congress further structured the implementation context by its requirement that the GAO monitor the implementation of employer sanctions and by the procedure and possible "sunset" provision in IRCA. The provision for the GAO assessment of the burden imposed on employers as one indicator the GAO was charged with measuring served as a possible constraint on the INS's implementation strategy and on how vigorously it could enforce sanctions. So too, the limited time period permitted by Congress served as a constraint on the way the INS could structure the legalization program.

Sometimes policymakers attempt to shape the implementation context by considering the possible interaction among different provisions and policies aimed at the same targets or implemented by the same agencies. With IRCA, Congress clearly saw some interaction among some of its provisions. For instance, Congress intended that the SLIAG funds would help implement the legalization program. In other cases, however, it seemed to take little note of possible interaction among IRCA's complex provisions or across other legislation involving the INS.

As we will see more fully later, one of the more glaring examples of such inconsistencies within IRCA's provisions were the different time frames and eligibility standards that applied to SAW applicants as compared to those applying through the regular legalization program. The major legislative actors in the IRCA drama were well aware of these discrepancies between the two programs, of course, but these discrepancies were allowed to remain for political reasons, as they embodied some of the critical compromises needed to secure passage of the bill.

Among major policies outside of IRCA that were likely to significantly affect its implementation were two laws passed around the same time. One was the Marriage Fraud Amendment and the other was the Omnibus Anti-Drug bill that authorized an increased drug-interdiction effort. Both laws significantly expanded the enforcement duties of the Border Patrol and Investigations Units within the INS—the very units that were so affected by the passage of IRCA. Yet little or no apparent consideration was given as to how these various policies would impact one another. As McDonnell and Hill succinctly put it:

> In sum, Congressional efforts to shape IRCA's implementing context were largely confined to its choice of the INS as the major implementing agency, and its imposition of implementation constraints in the form of the GAO reports and expedited procedures for employer sanctions and the limited time frame for legalization. It gave little consideration to questions of organizational capacity, and quite explicitly decided to allow inconsistencies across provisions within IRCA; its inattention to possible interactions between IRCA and other policies was less purposeful. (1989, 25)

It is to the implementation and to the various problems that developed during this stage of the policy process that the next chapter is concerned.

NOTES

1. "Immigration Bill: How a 'Corpse' Came Back to Life," *New York Times,* 13 October 1986, A16; *Congressional Quarterly Weekly Report,* 18 October 1986, 2595–2596; "Conferees Agree on Vast Revision in Law on Aliens," *New York Times,* 15 October 1986, A1, B11; "House Passes Compromise Immigration Bill," *Washington*

Post, 16 October 1986, A5; "Hill Revises Immigration Law," *Washington Post,* 18 October 1986, A1, 7–8; and LeMay 1987, 143–146.

2. For a further elaboration of views of the opposing members of the Hispanic Caucus members to the passage of IRCA, see the comments by then-chairman of the caucus, Matthew Martinez (D., Calif.), in Tomasi 1987, 1–5.

3. Described in Quirk 1989, 905–921. This section of this chapter also relies heavily on the application of that approach to the IRCA case as developed and presented by Professor Rosanna Perotti in her dissertation, "Resolving Policy Conflict: Congress and Immigration Reform" (Perotti 1989b).

4. This section draws heavily from an excellent paper by McDonnell and Hill of the Rand Corporation study of IRCA. See McDonnell and Hill 1989, 5–6; 9–25; and Bean, Vernez, and Keely 1989.

CHAPTER 4

Policy Implementation: Putting IRCA into Action

This chapter describes the process of implementing those Congressional strategies and intent that were enacted in IRCA. It describes the accomplishments achieved to date in implementing IRCA. It also discusses the many problems encountered during its early stages of implementation. Many of these problems resulted from the very nature of the law and the compromises necessary to secure its passage. It deals with the intergovernmental complexities inherent in implementing IRCA given the complexities of the law itself. It closes with a discussion of the somewhat unusual use of nongovernment agencies to assist with the implementation of IRCA—the special advantages and problems of employing QDEs to help administer the legalization program.

The chapter is based upon a thorough review of the relevant literature available on the topic, including various government reports.[1] It employs the results of dozens of interviews conducted by the author, many of which were with state government, QDE, and district INS officials who were the front-line troops in implementing IRCA (see Appendix B). Finally, it uses the information gained from survey questionnaires sent to over 800 offices. One version was mailed to 530 QDE offices that collectively were in the state of residence for just over 95 percent of all the legalization applicants processed via IRCA's amnesty programs. Another version was sent to 250 state offices that were involved in implementing IRCA. A third version was sent to all regional and district INS offices. Following are the results of those surveys:

IRCA Questionnaires from QDE Agencies
Total Sent: 530
Total Replies Received: 57
Percent Return: 11
Responses were received from Arizona, California, Colorado, Florida, Illinois, Idaho, Iowa, Maryland, New Jersey, New York, Oregon, Texas, Virginia, Washington, Wyoming, and Washington, D.C.

IRCA Questionnaires from State Agencies
Total Sent: 250
Total Replies Received: 82
Percent Return: 33
Responses were received from Alaska, Arizona, Arkansas, California, Colorado, Connecticut, Delaware, Florida, Georgia, Hawaii, Idaho, Illinois, Iowa, Kansas, Kentucky, Maryland, Michigan, Minnesota, Mississippi, Missouri, Montana, Nebraska, Nevada, New Hampshire, New Jersey, New Mexico, New York, North Carolina, Ohio, Oregon, Pennsylvania, Rhode Island, South Carolina, South Dakota, Tennessee, Utah, Vermont, Virginia, Washington, Wisconsin, Wyoming, and Washington, D.C.

IRCA Questionnaires from INS Offices
Total Sent: 37
Total Replies Received: 8
Percent Return: 22

Grand Total: 817
Total Replies Received: 147
Total Percent: 18

THE ACCOMPLISHMENTS OF IMPLEMENTING IRCA

This section summarizes the major results to date in implementing the complex IRCA law. Each of the law's major provisions will be briefly discussed.

Legalization

The passage of IRCA gave the INS primary responsiblity for implementing three legalization programs and the possibility of doing so for a fourth (the Replenishment Agricultural Workers, called RAWs). The three primary programs are: the regular program, referred to hereafter as the LAWs program; the Seasonal Agricultural Workers program, called SAWs; and the Cuban/Haitian Adjustment program. Together they involve the largest amnesty program ever granted by any industrial nation of the world (Kurzban 1989). These responsibilities were in addition to its new effort to implement employer sanctions as well as the continued work of its traditional services. Since passage of IRCA, the INS increased its staff by 45 percent, its overtime and holiday time by 400 percent, and its total budget by 42 percent.

In implementing the legalization programs, it accepted more than 3 million applicants. As of February 1992, the INS had processed 3,031,848 applications for amnesty. The two main such programs are the LAWs, for those undocumented aliens residing in the United States prior to January 1, 1982, and the SAWs, for seasonal agricultural workers having worked in perishable-crop agriculture for a specified period of time. Following is the breakdown of applicants:

LAWs, I-687: 1,759,705
SAWs, I-700: 1,272,143
Total: 3,031,848
Total Granted Permanent Residence: 2,482,348 (another 200,000–300,000 remain eligible) (Immigration and Naturalization Service 1992, 73, Table 23)

Both are one-time, temporary programs that would automatically end after permanent residency was granted, for which the last of eligible applicants was 1991. With no prior experience in such programs, the INS had but six months to plan, design, and implement the LAW program, beginning on May 5, 1987, and the SAW program by June 1, 1987. These programs involved a totally new approach for the INS, which prior to then had concentrated almost exclusively on enforcement and the deportation of illegal aliens. Now it was being asked to reach out and process the legalization of those undocumented aliens.

It managed the programs through its existing decentralized network of four regions and thirty-three district offices. The central office set general guidelines, directives, and program goals, but within those broad guidelines the regional directors had significant flexibility and, in fact, modified their efforts to fit needs within their respective districts. Early on, it was decided to physically separate the legalization offices from the INS's traditional enforcement offices, and the INS opened 110 new offices throughout the nation to handle the estimated 3.9 million applications.

In addition, applicants could also file at one of the networks of some 980 sites operated by roughly 200 QDE agencies. The INS had the authority and responsibility to review and approve applications processed at the QDE sites.

Table 4.1 shows where in the United States the applicants for both programs resided, detailing the top thirteen states that collectively accounted for more than 90 percent of the legalization applicants.

Review of all applicants took place at one of four regional processing facilities (RPF)—one in each of the INS regions. As of February 13, 1992, 5,826 legalization applicants had not received a final decision. Of the 1,753,879 who had been processed to a final decision, 1,655,676 (94.4 percent) had been approved for temporary residence status. Among SAW applicants, as of the same date, 1,272,143 had received a final decision, with 1,037,349 (or 87.8 percent) having been approved for temporary residence status. As of the end of fiscal year 1991, a total of 2,482,348 had gained permanent residence status under the IRCA provisions.

Employer Sanctions

The INS closely adhered to the phased-in implementation of employer sanctions as specified by Congress. The first six months, starting in December 1986, were the "public-education" phase. This was followed by the one-year period during which warning citations were issued for first-time offenders.

Table 4.1
State of Residence of Legalization Applicants: LAWs and SAWs as of February 13, 1992

	Total	LAWs	SAWs
Total U.S.	3,031,848	1,759,705	1,272,143
California	1,622,517	955,875	666,642
Texas	445,850	308,478	137,372
New York	171,083	118,210	52,873
Illinois	159,760	120,983	38,377
Florida	152,348	50,114	102,234
Arizona	82,649	29,261	53,388
New Jersey	45,439	29,146	16,293
Washington	37,539	9,850	27,689
New Mexico	28,085	16,287	11,798
Oregon	27,520	4,240	23,280
Georgia	24,118	7,247	16,871
Colorado	22,513	10,387	12,126
Nevada	20,244	11,160	9,084
Virginia	19,416	10,190	9,226
Massachusetts	18,128	9,859	8,269
All Other States	154,639	68,416	86,221

Source: Immigration and Naturalization Service 1992, 73, Table 23.

During this phase, the INS distributed nearly 11 million handbooks describing the program and detailing employer responsibilities under the new law. In addition, 1.8 million employers were contacted by the INS. During this phase, the INS was seeking voluntary compliance.

While in the education mode of implementing employer sanctions, the INS launched a multi-million dollar, national media operation explaining the new law and employer responsibilities to certify all new hires. At the urging of advocacy groups, the INS requested and Congress granted a three-month delay (from June 1 to September 1, 1987) in the requirement that employers complete the I-9 form used to certify employee work authorization. The INS allocated 50 percent of its investigative time and assigned Border Patrol agents to contact by telephone or in person over 1 million employers by June 1988 (Bean, Vernez, and Keely 1989, 42).

The INS continues in its responsibility to educate employers about IRCA. It established a new office of Employer and Labor Relations, headed by an assistant commissioner, to assist employers, labor and management groups, civic and community organizations, and others affected by the law. This office also manages a new service program of the INS, helping employers find legally authorized workers (Schroeder 1988; Bean, Vernez, and Keely 1989, 43).

The INS phased in enforcement action against employers who knowingly violated the law. The first citation was issued in August 1987 and the first Notice of Intent to Fine was served in October 1987. As of February 1989, over 15,000 were investigated, over 3,500 were cited or warned, and nearly 50,000 audits of employer I-9 forms were conducted by the Department of Labor (DOL). To assess the overall level of compliance, the INS is implementing an inspections program for which employers are randomly selected (LeMay 1989, 5; Bean, Vernez, and Keely 1989, 37). The first actual fine levied by the INS was against the Washington, D.C., area Wendy's fast food chain. DavCo Food Inc. of Crofton, Md.—the parent corporation running the Wendy's chain in the capital, Maryland, and Northern Virginia—agreed to pay a fine of $60,000.[2]

Inspections are initiated in one of two ways. Some begin as a result of tips based on local information. Others are the result of a random selection of companies conducted by the central office of the INS located in Washington, D.C. Half of those are to be businesses in the economic sectors known to traditionally employ illegal aliens (as determined by local district management), and half are from all other employers. As of February 1989, 75 percent of inspections were based on specific leads and 25 percent were random (Bean, Vernez, and Keely 1989, 43; General Accounting Office 1988b).

Enhancement of Border Patrol Enforcement Activities

The initial start-up activities for both the new legalization and employer-sanctions programs resulted in a temporary reduction of the other more traditional INS enforcement activities, such as border and interior enforcement. Table 4.2 shows selected INS budget, personnel, and workload data from 1985 through 1990.

The number of undocumented aliens the INS apprehended rose steadily until passage of IRCA. In the first year after its enactment, apprehensions dropped off by an impressive 30 percent. In 1988, the INS caught 992,308 illegal aliens, a decline of 16 percent from the previous year, and roughly a 42 percent decline from the pre-IRCA level. By 1989, however, they were back up to 1,954,243. In 1990, total apprehensions stood at 1,169,939, and 1991 were at 1,197,875—clearly back up to pre-IRCA levels (Immigration and Naturalization Service 1992, 146).

When passing IRCA, Congress authorized a 50 percent increase in Border Patrol staff for fiscal years 1987 and 1988. To date, that goal has not been achieved. The actual increase in Border Patrol staff from 3,600 personnel in 1986 to about 4,900 in 1989 falls about 500 agents short of the goal (or about a 37 percent increase instead of the 50 percent intended). The lag in the intended buildup reflects both a smaller budget increase in fiscal year 1988 than had been projected, as well as difficulties encountered in recruiting and expanding training staff and facilities. And as the INS's Bor-

Table 4.2
INS Budget, Personnel, and Workload: Fiscal Years 1985–1990

Budget and Selected Workload Indicators	1985	1986	1987	1988	1989	1990
Budget ($ Millions)	580	574	651	808	832	866
Personnel: FTE Employment	11,268	11,656	12,413	14,773	16,999	16,032
Selected Workload Indicators (Thousands) -Total Persons Inspected	307,657	328,042	297,020	341,078	350,000	350,000
Border Patrol Apprehensions	1,262	1,693	1,158	992	1,954	1,170

Source: Adapted from Immigration and Naturalization Service 1992, 146.

der Patrol has increased in size, so have its duties. As noted, the INS shifted some personnel from Border Patrol apprehension responsibilities to employer-sanctions education and enforcement. Also, in 1986 the interdiction of drug traffic across the borders became a prime focus of the Border Patrol (due to the 1986 Omnibus Anti-Drug Law). Border Patrol agents, then, shifted their emphasis from alien apprehension and smuggling to work with the Drug Enforcement Agency on Operation Alliance. Finally, the Border Patrol also expanded the number of staff being used to guard refugee camps and to identify, prosecute, and deport criminal aliens (e.g., from among the Mariel boatlift detainees housed in Atlanta's Oakdale camp) (Bean, Vernez, and Keely 1989, 44).

Thus, the intended 50 percent increase in Border Patrol crossing efforts has clearly not materialized. Actual "line-watch" hours have increased slightly over pre-IRCA years. In addition, the share of actual line-watch hours devoted to the interdiction of undocumented aliens, as opposed to drug interdictions, is not measurable in that slight increase. Moreover, the interdiction by immigration Border Patrol of illegal activities away from the immediate borders—that is, at airports, highway checkpoints, and bus stations, for instance—has declined. Table 4.3 details the number of Border Patrol staff, prosecutions, fines, and convictions for fiscal years 1985–1991. These data are striking in their uniformity. No appreciable improvement or even dramatic changes are noted as a result of the passage of IRCA and its increased support for the INS.

Table 4.3
Border Patrol Staffing, Prosecutions, Fines, and Convictions, 1985–1991

Indicators	Fiscal Years						
	1985	1986	1987	1988	1989	1990	1991
Number of Border Patrol Staff	3,473	3,687	3,643	4,689	4,919	NA	NA
Prosecutions Total Disposed	17,688	23,405	18,894	18,360	18,580	20,079	18,882
Prosecutions for Immigration Violations	16,976	22,751	18,200	17,590	17,992	19,351	18,297
Prosecutions for Nationality Violations	712	654	694	770	588	728	585
Aggregate Fines and Imprisonment Fines (Dollars in thousands)	930	1,123	1,490	2,528	1,831	2,936	2,623
Immigrant Violators (thousands)	903	1,117	1,463	2,523	1,827	2,872	2,508
Nationality Violators	26,785	5,973	26,550	4,375	1,900	63,385	114,575
Convictions Total	9,833	15,259	11,996	12,208	12,561	12,719	11,509
Immigration Violations	9,630	15,104	11,786	11,929	12,379	12,515	11,392
Nationality Violations	203	155	210	279	182	204	117

Source: General Accounting Office 1990, 165.

DIFFICULTIES IN THE INS's IMPLEMENTATION OF IRCA

This section highlights the many difficulties and problems resulting from the initial implementation of IRCA's many complex provisions, although several of the problems associated with the SLIAG and SAVE provisions of IRCA will be discussed in the following sections of this chapter dealing with intergovernmental aspects and the use of QDE agencies.

The sheer size and complex nature of IRCA and the programs it establishes pose challenges and problems of resources, manpower, and creativity for any organization, and especially for one as large, diverse, and decentralized as is the INS. The various legalization programs differ in their statutory and regulatory requirements, in their application dates, and in the application of the standard and nature of proof to establish a claim. That situation placed an extraordinary burden on the INS to hire and train personnel and to communicate often subtle changes in policy and practice. The statutory scheme outlined in Chapter 3 certainly contributed to the subsequent difficulties experienced by the INS in administering and implementing these programs. The Los Angeles office alone, for example, accepted 60,000 applications for the LAWs program on the last legal filing date for that program (from interviews with district office officials).

Legalization

A number of problems were associated with the legalization programs of IRCA, many flowing from the complex nature of the two main legalization programs, and from the fact that the INS had no prior experience in dealing with such programs. Indeed, they involved a 360-degree change from what had been the prevailing philosophy and tradition of the INS.

In setting up for the programs, the INS decided to establish separate offices away from their traditional enforcement-related district offices (Baker 1990, 63). While this decision probably helped to achieve the substantial numbers who came forward and applied, it also meant rather long delays in getting the program up and running as it was often difficult to find suitably located and sufficient office space to rent. The temporary nature of the program also contributed to some difficulty in finding owners of office space willing to rent such space to the INS (from interviews with district office officials).

The difficulty that the INS experienced in finding, renting, setting up, and staffing new offices to implement the legalization programs was closely related to another frequent complaint about the program cited during the interviews and from the responses to mailed questionnaires sent to QDE offices—the problem of transportation many applicants experienced in getting to the legalization offices. Getting from rural Illinois to an office in downtown Chicago can be difficult in terms of both time and money for migrant workers. Yet the attitude of some INS staff was reflected in the comments made to one QDE staffer interviewed who, when complaining of transportation problems faced by clients trying to get to the Chicago office, was told: "If they can get to Illinois, they can d— — — well get to our Chicago office."

The problem most frequently cited during the field interviews at QDE offices, and one cited in half of the mailed questionnaire responses from QDE agencies, was the tremendous difficulty involved in securing the proper documents. Undocumented aliens, especially the often poorly educated migrant workers, had a long tradition of avoiding paper documentation of their status in the United States. Suddenly, they were being required to provide various (and often changing) documentary proof of their continuous residency in the United States since 1982.

Other problems associated with the long delay in the program start-up concerned the difficulties that the QDE agency personnel and, more importantly, the legalization applicants experienced in dealing with INS employees who were themselves misinformed and poorly trained in IRCA's rules and regulations. This, in part, was exacerbated by the long period of time during which the INS had inconsistency in its rules and regulations. Naturally, the decision to decentralize legalization implementation meant that there would be differences from region to region and even from district office to district office within a region. Such confusion and delay was, in part, the result of the length of time it took the INS to develop and distribute the correct forms and to some rather frequent changes in the rules, regulations, or interpretations of the language used during the Phase I period of the legalization program.

One QDE official interviewed described the changes as "monthly." Another described the first phase as "chaotic . . . a real mess . . . the right hand didn't know what the left was doing." The INS released its preliminary working draft of the legalization regulations late in 1986. However, the *proposed* regulations were not first published in the *Federal Register* until March 1987, and the *final* regulations were not issued until May 1, 1987—a mere four months before the commencement of the application period. Perhaps the resulting confusion about the rules and regulations accounts for the frequent complaints that were made during the field interviews and the mailed questionnaire responses about INS adjudicators being "arbitrary and capricious," or of "front-desk staff" dismissing an applicant's case out-of-hand for some minor paperwork error or even due to their own misunderstanding of the proper rules, even before the adjudicator ever saw the applicant's documentation.

In part, these problems also reflected the review procedures established for legalization. As noted by one study:

> All cases recommended for denial by adjudicators were subject to a thorough RPF (Regional Processing Facility) review, however. As a result, local legalization office personnel in our field interviews noted that recommendations for denial became a strategy to "flag" what they considered questionable or thinly documented cases, ensuring that they would undergo close scrutiny at the RPF. In contrast, all SAW applications received an RPF review, regardless of the local adjudicator's recommendation, reflecting the INS's concern with fraud in the SAW application process. (Baker 1990, 108)

Inconsistency in the rules further resulted in the actual or apparent case of very subjective treatment of applicants by INS staff. Complaints about the discriminatory or subjective treatment of clients by INS staff, of their being "rude," "racist," or "insensitive," and treating clients in a very inhumane manner were among the most frequently cited during the field interviews and in the mailed responses from QDE offices. Indeed, INS employee "misinformation" or "bad attitude" were mentioned in one-third of the responses. District offices serving areas that had a variety of ethnic backgrounds among the applicants seemed more often to evidence such problems in their treatment of applicants. In New York and, to a degree, in Florida, for example, Haitians were clearly dealt with more harshly than were Cubans; in Illinois, Hispanics were not treated as well as Polish applicants; and in California, Iranians experienced harsher treatment (from field interviews). As one QDE staff member put it: "If you look brown, you're checked"—meaning the paperwork was given extra careful scrutiny for possible fraud.

Nearly 20 percent of the mailed questionnaire responses cited the long waiting periods for the INS to adjudicate applications, and roughly one-third cited the "lack of follow-up" by the INS and "insufficient training" of INS staff as significant problems they encountered in dealing with the legalization programs. Many cited cases where files were misplaced or lost—one referring to the local district office address as "that black hole on — — — street."

Confusing rules and complicated paperwork brought another associated problem—the fraudulent exploitation of applicants by unscrupulous immigration lawyers and other businesses that quickly set up storefront operations to assist often illiterate or poorly educated illegal aliens seeking to legalize their status. Such operations often charged considerable fees to perform routine, useless, or even totally unnecessary services for applicants. For example, one interview mentioned a local storefront operation that charged $80 simply to fill out a RAW program application card, and $500 to fill out Phase II forms. Mexicans who, by culture, had a completely different perception of what it is to have a document notarized, for instance, were especially susceptible to such economic exploitation.

Many respondents complained that their clients experienced real difficulty in finding access to affordable doctors or health officials to obtain necessary certification regarding various health requirements (i.e., the AIDS test requirement). Many also complained about the harsh situation that developed regarding the separation of families as a result of legalization rules wherein a parent, spouse, or children of qualified applicants would not themselves qualify, particularly with the January 1, 1982 residency requirement of the LAWs program. As one law professor and QDE agency official noted:

> The issue of "family fairness" indubitably played a part in limiting the number of applications that were submitted. Specifically, the lack of protection for ineligible

spouses and exposure of them to deportation was not required by statute and could have been obviated through a more humanitarian response to the problem. If the Attorney General had used his discretion to accord such individuals deferred action status, for example, it may very well have resulted in significantly more applications. (Professor Carrasco, in Tomasi 1989, 32; Baker 1990, 149)

And again, this issue evidenced wide variations across jurisdictions, from highly publicized and inclusive family fairness campaigns, as in Chicago, to what some immigration lawyers called "sting operations," in which family members applied, were denied, and were promptly subjected to deportation proceedings (Baker 1990, 147). Indeed, the issue was not really resolved until 1990.

In February 1990, over two years after the family fairness wire had gone to the field, a new INS Commissioner revised the policy and issued a new implementation wire. The new policy granted annually renewable voluntary departure to ineligible minor children and spouses of legalizing aliens, withdrew the condition of "compelling or humanitarian factors" from spousal eligibility, and provided for work authorization. The policy reflected a 180-degree shift from the position stated by the Department of Justice during IRCA debate, and reflected the broader trend toward slow but substantive liberalization throughout IRCA's implementation. (ibid., 149)

The cost to the legalization program was, by design, passed on to the applicants themselves. It was intended to be a primarily self-funded program. An application fee of $185 was to cover the implementation of the entire program, with a per-family cap of $420. The INS defended and justified this cost by comparing the fees of legalization versus the cost of a regular immigrant securing a visa. This comparison is shown in Table 4.4. But this cost was nearly prohibitive for many families in the eligible population. The actual cost of applying, of course, was much more when one considers the additional related costs of waivers, medical examinations, fingerprints,

Table 4.4
Comparison of Fees: Legalization versus Immigrant Visas (Sample Family of Five)

	Legalization Fees	Immigrant Visa Fees
Principal	$185	$185
Spouse	185	185
1st Child	50	185
2nd Child	0	185
3rd Child	0	185
Total	$420	$925

Source: Immigration and Naturalization Service, *INS Reporter,* January 1988, 10.

photographs, and legal fees often necessary. A typical family of four faced expenses of nearly $1,000, not $420. This cost is put into a more appropriate perspective when compared to the median household income, in 1986 census data, of Hispanic households of Mexican origin, which was $19,326. Undoubtedly, some who were eligible for legalization did not apply because they simply could not afford to do so (Tomasi 1989, 32).

In addition, the fact that Congress chose the January 1, 1982 cut-off date rather than a "date-of-act," had a deleterious effect on the program. By Congress selecting a date earlier than enactment and earlier than the employer-sanctions provision, IRCA created a new class of people afraid to come out of the shadows of illegal alien status. Those who entered the United States after January 1, 1982 and before November 6, 1986 (when the act became law), were likely to live and work illegally in the United States because their employers were not subject to sanctions under the "grandfather" clause of that provision. Similarly, people who entered before January 1, 1982 but became illegal aliens after that date (e.g., some visa overstayers) also fell into that category of this new class. In short, the specific date chosen by Congress created a new class of people who would likely remain in an underground illegal status—the very condition that the law intended to avoid. Moreover, the INS program of family fairness unfortunately did little to assuage these problems (ibid., 20).

Other detailed requirements Congress enacted in IRCA created barriers to applicants seeking legalization. IRCA's rules of exclusion concerning three misdemeanors and one felony, public charge, continuous residency, and continuous physical presence, or whether the applicant's presence was "known to the government," created obstacles. Congress also established special waivers for ineligible applicants.

These rules were exacerbated as problems or barriers to a successful generous legalization program by the interpretation that the INS gave to them. First, the INS defined Congressional terms in ways that were contrary to long-standing practice. This required court action fighting the INS's interpretation (see, for example, *Guitierrez v. Ilchert* and *Catholic Social Services, Inc. v. Meese,* both in 1988, which struck down INS's interpretation under IRCA regulations of brief, casual, and innocent trips as inconsistent with INS's long-standing interpretations). The INS also defined terms in a manner that was plainly inconsistent with Congressional intent, also requiring court action to overturn the interpretation (*Ayuda Inc. v. Meese,* 1988, in which "known to the government" was ruled not to mean "known to INS," all as cited and discussed in Kurzban 1989, 20–21).

The unnecessarily narrow or plainly incorrect reading of Congressional intent by the INS caused substantial confusion among potential applicants, as did the INS's frequent changes of position on a number of issues. These court-ordered or INS-decided rule changes undoubtedly confused and probably discouraged a number of potential applicants. The INS did not provide any clear definition, for instance, of how expunged convictions were to be treated and whether they could bar the use of convictions that would render the applicant for amnesty ineligible. Initially, the INS took the position that expunged convictions did not erase an applicant's conviction. Such applicant was therefore ineligible for legalization. But the INS, less than two weeks before the completion of the program, reversed its position (ibid., 21).

INS regulations often reflected very technical distinctions, making it difficult for immigration lawyers and examiners to follow, and impossible for the general public to comprehend. This type of a formal, legalistic, hair-splitting approach was seen in the way the INS treated questions of "public charge." Yet such cases were precisely those in which the applicant had little knowledge about the program and less access to legal assistance. Such legalism leaves the applicant confused, and hampers a program intended to reach a socially and economically underground population with marginal education and English language skills and no legal training. A simpler and more generous approach to Congressional terms would have been more consistent with the program's stated goals.

Virtually everyone interviewed stated that the INS's media and outreach campaign was too little and too late. It did not really get under way until the legalization program was nearly over. The media outreach was more evident and effective for the Spanish-speaking population, but was far less so for nearly all other language groups. Followup and outreach to those in Phase I to ensure their continued action to successfully complete Phase II was also highly criticized as too little and too late.

The Cuban/Haitian Adjustment Act is a generous amnesty program. Most of the Cuban entrants, including those from Mariel, have applied or could apply under the Cuban Refugee Adjustment Act of 1966. Thus, IRCA's legalization program is best judged by its treatment of Haitian applicants. Interviews with QDE agency staff in Florida cited more difficulty in the INS's treatment of Haitians than they experienced with Cuban clients. One knowledgeable source, however, rather positively evaluates the Florida implementation of the program in which it processed nearly 40,000 applicants as Haitian entrants:

> To the agency's credit, it addressed those applications in an expedited program lasting only several months that caused little disruption of the rest of the district office's work. The program was conducted in a courteous, professional environment that emphasized the generous nature of Congressional intent. As a result of those efforts well over twenty thousand Haitians have become residents and are now able to apply for citizenship and become full members of our political and economic community. (Kurzban 1989, 22)

By contrast, the New York district office took a more negative approach to the whole program:

> The climate of harassment, intimidation and hostility faced by Haitians in New York who were seeking permanent residency under this special act was also in sharp contrast to the courteous and professional treatment they received in Florida and other places in the United States. As a result of the overtly hostile treatment Haitians received in New York City, litigation has been initiated against the district director and his staff. (ibid., 23)

The Haitian Adjustment program in New York, Florida, and elsewhere have been plagued by problems for Haitians not registered in the INS computers or for whom files do not exist. Under IRCA, a Haitian who was documented by the INS is entitled to the adjustment to permanent residency. But there are many cases where no file exists, where the Haitian's alien registration number was mistakenly assigned to another person, or where the Haitian is simply not listed in the INS computer. The legislative history of IRCA recognized the problem of lost files and lack of current documentary evidence because many such files were lost during the course of the *Jean v. Nelson* case (1985), or simply as a result of the passage of time since 1972. Yet the INS's position was to refuse to grant status to the applicant even when he or she presented secondary proof in the form of affidavits and live testimony. The agency granted permanent residency only if its own records reflected that the file had been lost or destroyed. This approach caused much hardship and the Haitian Refugee Center and other organizations began litigation on the issue.

The SAW legalization program also involved a history of more problematic interpretation. Local INS offices looked upon SAW applicants with a high degree of suspicion and skepticism (Baker 1990, 138–139). The SAW program allows for the temporary residency of aliens who have performed field labor in perishable agricultural commodities for at least 90 days during the year ending May 1, 1986, and are otherwise admissible as immigrants. The eighteen-month application period began on June 1, 1987 and ended on November 30, 1988. Up to 350,000 aliens who worked ninety days in each of the three years preceding May 1, 1986 were eligible for Group 1 temporary resident status. Adjustment to permanent residence was essentially automatic for both groups; however, aliens in Group 1 were eligible on December 1, 1989 and those in Group 2 were eligible one year later. IRCA also provides for the temporary residence and later permanent residence of agricultural workers under the Replenishment Agricultural Worker program (RAW).

Initially, problems developed around INS's interpretation and rulings as to which crops constituted perishable agriculture. The SAW applicant, moreover, had to provide a preponderance of evidence that he or she had worked the ninety man-days of farm labor. No specific kinds of proof were mandated for SAW applicants. Rather, Congress recognized the extreme difficulty migrant farm workers would face to obtain standard employment records. It therefore made the Fair Labor Standards Act (FLSA) case law applicable to SAW cases. This provided an exceptionally lenient standard of proof that allowed even uncorroborated testimony alone to create a just and reasonable inference that shifted the burden of disproving that inference to the other party. INS regulations also provided that proof other than standard employer records, including affidavits from crew leaders and co-workers, might be submitted. Yet despite these very liberal standards intended by Congress, the INS applied standards of proof that undermined the Congressional intent. Because the INS was so concerned about fraud in the SAW program (and it undoubtedly was extensive), it set standards for SAW cases that included payroll and like employment records that farm workers found difficult if not impossible to produce, resulting in a much slower processing of application.

Many immigrant advocacy groups and QDEs felt uncomfortable representing cases whose entire documentation consisted of an affidavit from a single farm-labor contractor. Soon, local for-profit immigration and *notarios publicos* reported the bulk of SAW clients rather than the established QDEs. The perception of the SAW program as being fraud-ridden led many of the most credible agencies to cease assisting SAW applicants, who then increasingly turned to the *notarios* who were themselves the targets of INS fraud investigations. By the fall of 1988, the SAW program became synonymous with fraud in the local INS lexicon (ibid., 139). This criticism was especially the case for those SAW applicants who applied within the final six months of the program, who numbered more than half to the total SAW applicant pool.

Local INS suspicions of fraud resulted in the agency taking actions to prevent or detect it. In San Jose, Calif., applicants who were suspected of using fraud were videotaped during their interviews. In New York, INS investigators cited massive fraud and denied some 5,000 SAW applications employment authorization cards until court action forced them to call the applicants back and issued them work cards. They also issued "notices of intent to deny" to the applicants. This action averted a lawsuit in the Eastern region similar to the class-action suits that won the issuance of work authorization cards and revision of SAW adjudication procedures in the West and the South (ibid., 140).

At first SAW approval rates were relatively high (about 85 percent). As suspicion of fraud grew, denials began to rise. In the South, where they first rose, class-action court cases won challenges of the evidentiary standards that led to the denials. The INS had difficulty proving the fraud to the satisfaction of the courts.

The district court had ordered a sweeping injunction requiring the INS to readjudicate all applications where improper procedures were utilized (*Haitian Refugee Center, Inc. et al. vs. Nelson et al.* 1988). That led to a review of approximately 21,000 SAW applications by the Southern RPF (cited in Kurzban 1989, 25; Baker 1990, 141).

Another source of difficulty in the SAW fraud situation was the INS's lack of resources to deal with the size of the investigative task—in each region a half-dozen or so investigative agents were assigned hundreds of thousands of cases.

These difficulties with processing fraud at the regional level led some local INS operations to undertake their own effort to deal with the problem. Probably the best example of this was the Houston case. After months of work and apparent failure at the regional level, the Houston office simply held up the last 140,000 applicants in its SAW pool, and assigned a fraud officer to interview everyone in the pool. It set up its own SAW Fraud Task Force in early 1989 out of the Houston legalization office (Baker 1990, 141–145).

The SAW program had unquestionably been troubled with many more cases of fraudulant documents. By October 1989, the INS had placed 390,000 SAW applications on hold because of suspected fraud and had arrested about 750 people for selling phony labor documents. Packets of such documents were selling for up to $2,000 in central Texas, and $1,500 to $3,000 in California (from field interviews with INS district offices).

The SAW fraud problem further illustrates the often poor coordination within the INS bureaucracy—the lack of communication between the INS agent who investigates fraud and employees who process applications. Names of people convicted of selling reams of false documents were often not distributed to other INS offices. In some cases, even when applicants admitted to investigators that their documents were fraudulent, the processing centers approved the applications. The deputy district director of the Houston INS district office claimed to have over 1,000 sworn statements of aliens admitting to the use of phony papers, yet whose applications were still approved at the regional-level office.[3]

By the end of the program, the INS had granted an approval rate of roughly 93 percent, quite comparable to the LAWs program (with an approval rate of 95 percent).

Employer Sanctions

Before passage of IRCA, its proponents viewed employment as the magnet drawing aliens here and employer-sanctions provisions as designed to close the job market to undocumented workers. The major controversy with these provisions centered on a fear that such sanctions would lead to widespread discrimination against authorized aliens and even native-born Americans who appeared "foreign" (principally Hispanic Americans). To address those concerns, IRCA makes it illegal to discriminate against any individual on account of national origin or citizenship status; however, it is not illegal to select a U.S. citizen over an alien for employment if the two are equally qualified. In addition, an Office of Special Counsel was established to investigate and prosecute charges of immigration-related employment discrimination. In the event that these measures proved ineffective and there was evidence of widespread discrimination (as was subsequently determined by the final, of three, report of the General Accounting Office), then the employer-sanctions program could have been terminated by Congress (LeMay 1989, 4).

As was the case with the legalization program, and despite intensive effort by the INS, almost every field interview and half of the mailed questionnaire responses cited a lack of information about the sanctions program among employers as one of the most significant problems they faced in dealing with it. Numerous instances of *misinformation* given to employers by poorly-trained INS staff were recounted. Border Patrol agents who shifted from their regular duties to temporary service in the employer-sanctions program were frequently mentioned as part of the problem, as there was such an inconsistency between the Border Patrol's normal police enforcement attitude and the basic idea behind the law. Their misinformation led to such practices as business personnel staff ignoring the "grandfather clause" and firing undocumented workers, some of whom were in the process of having their status legalized.

Most of the QDE officials interviewed, and half of the mailed responses, cited increased discrimination by employers as a significant problem with the program. Haitians, Hispanics, and women workers particularly seemed to be the targets of such employer discrimination.

Rumors and a general fear of the INS by legalizing applicants seeking or keeping jobs and by employers afraid they would be fined was a problem the INS staff experienced in implementing employer sanctions. As part of the public education task, the INS did have to do some image changing (from field interviews).

Those problems, of course, in large measure flowed from the sheer volume or size of the education task confronting the INS in implementing the sanctions program. IRCA affects in excess of *7 million employers,* and, of course, scores of millions of newly hired employees every year. IRCA requires employers to maintain on file for three years the I-9 forms attesting that they have inspected specified work eligibility and identification documents submitted by the employee. Informing so many employers, especially the smaller companies that had only a few employees, was a monumental task and one should not be surprised that many employers still do not understand the law or the requirements under it despite the INS's strenuous efforts to so inform them.

That there exists a fairly sizable population of employers who do not fully or properly understand their obligations under IRCA, and particularly the antidiscrimination provisions of the law, was substantiated by the 1988 GAO report on the results of its survey of employers (GAO 1988b, 46–53).

The GAO survey showed that two major provisions of the law with respect to discrimination were clearly not well understood. Similar results were found in the state government task force reports as well. Of the estimated 1.7 million employers who were aware of and received information on IRCA, the GAO estimated that about 20 percent (about 332,000) were unclear about the authority to hire a U.S. citizen rather than an authorized alien when both were equally qualified, and that 15 percent (about 248,000) were unclear about the penalties for employers who discriminated. In addition, the GAO survey found that about 16 percent (an estimated 528,000) of the 3.3 million employers who were aware of the law reported beginning or increasing policies or practices that might not have been permitted under the law. For example, they specifically said that they: (1) asked only foreign-looking or foreign-sounding job applicants for work-authorization documents, (2) asked only current workers who were foreign-looking or foreign-sounding to present work authorization documents, and (3) began a new policy to hire only U.S. citizens.

The GAO survey found that unfair hiring practices were generally not related to the employer's state, industry, or business size. Instead, such practices seem to be related to the employer's knowledge of IRCA's I-9 verification requirements and previous INS visits. Also, those employers who responded that they had fired "grandfathered" employees for not having work authorization documents were located in the five high alien-population states. Most of the employers who did report beginning or increasing such practices indicated that they did so *because of employer sanctions.*

Several state government studies, discussed more fully in the next chapter, found widespread employer ignorance of IRCA. Studies by Arizona, New York, and Oregon found sufficiently "widespread discrimination" that they essentially concluded that "for the purposes of Congressional review of the impact of employer sanctions as currently implemented a 'widespread' pattern of discrimination had been documented."[4]

A DOL report on its audits of I-9 forms shows comparable rates of compliance: a 57 percent apparent full or partial compliance of companies it inspected during fiscal year 1988, and a 62 percent rate for the first part of fiscal year 1989. As one would expect, such compliance was higher among employers randomly selected for investigation (93 percent) than among those investigated while following up on a specific complaint (60 percent). Noncompliance seems to be correlated with: (1) INS administrative problems, such as an inadequate supply of I-9 forms or a misunderstanding of the verification requirements of the I-9 process; (2) the employers' perceptions of how likely or not they were to be inspected; and (3) how difficult it was for the employer to locate authorized workers (Bean, Vernez, and Keely 1989, 51–52).

Unquestionably, the *major problem* relating to difficulties in effectively enforcing sanctions provisions was that of the availability of fraudulent documents. The widespread access to and use of counterfeit documents was often cited in response to our survey questionnaire—over 40 percent of whom replied that they noted an increase in the use of phony documents. These results closely parallel those of other studies. In a survey conducted by the GAO of employed but unauthorized aliens hired between September 1987 and October 1988, 39 percent had provided or were suspected of using fraudulent documents, mostly fake Social Security and Alien Registration cards. Likewise, a 1987–1988 survey of undocumented aliens on street corners in San Diego found that 41 percent acknowledged that they had either purchased phony documents or borrowed such from a friend or relative in order to gain employment (in Bean, Vernez, and Keely 1989, 53).

This was confirmed in our interviews with INS district enforcement officials in the field. They noted that as the employer-sanctions program progressed, the use of phony documents increased. Counterfeit Social Security cards and "green cards" routinely sold for $40 to $100, and after IRCA the "number of phony documents skyrocketed" (field interviews with INS enforcement officials in California and Arizona). The fact that 18 different variations of the I-551 "green cards" exist complicated enforcement more than anything else. One district office arrested 121 vendors in a ten-month period, and yet such arrests failed to make a dent in the availability of documents, judging from the supply and demand prices for such. Both the Social Security and "green card" documents are easily forged. Small "mom and pop" printing operations can readily produce them and such businesses spring up as fast as the INS puts others out of the market. While trained agents can easily spot such phony documents, most employers cannot.

This problem was noted in a 1988 study by the GAO that concluded that there were simply too many such documents that could be used for employment eligibility purposes to realistically expect employers to control unauthorized employment. Many of those documents are very easy to counterfeit. It recommended reducing the number of documents that could be used for employment authorization, and making the Social Security card, after suitably improving its issuance process and making it considerably more tamperproof, the only authorizing document (General Accounting Office 1988a).

Enhancement of the Border Patrol

To date, the most significant problems involved in implementing IRCA's provisions to strengthen the role of the Border Patrol have been: (1) the lag in actual appropriations of funds to accomplish that effort; (2) the difficulty the INS has experienced in recruiting new Border Patrol staff; and (3) problems centering on the need to expand training staff and facilities.

Increasing actual border-enforcement activities has also been complicated by the INS's new responsibilities, particularly those of educating employers about IRCA-related requirements, and the need to enforce such requirements, and the above-mentioned new responsibilties associated with the drug interdiction effort.

INTERGOVERNMENTAL ASPECTS OF IRCA

One of the more interesting aspects of IRCA, and certainly one of the more problematic for implementation purposes, is the complex set of intergovernment relations it establishes. These include both federal-to-federal agency relationships, federal-to-state and federal-to-local relations, and state-to-state and state-to-local relationships. When a law as complex as IRCA launches an entirely new approach to a policy area, and particularly when it divides the responsibilities for conducting that new policy among a host of government levels and agencies, it necessitates the development of new bureaucratic relationships between and among the various agencies affected by the new law. Establishing such new interbureaucratic working relationships takes time and inherently involves implementation problems.

Intra-Federal Relations

A number of federal departments and agencies have already been alluded to above. But those are just agencies *primarily* impacted. Following is a list of all the federal agencies impacted by IRCA, giving one a better sense of that complexity:

Department of Justice

- Immigration and Naturalization Service
- Office of the Special Counsel for Immigration-Related Discrimination

Department of Health and Human Services

- Health Care Financial Administration
- Division of State Legalization Assistance
- Office of Refugee Resettlement
- Family Support Administration
- U.S. Public Health Service, Office of Refugee Health

Department of Labor

- Office of Federal Contract Compliance Programs
- Wage and Hour Division

General Accounting Office

Federal Social Security Administration

Department of Education

Federal Equal Employment Opportunity Commission

Department of Agriculture—Food and Nutrition Service

Census Bureau

Department of Housing and Urban Development

Department of State—Bureau of Migration and Refugee Affairs

Federal District Courts

IRCA impacted on the Immigration and Naturalization Service within the Justice Department, of course, in myriad ways—from increasing its funding, staffing, and responsibilities to even the nature of its relationship with its parent department. For example, IRCA created an entirely new office and operation within the Justice Department—the Office of Special Counsel for Immigration Related Unfair Employment Practices.

The special counsel's office recruited and was staffed by sixteen attorneys and fourteen administrative and support staff members. It had to create new forms, and develop and put sense into the various procedures to assert citizenship-status discrimination claims. It developed Form I-722, the Declaration of Intending Citizen, to claim discrimination. But that form became an INS form. Originally, it could only be filed with the INS. But as its purpose was to meet the law's requirements to file a discrimination charge based on citizenship status, many aliens logically concluded and assumed it should be filed with the Office of Special Counsel. Misfiled forms delayed processing of charges. Thus, a formal agreement was worked out and announced in the *Federal Register,* completed only by mid-October 1988, under which the INS agreed that the Office of Special Counsel could serve as its agent for receiving I-772 form charges.

Attorney General Edwin Meese had to issue regulations announcing that successful legalization applicants were protected from citizenship-status discrimination *from the time they applied.* This afforded protection to the over 1.7 million aliens who had applied for legalization, covering them during the processing period.

Moreover, the Office of Special Counsel and the Equal Employment Opportunity Commission (EEOC) had to develop and enter into an interim Memorandum of Understanding that each agency would be the agent for the other for the purpose of filing charges under Title VII and Section 102. Unless this was done, a timely charge filed with the wrong agency would have negated a claim. The special counsel's office invited similar agreements with 114 state and local civil rights enforcement agencies (from statement of the counsel, Lawrence Siskind, to the U.S. House Committee on the Judiciary, 10 May 1989; U.S. Department of Justice 1989, 195). The Office of Special Counsel also dealt with the Chief Administrative Hearing Officer of the Department of Justice with whom it files its charges.

The INS shared its responsibility for inspecting employer's I-9 forms with the Department of Labor. That department added responsibility for such to its Wage and Hour Division (WHD) and its Office of Federal Contract Compliance Programs (OFCCP). By January 1989, the DOL also began implementing the H-2A Temporary Agriculture Workers Program, which was similar to the old H-2 program. It allowed individual growers wider use of temporary foreign workers when labor shortages were certified by the DOL. IRCA streamlined the program by requiring DOL determination to be made within set time periods. It was projected to increase to as high as 200,000 workers, but the volume under H-2A did not differ from the previous H-2 program of about 20,000 temporary farm workers authorized for admission to about 1,700 employers, mostly East Coast and Mid-Atlantic growers (Bean, Vernez, and Keely 1989, 247).

Another federal agency involved in a major way in the implementation of IRCA was the Department of Health and Human Services (DHHS) which administered the State Legalization Impact Assistance Grant (SLIAG). It administered federal funds set in law at one billion dollars for each of four years beginning in 1988. These funds were to compensate state and local government for the increased costs of providing certain services to the newly legalized population. More will be said of the myriad intergovernmental relation problems of this program in the subsequent section of this chapter dealing with state and local government involvement.

Additionally, DHHS's Office of Refugee Health (ORH) administers a program for medical consultation to the INS, detention, and deportation, and provides medical services to undocumented aliens at selected service-processing center sites throughout the United States. The ORH coordinates the mental health services for the Department of Justice (DOJ) for Cuban entrants at the INS Detention Facility at St. Elizabeth's Hospital in Washington, D.C., and oversees a DOJ outplacement residential community program for Cuban entrants (Tomasi 1989, 139; and *Governing,* May 1989, 25–30).

The General Accounting Office was charged in IRCA with conducting three annual reviews of the impact of IRCA, primarily to determine whether its employer-sanctions program constituted an undue burden on business to comply with the law, and whether that program resulted in a "widespread pattern of discrimination." In order to implement its charge, of course, the GAO was required to deal with literally hundreds of federal, state, and local governments as employers and to assist it in data-gathering on the impact of the law. The GAO also, of course, surveyed thousands of businesses, and dealt with hundreds of community service organizations and immigration policy scholars.

The Social Security Administration deals with businesses and with state and local governments in certifying the authenticity of people's work eligibility.

Federal courts become involved whenever a new law is implemented as well, especially when the new law launches a radical departure in policy and is such a complex law as is IRCA. Whenever a new law is passed and its implementation begun, its legislative policies and the "intent of Congress," must be established as a new set of operational rules and regulations developed by the federal agencies involved in the implementation process. As we have seen, such rules develop over a period of time. Draft regulations elicit public comments, during which time interested parties can challenge the agency's interpretation of the law. Final rules are then published in the *Federal Register* and become the operating guidelines for implementing the new law. These can, and routinely are, challenged in the courts. Such court challenges to INS regulations were filed almost as soon as the regulations were published and resulted in dozens of lawsuits filed in various federal courts around the nation. Most were class-action suits seeking liberalization of rules and regulations of the two main legalization programs. Some were national in scope, although several challenged regional INS practices. The courts generally overturned the administration's position and granted the relief being sought. Advocates argued that the INS, however, was slow in implementing such court-ordered remedies (Bean, Vernez, and Keely 1989, 49–50).

State and Local Intergovernmental Relations

As with the federal level, IRCA impacts upon a great number of state and local agencies in several ways. State and local governments are collectively among the largest employers in the United States. There are also numerous state agencies that regulate or assist in employment services, all of which are potentially impacted by IRCA. Perhaps the most complicated and significant impact of IRCA on state and local relationships, involving state-to-federal, local-to-federal, state-to-state, and state-to-local intergovernment relations flows from the SLIAG and SAVE provisions of IRCA. The very newness of the law and the novel approach to federal grants entailed in the SLIAG program meant that the various states were all required to "reinvent the wheel" in how to work with this program. Much state-to-state consultation resulted as various states thrashed out the nitty-gritty working relationships with DHHS on how to apply for SLIAG funds.

Passage of IRCA impacted upon many state governors' offices, state offices of planning and budgeting, general administration, state offices of federal or local relations, state departments of health, welfare, education, employment, economic development or security, agriculture, vocational boards, human rights commissions, and offices of community services, to name the most obvious. Precisely how and with which such state agencies IRCA impacted varies greatly from state to state, of course, given the United States' highly complex federal system. Indeed, in addition to impacting upon numerous state agencies, the passage of IRCA spawned the development, in many states, of variously organized and informal to formally created task force bodies or commissions set up to help coordinate the work of the many state and local governments involved. In New York state, for example, a total of thirty-three state and local agencies are regularly involved in one or another aspect of implementing IRCA's complex provisions.

A number of problems flow from the intergovernment complexities of IRCA. In responses to our survey of state and local agencies, for instance, any number of them noted and complained about the difficulty of dealing with the various rules and regulations emanating from other agencies, of coping with the natural confusion brought about by a different language being used by those agencies, or simply by the newness of the approach established by IRCA. Many complained that the DHHS had "no idea about how we operate; how we keep our records." Funding has been awkward and slow, both from the federal level and sometimes at the state level. Several complained that the reporting requirements were "strange."

The SLIAG program, especially, elicited complaints about how long it took for the DHHS to finalize its rules and regulations, long after the program had already started. The need to satisfy requirements of both the INS and DHHS, which sometimes seemed in direct contradiction, was often mentioned as being an especially problematic aspect of the SLIAG program. Clearly, it would have been easier if one department had administered the program. Rules and regulations were often referred to as "nebulous."

As with the legalization program, many agencies dealing with SLIAG complained about the lack of knowledge among INS and DHHS staff regarding aspects of IRCA. They found it exceedingly difficult to educate applicants about all the rules and regulations. One such response, for example, complained: "This agency deals only with SLIAG. The paperwork could be a plot for a grade B horror movie. It should have been a simple block grant."

That so many agencies were involved contributed to confusing regulations, to uncertainty as to whether applications for refunding of certain expenses would be accepted, and to cases wherein the alien applicants were exploited. Many state education agencies complained that only being allowed 1.5 percent to administer the program was not enough. Others complained that the 40-hour course (civics and English) was far too short to be of much value. In addition, the intergovernment complexity contributed to complaints of SLIAG being "top heavy" from DHHS on down, with far too much red tape, and a resulting waste of a lot of money in data-collection systems and in developing a new management system for such a short-term grant.

State governments, in part, attempted to coordinate such complexities, at least from the state level downward, by setting one agency as the "single point of contact" (SPOC) for SLIAG programs in the state. While the use of the SPOC undoubtedly helped with coordination, it also created problems of its own.

> The major problem our office faces is California's organization for implementing the program. The Governor designated the Health and Welfare Agency as the lead agency

for the division of available federal dollars. By placing authority to divide education, health, and social welfare funds in an executive agency under the Governor's authority, it sets the stage for governance conflict over program funds in California. One example of this problematic organization scheme is that the proportion of funds on education in California is next to the lowest among the five states with the largest amnesty population. (Field interviews)

The SPOC aspect of the SLIAG program often means a difficult task for the coordinating agency, one of which noted, "We deal with several human resource agencies that are responsible for delivery of the approved programs as well as the State Department of Education, the community college system, community-based agencies, migrant health clinics, etc. In total, we have direct and indirect contact with 14 state agencies and numerous subcontractors" (Field interviews).

The newness of the SLIAG approach meant that an entirely new system of grant management had to be devised. In the past, federal grant programs were typically block grants in which the grant was announced, state or local agencies applied to the specified government agency, and if awarded the grant, were allocated the money. Money in hand was used to provide the service. The SLIAG approach turned that typical system on its head. In IRCA's case, the state and local agencies spent the money providing the services, then had to apply to be refunded, thus needing to develop a new management system to prove to the DHHS that the money already spent was for eligible services performed for eligible clients, that is, for those certified as eligible legalizing aliens (ELAs). That meant there would be new problems and delays in getting the new approach to grants off and running. To cite from one agency response that reflects this problem:

The Bureau of Refugee Services, Department of Human Services had to enter into letters of agreement with the Department of Health and the Department of Education and into contracts with the — — — State Association of Counties and County Boards of Supervisors. A monitoring system had to be established with all these agencies. Training had to be provided on how to document ELAs and SLIAG reimbursement costs. (Questionnaire responses from State Agency)

Naturally, setting up a new system of management involved delays. And as yet another state agency questionnaire respondent noted:

Delays on the part of federal agencies in promulgating and posting final rules and regulations governing various aspects of IRCA have caused problems for the state. To further compound the problem, INS is months if not years behind the projected timetable for processing all the ELA applications, especially those seeking adjustment under Section 210 of IRCA. These delays and the lack of swift adjudication of the SAW applications have severely hampered the state's ability to claim the SLIAG funds available for reimbursement for allowable service costs. (Questionnaire responses from State Agency)

Another state agency respondent, also dealing with the SLIAG grant system, recognized similar problems but reflected a more tempered tone, recognizing more explicitly the fact that such problems, while typical of any such new program, were also somewhat temporary:

> We deal almost exclusively with SLIAG-related topics. The communication dealing with the implementation of this program in its incipient stages was somewhat confusing. However, as the program matures and the rules and regulations become rational and easy to work with and the communication improves, SLIAG will undoubtedly be much easier to administer and implement. All new programs seem to go through such a sorting out phase during which communication of regulations and the interpretation of those regulations produce some confusion. The SLIAG program ORR personnel seem committed to reducing this confusion however. (Responses to mailed questionnaires to State Agencies)

Yet another view of the problem was presented in a response from a state with a small population of legalizing aliens. For them, participation in the program was often prohibitive because the costs involved in documenting their few cases of ELAs exceeded whatever refunds they could likely receive. One such agency noted:

> Kentucky has such a small alien population that the value of many provisions of IRCA is questionable. The alien status verification requirement has not resulted in any illegal aliens being identified. The declaration of citizenship or satisfactory immigration status requirement is burdensome since we verify citizen or alien status. Legalized aliens in Kentucky are less than 700. All but one agency, Public Health, declined to apply for SLIAG, reasoning that the population was too small, and the program requirements too burdensome. (Responses to mailed questionnaires to State Agencies)

A Minnesota respondent, another state with a small impact from IRCA, noted a related yet somewhat different aspect of the new law:

> IRCA requires that *all* new employees be "certified" to work in the U.S. As the public employment service, many employers would like us to handle the certification issue, especially for those individuals we refer to employers. This would reduce the cost of recruitment for employer, reduce the employer's paperwork, and relieve the employer of his/her liability in terms of IRCA's provisions. While we are a logical provider of this service, Minnesota decided not to become involved in the IRCA certification process. We would only have been able to provide this service by eliminating other services we regularly provide. (Responses to mailed questionnaires to State Agencies)

Finally, a report by the Refugee Policy Group for the American Public Welfare Association pointed out numerous problems associated with the SLIAG program. Many of those will be dealt with in the next chapter concerning an evaluation of the effectiveness of IRCA. Two points from that report, however, are especially appropriate to our discussion here. Both relate to problems flowing essentially from the complexity of our federal system and its myriad intergovernment variety. The first concerns the *difficulty for planning* for SLIAG because state and local governments had such poor advance knowledge about their legalizing population. As their report noted:

> The aliens who have applied for legalization have been living in an undocumented illegal status. For the most part, they have avoided contact with U.S. institutions because of their fear of apprehension and detention by the Immigration and Naturalization Service. As a result, there has been little accurate data about their service needs or likely utilization patterns. (American Public Welfare Association 1988, 4–5)

A second and related planning and implementation problem for SLIAG noted in the APWA Report centered on the *variety* between and among the states with regard to the demographics of the ELA population. Some states had one overwhelmingly large group from a single national origin. Mexicans, for example, comprise about 96 percent of the ELAs in Oregon, 87 percent in Texas, 81 percent in California, and 80 percent in Illinois. Other states exhibit a pattern in which no single country predominates, but where most of the legalizing alien population come from a single region. In Florida, for instance, the ELA population was from North America, with 45 percent coming from the Caribbean, 25 percent from Mexico, and 8 percent from Canada. Still other states had to cope with a great variety of national origins among its legalizing population. In New York, for example, 153 nations comprised the origins of its ELAs, with the largest group—Haitians—comprising only 8 percent of the total. In New York, the top ten nationalities nationwide in the legalization program accounted for only 40 percent of its total. In other states, those same top ten averaged 95 percent or more of the legalizing aliens (ibid., 13).

Such variety in the demographics of the ELAs between and within states generated problems for planning and programming to serve their needs; for instance, problems flowing from the distribution of the legalizing population within the state, and with the need for outreach and dissemination of information about their rights and responsibilities under IRCA.

NONGOVERNMENT AGENCIES AND IRCA

Certainly one of the more innovative and interesting aspects of IRCA was its provision for the use of QDEs to assist in implementing the legalization programs. In applying for legalization, applicants could file directly with the INS or through a "qualified designated entity." This was mandated by Congress because it recognized the extensive distrust and pervasive fear of the INS among the target illegal alien population. In terms of the implementation of legalization, the Congressional decision to use QDEs involved both advantages and problems for the implementation of IRCA.

Hundreds of state, local, and community organizations and a host of voluntary organizations were designated by the INS to receive applications and advise applicants. The QDEs, in turn, sent applications to the INS. Because of concern for privacy, IRCA specifies that any information on any application may be used solely for the purpose of judging the application. Data on the application are strictly confidential, and the law restricts their use to determination of the validity of the legalization claim. All QDE files and records are thus confidential. The Attorney General, and even local police departments, are barred from access to them. Organizations seeking QDE status had to show previous immigration counseling experience or the support of people with recognized immigration law experience. National and local QDEs were selected with 977 locations nationwide. A massive training program was conducted by the INS between April and December 1987. A total of 4,310 participants attended 124 training sessions (LeMay 1989, 25).

Use of the QDE approach unquestionably helped in the success of the program. Approximately 20 percent of all applications came through the QDE agencies, and many of those who formally applied through the INS did so only after some advice and consultation with a QDE agency. The INS's outreach program to educate the relevant population on the legalization program was, moreover, enormously aided by various QDE agencies and their efforts. Such agencies frequently translated forms and various media appeals into the appropriate foreign language. They greatly assisted in overcoming fear within the target populations as to the safety and legitimacy of the amnesty program. Literally hundreds of thousands of applicants were successfully processed through the program because of the actions of the various QDE agencies. They effectively expanded the staffing, office location, and other outreach of the INS.

But there were unintended problems with such an approach as well. The use of the QDEs complicated an already complex program. It took the INS considerable time to complete its selections of QDEs and to approve them as designated sites. Their staff frequently had to be expanded and new hires trained in the complexities of IRCA in general, and the legalization programs in particular.

Many QDEs were selected as such precisely because they had long-established traditions and programs of welfare work and assistance to specific target groups. Yet precisely because of that fact, there often existed an adversarial relationship with the INS that had to be dealt with and, if possible, overcome. Staff members of both the INS and the QDE had the difficult task of overcoming mutual distrust and suspicion, if not open antagonism. That meant a period of time during which trust had to be built. Attitudes toward one another had to be changed over time, and frankly were not always accomplished. The adversarial relationship was exacerbated in some cases when the QDE agency became the prime mover or at least a supporting party to class-action litigation against the INS. Sometimes applicants became frustrated with being told one thing by a QDE staffer and something quite different by an INS staff person. Sometimes such frustration undoubtedly led to an undocumented alien's decision not to further pursue amnesty.

But on balance, the various QDE agencies and the INS did work out effective, if not always amicable, relations. Their use not only expanded the success of the amnesty program in terms of reaching out and processing successfully the millions of applicants in Phase I, but many continued to operate and assist in outreach again to ensure that those applicants would likewise proceed through Phase II. More will be discussed about the INS and QDE relationship in the next chapter, when we turn our attention to an analysis evaluating the successes and failures of IRCA.

NOTES

1. State reports include Arizona Civil Rights Advisory Board, two by the New York State Department of Social Services, the Oregon Governor's Immigration Coordinating Committee, and the Pennsylvania Human Relations Commission. Nongovernment reports include the Refugee Policy Group, Center for Policy Analysis and Research on Refugee Issues of the American Public Welfare Association, and the Mexican American Legal Defense Fund (MALDEF). This chapter also used extensively the Bean, Vernez, and Keely book, *Opening and Closing the Doors,* a report of the Program for Research on Immigration Policy of the Rand Corporation and the Urban Institute; the McDonnell and Hill paper (1989), also based on the Rand Corporation study; and *In Defense of the Alien,* Volumes 10 and 11, of proceedings of the Annual Legal Conference on Immigration and Refugee Policy sponsored by the Center for Migration Studies (volumes for the 1986 and 1987 conferences published in 1987 and 1988, respectively). National government reports include several by the INS, the three annual reports of the GAO, plus a few other reports issued by the GAO on relevant aspects of IRCA, and one by the Department of Labor. (See also Baker 1990; and Crane et al. 1990.)

2. Immigration and Naturalization Service, *INS Reporter,* January 1988, 3; "Wendy's Pleads Guilty to Hiring Illegal Aliens," *USA Today,* 3 November 1988, p. 1; and LeMay 1989, 5.

3. "INS Finds False Filings Pervasive," *Austin American Statesmen,* October 1989, A1–12. Several district officials interviewed stated that SAW fraud was widespread. Their estimates of the number of SAW applications that were bogus in part at least ranged from 40 percent to as high as 75 percent.

4. From the report of New York State, Department of Social Services 1988. Similar conclusions were reached in the report of the Arizona Civil Rights Advisory Board 1989; and by the Oregon study, Governor's Immigration Coordinating Committee 1989.

CHAPTER 5

Policy Evaluation: An Assessment of IRCA

Assessing the impact of a law as complex as IRCA is at best a difficult task.[1] The debate since its passage as to the effectiveness of IRCA has been nearly as strenuous as the debate prior to its enactment on the anticipated merits of the proposal. Now that a number of years have passed since its enactment and implementation, a thorough examination is in order. Assessing IRCA, however, is complicated by a lack of agreed-upon indicators to measure some of its effects. But with that caveat firmly stated, this chapter will present an assessment of IRCA. As with the preceding chapter, this one discusses, in order, the major provisions of IRCA. It attempts to assess for each: (1) the degree to which that provision seems to have achieved its intended goals; (2) whether shortcomings in achieving those goals reflect problems in implementation or are the result of faulty assumptions in the policy's legislative strategy; and (3) whether a provision has engendered any unanticipated consequences.

As with Chapter 4, this chapter relies heavily upon the following sources of information: (1) field interviews conducted by the author with over forty individuals who were in the front line of implementing IRCA (see Appendix A); (2) responses to the nearly 800 questionnaires sent to state agencies, district INS offices, and various QDE agencies; (3) several Rand Corporation/ Urban Institute study results that were, in turn, based on hundreds of interviews, some 150 of which were with employers (McDonnell and Hill 1989, 26); (4) the White, Bean, and Espanshade report; (5) assessments made in *In Defense of the Alien, Vol. 11* (Tomasi 1989); (6) the series of GAO and DOL reports on the subject; and (7) the several state government task force reports and studies already cited in Chapter 4.

EMPLOYER SANCTIONS AND DISCRIMINATION

Impact on the Illegal Alien Flow

In measuring the effectiveness of the employer-sanctions provisions of IRCA, we need to examine two important aspects: (1) whether sanctions have demagnetized the pull of the U.S. labor market; and (2) whether the law has resulted in increased and widespread discrimination.

With the phased-in approach to sanctions, its proponents did not expect to see immediate results (McDonnell and Hill 1989, 28). Advocates of employer sanctions had hoped to see an approximately 30 percent reduction in the number of illegal aliens entering the United States as a result of IRCA's passage. Initially that goal seems to have been reached, at least if measured by the decline in the number of undocumented aliens apprehended at the borders. For example, INS data show that total INS apprehensions, including Border Patrol and Investigations Unit apprehensions, declined from 1,767,400 to 1,008,145 between fiscal years 1986 and 1988. That represents a 30 percent decline in border apprehensions in 1987 (from the pre-IRCA 1986 total), and a 42 percent decline from the pre-IRCA level by 1988. In 1989, however, that figure rose again to 1,954,243. In 1990, it was at 1,169,939, and in 1991, was at 1,197,875. The trend line in aliens apprehended (fiscal years 1951 to 1991) is presented in Figure 5.1. The overall impression is that IRCA has had little sustained impact on illegal migration at least as measured by apprehension data.

Such data, however, cannot be so simply interpreted as a direct result of the law. Several scholarly studies have tried to measure the degree to which IRCA has resulted in a significant decrease in the undocumented alien migration. They show how complex it is to measure, and concluded it was too early to tell, or that the law had not reduced the flow to any significant degree.[2]

Two somewhat controversial but sophisticated assessments of the impact of IRCA on the flow of undocumented aliens found substantial decreases.[3] One study employed a monthly time-series of Border Patrol apprehensions from January 1977 to September 1988 to develop a multivariate statistical model (White, Bean, and Espanshade 1989). It found that allocation of INS resources, Mexican population growth, comparative economic conditions, and seasonal factors were all determinants of border apprehensions and thereby the flow of undocumented aliens into the country. In summary, the study found that

> the effects of IRCA on the reduction of apprehensions operates through shifts in INS resources, the agricultural legalization program, and a deterrent effect. Our analysis indicates that the effects of IRCA are smaller than is sometimes inferred,

Figure 5.1
Aliens Apprehended, Fiscal Years 1951–1991

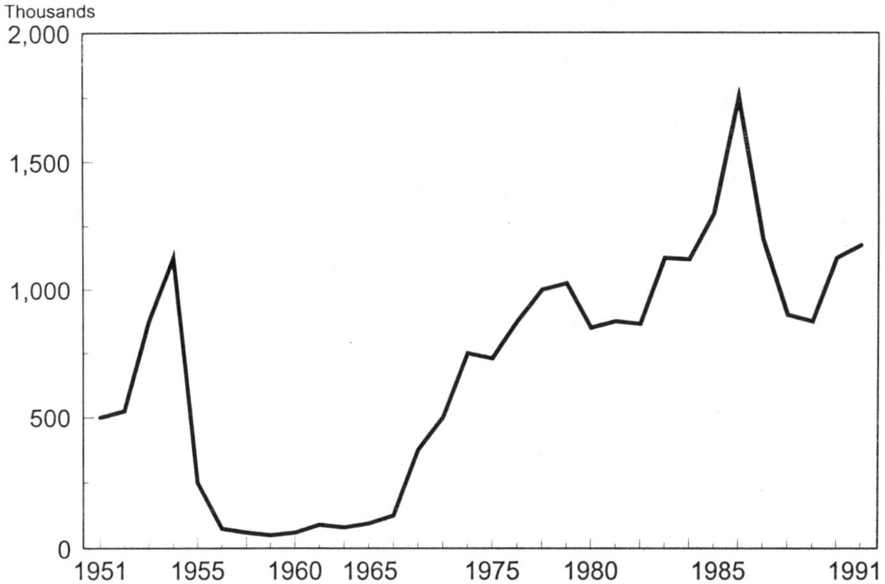

Source: Adapted from Immigration and Naturalization Service 1992, 144.

but are still associated with a cumulative net reduction of apprehensions of nearly 700,000 or 35 percent below what would have been anticipated if circumstances had not changed, in a 23-month period following enactment of the law. (White, Bean, and Espanshade, *Report,* 19 July 1989, Abstract)

A second report (Crane et al. 1990) likewise used multivariate analyses. While the study concluded that none of the data sets provided conclusive evidence that employer sanctions reduced the illegal alien flow, the preponderance of evidence pointed to some decline. Based on their best judgment, the study concluded that estimates indicated a decline of about 20 percent that could be attributed to IRCA's employer-sanctions provision (ibid., 71).

Apprehension data do not assess the degree to which proponents of employer sanctions were correct in their assumption as to the pull of the U.S. labor market as the primary force toward illegal migration. Again, studies of that factor have shown mixed results.

A *Los Angeles Times* poll of a nationally representative sample of Mexicans found that while 62 percent believed that sanctions had discouraged illegal immigration, another 22 percent said they would likely try to emigrate to the United States the next year.[4]

Various demographic and mobility studies have argued that both push and pull factors can substantially explain the motivation of migrants for moving back and forth between the country of origin and that of destination. One such study (Cheng and Nitz 1989) attempted to empirically measure the determinants of Mexican migration to the United States using aggregate data applying a variation of the Suits model (1985) to measure observed migration flows and determinants of migration simultaneously. It tests for both push and pull factors. Aggregate data in that study showed that strong pressures brought about by the decreasing employment opportunities in Mexico led many to choose to leave even under the circumstances that unemployment in the United States was rising.

The fact that the post–1920s immigration to the United States reached its peak in the late 1970s and early 1980s, as we saw in Chapter 1 (which was also when unemployment was growing rapidly) supports that argument. The period from 1970 to 1982 was one of a rising unemployment rate both nationally and in California. Yet, that is the period when millions of foreign-born people accounted for a nearly 20 percent increase in California's population (Muller and Espanshade 1985). The study concluded that while both push and pull factors are important determinants of population mobility, they found that the *push* factors took the leading role in the case of Mexican migration to the United States. In their words, "The job-seeking pressures generated from the origin appear to have greater effect on the migration across the border" (Cheng and Nitz 1989, 10).

Clearly, illegal immigration responds not only to the opportunity of jobs in the United States drawing aliens here, but also to social reasons (e.g., family reunification), and in response to economic and political pressures in their country of origin that propel them to leave—pushing them here.

The Mexican population is growing exponentially—at an annual rate of 3.2 percent compared to the 0.9 percent annual growth rate of the United States. Mexican per capita income is $740, while the U.S. per capita income is over $6,000. Demographic projections estimate that Mexico will double its population every 20 years. It is expected to reach 150 million by the turn of the century. The continued political instability in Central America is pushing migration northward, further increasing pressure on Mexico. Clearly, it is becoming increasingly attractive to cross the Rio Grande, legally or not, and work for whatever wages are available, as even the lowest U.S. wages are far above those in Mexico. Mexican legislators predict that with each passing year IRCA will increasingly fail to stem the flow north, and may further strain U.S.–Mexican and possibly even U.S.–Canadian relations. IRCA represents a compromise that allows for the reinforcement of antiimmigrant sentiment, while avoiding any substantial change in the economic realities that propel the immigrant to seek employment, legally or illegally, in the United States.

Another point regarding the effectiveness of IRCA's employer-sanctions provision that needs to be discussed here focuses not upon whether *new illegal aliens* are continuing to enter the United States, but upon whether those already in the United States remain so, despite sanctions, or whether the IRCA-caused "demagnetizated" labor market has forced them to return to their countries of origin. No firm aggregate data is yet available to answer that question. Only impressionistic data can be cited. Our survey questionnaire to QDE agencies, the front-line troops who daily dealt with the various ethnic groups that made up the target population of the sanctions provision, provide some interesting, if impressionistic, data. When asked if in their dealings with client groups as a result of IRCA's passage, they had noted a decline in the number of illegal aliens still in their communities, only 33 percent noted a decline. Most of them based their estimates on the number of former illegal alien clients they knew who were in the process of legalization. Forty-eight percent answered that they saw no decline at all, and another 20 percent saw an *increase* since IRCA's enactment.

The survey asked the same question of state officials. Of those respondents, the results closely parallel the QDE agency responses: 44 percent of those making an estimate noted some decrease in the number of illegal aliens—most of them basing the response on the number of ELAs in their state, arguing that those numbers of legalizing aliens decreased the number of illegals. Another 48 percent of those answering felt there was no decrease, that the number of illegal aliens in their geographic area remained about the same. And 8 percent of those answering estimated that the number of illegal aliens had actually increased. As one respondent from Oregon put it when asked if his office had noted a decline in the number of illegal aliens since passage of IRCA: "No. In fact, due to misinformation regarding the RAW program, we believe that more undocumented aliens are remaining in our geographic area longer than they would have pre-IRCA." These data are summarized in Table 5.1.

A majority of the QDE and local INS staff members we interviewed also felt that the illegal aliens who were in the United States and who did not or could not apply for amnesty had remained. An INS enforcement official in California noted the increase in the number of persons on street corners looking for day work. QDE staffers in Arizona, California, Florida, and Illinois all responded that they personally knew of many illegal aliens who had chosen to remain despite their illegal status. None of them knew, personally, of anyone returning to his or her country of origin because of the passage of IRCA.

As the Rand Corporation/Urban Institute study notes of this population:

> There are at least two reasons to expect that many (possibly most) ineligible workers will remain here. First, the growing disparities in job opportunities and wages be-

Table 5.1
Number of Illegal Aliens Post-IRCA, by State Officials and QDE Respondents

	State Officials	QDEs	Totals
Noted Some Decline in Illegal Aliens Post-IRCA	34 (44%)	18 (33%)	52
No Decline Seen Post-IRCA	37 (48%)	26 (48%)	63
Increase in Illegal Aliens Post-IRCA	6 (8%)	11 (20%)	17
Total	77 (100%)	55 (100%)	132

Chi Square = 5.14; df = 2; .10 level of significance

tween the United States and the various countries of origin, as well as political and social unrest in some of these countries make undocumented immigrants unlikely to leave voluntarily, even if their job opportunities or wages fall here. A second reason is the family ties that some remaining undocumented individuals have with legal or IRCA-legalizing immigrants. As noted earlier, 40 percent of the applicants for legalization are married. Those "grandfathered" by IRCA have the option of remaining with their employers. Others who remain have several adjustment options available—increased self-employment; accepting employment in firms that are willing to risk sanctions, possibly on substandard terms; accepting longer periods of unemployment or underemployment; and/or obtaining fraudulent documents, thereby satisfying, albeit illegally, the employer requirements. Many ineligible workers have relatives here, some of whom have been legalized from whom they may get some support. Hardships are likely to fall more heavily on family members remaining behind in the sending countries, as the remittances they receive decrease or become more irregular. (Bean, Vernez, and Keely 1989, 72–73)

Job Discrimination

As with the measurements of the impact of IRCA on the flow of illegal aliens, assessing the impact of the law on discrimination is likewise a difficult task and shows mixed results. A number of studies and data, however, allow one to make at least a degree of assessment. This section discusses the degree to which IRCA's employer-sanctions provisions have contributed to an increase in job discrimination experienced by the relevant target populations.

In the first of a series of studies on immigration and the labor market, the U.S. Department of Labor (1989) did an exhaustive review and balanced evaluation of the research evidence on immigration's impact. It concluded the presence of immigrants in the U.S. labor market benefited employers, consumers, and the U.S. international position. The report notes that between 1950 and 1988 the number of immigrants to the United States more than doubled, while U.S. birth rates declined. This resulted in an increasingly large role played by immigrants in both the growth of the U.S. population and the labor force. Whereas in the 1970s immigrants accounted for 11 percent of the labor force growth, DOL estimates that during the 1980s they contributed about 22 percent to the annual increase in the civilian labor force. Its review concluded that neither U.S. workers in complementary jobs nor most minority workers appear to have been adversely affected by immigration. Indeed, while immigration may initially challenge U.S. workers at a variety of levels, ongoing economic and labor market adjustments appear to effectively incorporate immigrants into local economies.

The tendency of immigrants to concentrate in a few locations suggests that they have disproportionate effects in such local labor markets. The DOL study employed two types of analytical approaches to measure such effects: macrolevel regional and key metropolitan area labor markets and case studies focusing on specific industries in a given locality.

Macrolevel regional analysis indicates that the *aggregate effects* of immigration on the employment, wages, or working conditions of native-born workers are small. Research in such metropolitan areas as New York, Los Angeles, Miami, Chicago, and San Antonio showed considerable substitution and displacement occurring, especially among low-skilled occupations. But clear beneficial effects were also noted. The DOL report concludes that the market forces that characterize dynamic labor markets seem to effectively absorb and integrate immigrants—both legal and illegal—in a manner that makes their effects indistinguishable from those of other workers at the aggregate level. Indeed, the report concludes that an exhaustive group of studies reviewed by DOL showed that the group of workers most disproportionately impacted by new immigrants were earlier, more settled immigrants. New and older immigrants move into the same markets and are distinguished mainly by their knowledge and experience in the U.S. labor market, as well as by their expectations. In this process, earlier arriving immigrants often found themselves competing with the more recent arrivals who may have had more modest expectations about wages and working conditions.

The DOL review shows few instances of outright displacement of native workers. In such instances, once employers began to focus their recruitment efforts on immigrant workers, the participation of native workers tended to diminish. Since such effects are invisible at the higher levels of aggregation, it is likely those native workers directly or indirectly displaced are absorbed elsewhere in the labor market.

Another indicator to measure IRCA-related job discrimination is the incidence of formal charges of such. Several studies will be discussed here that have documented various types of discriminatory behavior by employers, including the following:

1. Giving preference to U.S. citizens
2. Hiring only citizens or "green card" holders
3. Refusing to hire or even to pre-screen someone who looks foreign
4. Failing to recognize authorized documents
5. Demanding documentation only from foreign-looking or foreign-sounding applicants
6. Dismissing or threatening to dismiss "grandfathered" or other authorized workers
7. Loss of seniority or other benefits
8. Giving preference to undocumented workers
9. Requiring too many or only specific documents from applicants
10. Applying higher standards of documentation or employment qualifications from anyone foreign-looking or foreign-sounding
11. Hiring only after appropriate documentation has been provided, although the law requires that job seekers be hired regardless of their immediate ability to produce acceptable documents. (Bean, Vernez, and Keely 1989, 74)

Perhaps the most important of the various government studies was the third report of the GAO, entitled, "Immigration Reform: Employer Sanctions and the Question of Discrimination: Report to Congress" (General Accounting Office 1990). As noted, Congress had mandated that the GAO determine whether widespread discrimination had resulted as a result of IRCA specifically. For its report, the GAO reviewed federal agency implementation of IRCA, reviewed discrimination complaints filed with federal agencies, reviewed data from groups representing aliens, and surveyed over 9,400 of the nation's employers, projecting to a universe of about 4.6 million employers. In collaboration with the Urban Institute, the GAO also did a hiring audit in which pairs of persons matched closely on job qualifications applied for jobs with some 360 employers located in two cities. One member of each pair was a "foreign-appearing, foreign-sounding" Hispanic and the other was an Anglo with no foreign accent (ibid., 29). In brief, the GAO found that there was widespread discrimination that was a direct result of IRCA (ibid., 3).

The GAO estimated that 461,000 employers, or 10 percent of all those surveyed, reported national origin discrimination as a result of the law. It concluded that many employers discriminated because of the law's verification system, which lacked a simple and reliable method to verify a job applicant's eligibility to work. It saw three options for Congress as a result: (1) leaving IRCA as is for the present, (2) repealing the employer-sanctions and antidiscrimination provisions, or (3) amending IRCA with regard to verification in order to reduce its discriminatory effects (ibid., 4).

The GAO study noted that 227,000 employers reported that they began a practice, as a result of IRCA, not to hire job applicants whose foreign appearance or accent led them to suspect them to be illegal aliens. And contrary to IRCA's provisions, an estimated 346,000 employers said they applied IRCA's verification system only to persons who had a foreign appearance or accent. Some employers began both practices.

Employers engaged in practices that the law classified as discriminatory verification and hiring practices ranged by geographic location from 3 percent to 16 percent, and were higher in areas with high Hispanic and Asian populations. Such practices were new and would not have occurred without IRCA, leading the GAO to conclude there was a "widespread pattern of discrimination that was a direct result of IRCA." Likewise, its "hiring audit" of 360 employers in Chicago, Ill., and San Diego, Calif., showed that the foreign-appearing, foreign-sounding Hispanic member of the matched pair was three times more likely to encounter unfavorable treatment than the Anglo nonforeign-appearing member of the pair. The Anglo members received 52 percent more job offers than the Hispanic members (ibid., 6).

The GAO report also indicated that the law resulted in citizenship discrimination. It estimated an additional 430,000 employers (9 percent) said that because of the law they began hiring only persons born in the United States or not hiring persons with temporary work eligibility documents. Thus, in total, the GAO estimated that 891,000 (19 percent) of the 4.6 million employers in the survey population nationwide began one or more discriminatory practices as a result of the law (ibid., 7).

Undoubtedly, much of this discrimination reflected employers being confused and uncertain about the law's verification system and that a simpler system using fewer documents would reduce such discrimination. Indeed, 78 percent of the employers responding to the GAO wanted a simpler or better verification system. Part of the problem arose from the variety of documents, seventeen in all, and the prevalence of counterfeit documents.

To establish whether there was a widespread pattern of discrimination against authorized workers, the GAO relied on several methods. It surveyed, as mentioned, a stratified random sample of 9,491 employers about their hiring practices. It conducted a hiring audit of 360 randomly selected employers in two cities using matched pairs of people who applied for a job advertised in the newspaper. It surveyed 300 judgmentally selected persons who had applied for a job in person since January 1, 1989 in Miami, New York, Chicago, Dallas, and Los Angeles. It then compared the experiences relayed by the foreign-sounding and nonforeign-sounding applicants regarding the employers' hiring practices. It analyzed the national origin discrimination charges filed by the EEOC from fiscal year 1979 to May 1989. It reviewed discrimination charges filed with the OSC from May 1988 to May

1989 to identify those that appeared to be related to employer sanctions. And it analyzed state employment data from Illinois, Florida, and Texas to compare the percentages of Hispanic and other minorities who found jobs through state employment services with that of Anglos and blacks before and after IRCA (ibid., 25).

IRCA specifically prohibits selective application of the law's verification provisions. If foreign-appearing people are asked to meet requirements that nonforeign-appearing people are not required to meet, it can result in reduced hiring of such foreign-appearing workers. The GAO study found ample evidence of such. The levels of discrimination it found are presented in Figure 5.2.

As IRCA's verification system is unique to that law, any evidence that shows it is being applied selectively for foreign-sounding or foreign-looking people can only be interpreted as new discrimination that would not have existed without enactment of IRCA.

Further evidence of such discrimination comes from charges filed with the Office of the Special Counsel (OSC) in the Department of Justice. From the law's enactment in 1986 until October 1989, the OSC had received 708 discrimination charges, which included 81 filed with the EEOC. By far the most common charge was that the potential employer refused work authorization documentation (55 percent). Another 25 percent charged they were refused being hired or were fired because of their immigrant status, and 16 percent charged the employers had a policy to hire only U.S. citizens (ibid., 53). As of March 1990, 708 cases were settled, some of which affected entire industries and engendered widespread reforms.

This is particularly the case with airline and defense industries. Negotiated settlements with four major airlines (Pan Am, United, Northwest, and American) ended industry practices of hiring only citizens or permanent residents with "green cards" as flight attendants or pilots. Those industry-wide practices have been changed as a result of the settlements. In the defense industry cases, employers erroneously were using a blanket citizens-only hiring policy. Settlements in cases involving a variety of defense contractors and the airlines led to "tens of thousands of jobs in the defense and airline industries are now open to aliens who intend to become citizens" (U.S. Department of Justice 1989, 7–11).

The GAO report also noted the results of its survey of private, state, and local agencies regarding complaints about employment discrimination they had received, using EEOC criteria to describe and identify the discrimination complaints related to employer sanctions. A total of fourteen organizations responded to the GAO survey. The results of that survey showed 876 complaints had been filed (General Accounting Office 1990, 82).

The GAO study reported on hiring audits in New York City showing discrimination, as did a survey of San Francisco employers (ibid., 82–83). The California Fair Employment and Housing Commission held hearings in 1989 and reported that IRCA had, indeed, resulted in a widespread pattern

Figure 5.2
Levels of Discrimination across the Nation

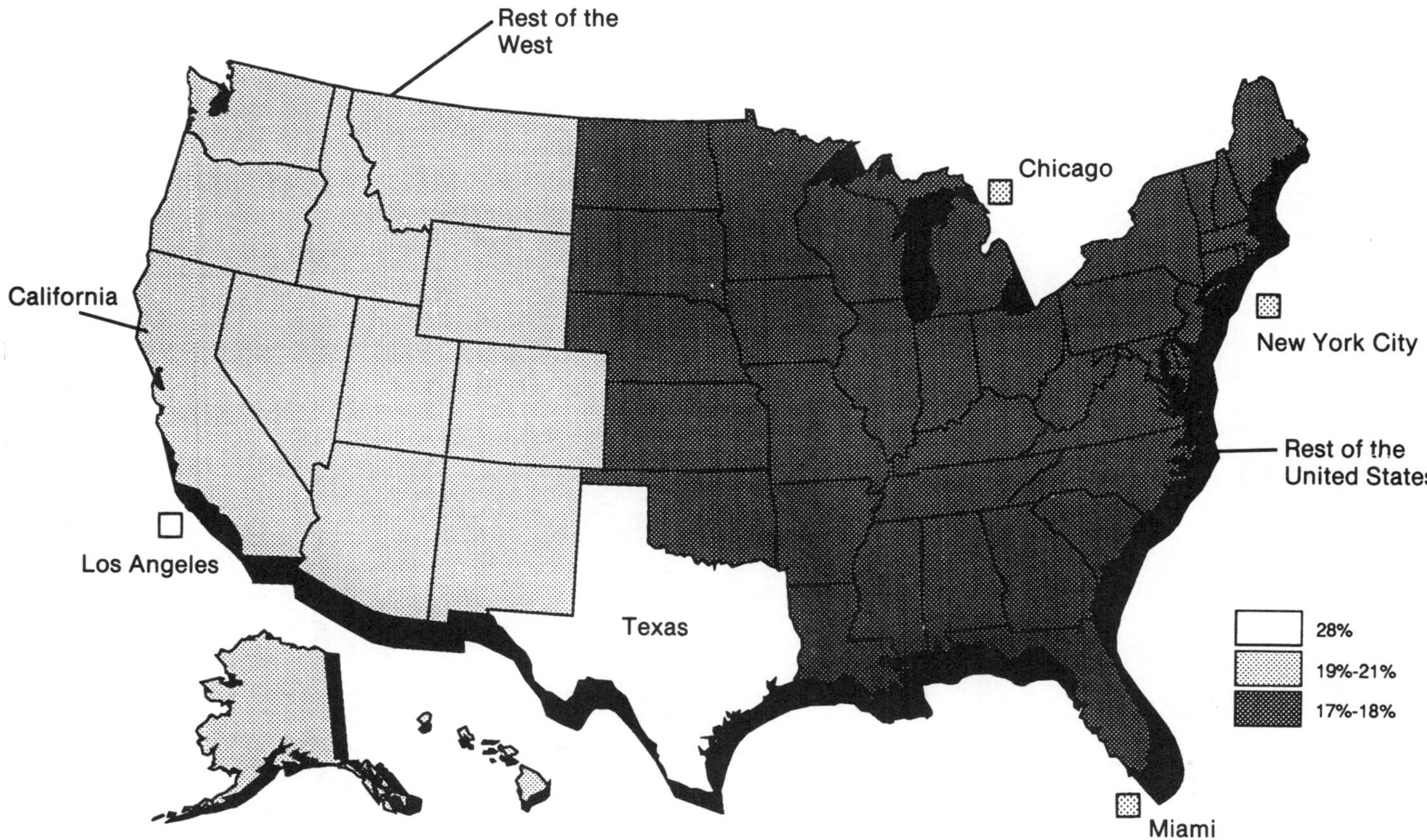

Source: Adapted from GAO 1990 Report, 40.

of discrimination in that state (ibid., 84). These results were similar to a MALDEF study reported on in the second of the GAO reports (1988b).

MALDEF reported a Los Angeles-based coalition concerned with immigration reform had received 194 complaints about IRCA-related discrimination between November 1986 and September 1988. The types of employers' actions complained about included penalizing employees for previous use of false documents and aliases, requiring work documents of "grandfathered" individuals, accusing employees of using fraudulent documents that were valid, and favoring U.S. citizens over noncitizens. According to the project report, in 73 of the cases the employers demanded more documents than the law required or requested ones that the law did not permit. Forty-four cases were filed with the OSC, EEOC, state or local antidiscrimination agencies, unions, or other organizations. In addition to the 194 cases in Los Angeles, MALDEF's Chicago office provided data on 58 discrimination charges filed there from April 1987 through August 1988.

Similarly, a report by MALDEF and the ACLU released in November 1989, entitled *The Human Cost of Employer Sanctions,* found IRCA clearly to be a source of increased discrimination against foreign-looking and foreign-sounding people. The report documents the experiences of individuals who had suffered various types of discrimination under employer sanctions, and assesses IRCA's discriminatory effects to have been felt by people who should not have been affected by the law—including U.S. citizens and legal permanent residents or temporary residents. It found discrimination to be pervasive.

The New York State Assembly Task Force on New Americans sponsored a public hearing on November 2, 1987 to assess the effects of employer sanctions in New York. During the hearings, numerous advocacy groups and individuals testified to evidence that sanctions were leading to discrimination against legal immigrants, to widespread employer ignorance of acceptable documents, and to discrimination against citizens, particularly Puerto Ricans, who many employers did not know were citizens. They also testified that employers made fearful by IRCA were not aiding current and past employees with their legalization applications. They charged the INS with failure to do an adequate job of education about IRCA and its antidiscrimination provisions.

Indeed, Governor Mario Cuomo was sufficiently concerned that he established an Inter-Agency Task Force on Immigration Affairs to investigate. Their study, released in November 1988, concluded that at least 22,262 persons who were U.S. citizens or aliens authorized to work had been denied employment and that "for the purposes of congressional review of the impact of employer sanctions as currently implemented a 'widespread pattern of discrimination' has been documented in New York."[5] (See also General Accounting Office 1990, 85.)

The results of the extensive Rand Corporation survey found a similar compliance rate to the GAO study; just over 60 percent were in compliance. That study also found that a significant minority of employers still do not understand fully all of IRCA's requirements. Small, informally organized companies were found to be less likely than larger companies to have learned about IRCA or to have implemented its employee screening and record-keeping requirements. That study concluded the major reasons for such failure to be twofold: (1) the INS's employee education effort has not been as extensive as Congress anticipated, and (2) limits on the number of inspections and the affirmative defense for employers make the avoidance costs for some firms much lower than the costs of full compliance (McDonnell and Hill 1989, 29).

The results of the questionnaire survey sent to state agency officials and QDE agencies were similarly varied and comparable to the other studies cited here. Those survey results are shown in Table 5.2.

To cite one response from a QDE agency, "Discrimination is rampant. People with 'foreign' looks are treated as suspicious illegal aliens, and in documented cases, employment hiring and even interviewing have been denied *ipso facto*."

Virtually all involved in implementing IRCA recognize the need for greater public education regarding its provisions to further reduce the discrimination which is undoubtedly occurring. In the words of Lawrence Siskind, the Special Counsel,

Table 5.2
State Official/QDE Survey Results on Discrimination

	State Officials	QDEs	Total
Saw Increased Discrimination Post-IRCA	12 (16%)	12 (21%)	24
No Increased Discrimination	35 (54%)	13 (24%)	48
Not Able to Answer Item	30 (39%)	30 (55%)	60
Total	77 (100%)	55 (100%)	132

Chi Square = 6.59; df = 2; .05 level of significance

Most employers do not want to discriminate, and will not, once they understand the law. In fact, of all the charges and investigations where we found discrimination, only three resulted in trials. In all the others, we achieved our results through persuasion rather than litigation. The problem, as the General Accounting Office (GAO) pointed out in its second annual report on the implementation of employer sanctions, is that too many employers are unaware of their antidiscrimination responsibilities. . . . The GAO recommended that the Attorney General direct the Special Counsel to set up a task force of federal agencies to develop a coordinated strategy for educating the public about IRCA's antidiscrimination provisions. (Siskind 1989, 12–15)

THE LEGALIZATION PROVISIONS

The legalization provision was one of the most controversial sections of IRCA. As the reader will recall, the Select Commission recommended the date of January 1, 1980. Although leaving the decision of the cut-off date to Congress, the commission estimated that a two-year residency requirement would include about 60 percent of the illegal aliens in the United States, and that a three-year requirement would include about 45 percent. Under IRCA, Congress settled upon a residency requirement of almost five years. Legalization consists of two stages—temporary and then permanent residency. The one-year application period for temporary residency, often referred to as the amnesty application period, began on May 5, 1987 and ended on May 4, 1988. The application for permanent residency began on December 5, 1988 and ended on December 4, 1990. Those granted temporary status had to apply for permanent residency within a one-year period beginning nineteen months after their initial application. If they failed to do so, then their temporary status could be revoked. In order to adjust to permanent status, they must have had continuous residency in the United States, be admissible as an immigrant, and demonstrate minimal understanding and knowledge of English and of U.S. history and government.

IRCA also has two special provisions allowing several groups of aliens to adjust directly to permanent residents. Aliens who have continuously resided in the United States in an unlawful status since January 1972 are one such group. Aliens classified as Cuban/Haitian Entrants—nationals of Cuba or Haiti who entered the United States without inspection and have continuously resided here since January 1, 1982—may also apply directly for permanent resident status.

In order to assess the success of legalization, one needs to have a fix on the number of illegal aliens in the United States prior to IRCA's enactment to serve as a benchmark. But therein lies a severe problem for accurately and empirically measuring the success or lack thereof of the legalization effort. Throughout the 1970s, a debate over the size of the illegal alien population raged, with highly speculative claims ranging from 4 to 12 million.[6] The 1980 census counted 2.1 million undocumented immigrants nationwide (Baker 1990, 162). More empirically based estimates during the 1980s were lower than the 4 to 12 million figure, but they were also somewhat imprecise. They were essentially based on indirect measures and thus sensitive to several assumptions. The best available research to date puts their numbers at 3 to 6 million as of 1986 (Hoefer 1988, 1).

The INS had anticipated about 3.9 million applicants in all. Congressional policymakers assumed that there would be no more than 350,000 applying for the SAW legalization program. INS planning estimates anticipated no more than 800,000 SAW applicants. In fact, as seen in Chapter 4, there were over 1.3 million SAW applicants. As of July 1989, nearly 94 percent had been processed and almost 95 percent of those approved.

Estimates of those eligible to meet the LAWs requirements of IRCA ranged from 1.3 to 2.7 million. The 1.7 million who applied thus represent a substantial majority of the target population (McDonnell and Hill 1989, 30). As we have seen in the previous chapter, the approval rate has been high.

There are several reasons why so many more SAW applicants than were anticipated actually came forward. As has been discussed, the standards for documentation for SAWs were lower than for LAWs. Also, the SAW program's closing date was six months later, and roughly half of the SAW applicants filed during those last six months. Thus, it would seem that many of those who could not qualify for the main legalization program applied under the SAW provisions. As we noted previously, the INS has charged that use of fraudulent documents has been much higher in the SAW program. There seems to be a consensus in local communities and among QDE agencies that the discrepancies between the LAW and SAW programs in application criteria, timing, and the lack of civics and language requirements for SAWs violate basic equal treatment standards and have undermined the legitimacy of the entire process. Proponents of IRCA, in their eagerness to secure its passage, and those pushing for the rights of farm workers, may have found common cause with growers in supporting the SAW provision, but in doing so they let 8 to 10 percent of the problem become 40 percent of a very troublesome solution (ibid., 33).

How well has the total legalization program achieved its target? The INS estimates had been for a total of 3.9 million. If the total number of eligible aliens in the United States was near that number, the total IRCA legalization applicant pool is indeed a significant success. If, however, the total of eligible aliens was actually nearer the highest ranges of those estimated (closer to 6 million), then the program was far less successful.[7]

In any event, for the INS to have successfully reached and processed over 3 million applicants in the limited time set by Congress, particularly with the complexities of the application process as set by the law, is an accomplishment that few of the critics of the INS would have believed it capable of performing.

Another interesting aspect of the legalization application data concerns the relative number of applicants from various national-origin groups who have applied. The INS undertook a comprehensive, but highly criticized, advertising effort to reach eligible illegal aliens. These were developed in several languages and were put into motion between July and October 1987. The INS complemented the television and radio campaign with press conferences and interviews; ethnic media press releases and counseling; special television programming by cooperating Spanish language stations; visits to employers; mobile van programs; educational cassettes for community groups interested in the legalization program; public service announcements for local media, subway, and bus cards; and similar efforts to get their message across (LeMay 1989, 25).

Table 5.3 presents data on the number of applicants from various countries of origin and their percentage of the total applicant pool. These data are compared with that group's estimated percentage of those aliens within the 1980 census data.

Most of the data available describing the illegal aliens residing in the United States are based on estimates counted in the 1980 census. Warren and Passel (1983) estimated the number and characteristics of undocumented aliens by comparing two sets of data: (1) estimates of the alien population counted in the census derived from census data on the foreign-born and INS records on naturalization; and (2) estimates of the legal resident aliens derived from INS administrative records. They produced estimates by country of birth, period of entry, age, and sex. Passel and Woodrow (1984) used the same methodology and data sources to produce estimates for states of residency by country of birth, period of entry, age, and sex (Hoefer 1988, 9).

The characteristics of the aliens applying for legalization and those estimates from the 1980 census data are compared in Table 5.3. One should expect some differences between the two populations, of course, because there will be differences in the aliens eligible for legalization and those actually applying. The eligible population is not identical to the census population due to the passage of time; that is, the census counts do not include illegal immigrants who came between April 1980 and January 1982. Also, the characteristics of those who stayed and those who left before 1986 would affect the legalization population. Therefore, these data should not be construed as an evaluation of the completeness of the legalization program. The data are suggestive, however, as to relative numbers of potential groups who were reached by and participated in the legalization program, and do illustrate some interesting points regarding which minority groups apparently received the greater benefits from the amnesty program's approach and implementation.

Note, for instance, the Mexican group. While it was estimated to make up only 55 percent of the illegal alien population in the 1980 census, it comprised 74.9 percent of the applicants in the Legalization Applicant Pool (LAP) database. Likewise, immigrants from El Salvador comprised an estimated 2.5 percent of the 1980 census population, but were 5.5 percent of the appli-

Table 5.3
Legalization Applicants by Selected Country of Birth, as of 7/20/89, and Estimated Percentage of 1980 Census Population

Country of Citizenship	Total Numbers	Percentage in Pool	Percentage in 1980 Census Data
Mexico	2,299,900	74.9	55.0
El Salvador	168,400	5.5	2.5
Guatemala	71,800	2.3	1.4
Haiti	62,200	2.0	2.1
Colombia	34,600	1.1	6.2
Philippines	30,100	1.0	0.8
Dominican Republic	28,100	0.9	0.9
Pakistan	22,200	0.7	X
India	22,000	0.7	0.9
Peru	19,900	0.7	0.7
Jamaica	19,300	0.6	1.9
Honduras	18,200	0.6	X
Nicaragua	16,800	0.5	X
Ecuador	16,300	0.5	0.7
Poland	16,200	0.5	7.3
Nigeria	15,900	0.5	X
Iran	15,400	0.5	1.2
Canada	11,800	0.4	1.2
Korea	11,700	0.4	X
China, Mainland	11,400	0.4	1.2
Bangladesh	8,000	0.3	X
United Kingdom	7,800	0.3	1.8
Brazil	7,600	0.2	X
Ghana	7,100	0.2	X
Belize	6,300	0.2	X
Argentina	6,000	0.2	0.5

Source: Data on country of birth and percentage of applicants as of 7/20/89 from INS Statistical Analysis Branch Report; data on percentage of 1980 census data from Hoefer 1988, Table 1.

cant pool. Those from Guatemala were 1.4 percent of the 1980 census pool but were 2.3 percent of the applicant pool. These groups, then, are significantly over represented in the applicant pool for those seeking legalization. Other groups are likewise underrepresented in these data. Those from Asian countries were 10.4 percent of the 1980 census population data, but only 5.5 percent of the applicant pool. Those from European nations were 7.3 percent of the 1980 census population estimates, but were less than 2 percent of the applicants. Other specific countries underrepresented in the applicant pool as seen in Table 5.3 are the Colombia at 6.2 percent in the 1980 census column, but only 1.1 in the applicant pool; Poland at 7.3 in the census but only 0.5 percent of the applicant pool; Iran at 1.2 in the census and only 0.5 in the pool; Canada and mainland China, both at 1.2 in the census and only

0.4 in the pool; and the United Kingdom at 1.8 in the census but only 0.3 in the applicant pool.

While these data must be taken with caution, they do suggest that those groups that had been the most visibly organized against the passage of IRCA and had been the most vocal and organized during its early implementation stages (often supporting court-based challenges to INS rules and procedures, for example), are precisely those groups most over represented. That is especially the case with the Mexican group. They, largely through the efforts of the Hispanic Caucus as we have described in Chapters 2 and 3, had forced the key compromises in the IRCA bill in order to enable its ultimate passage. When the INS began to implement the legalization program, it was aware of that opposition. It worked extra hard in the implementation stage of the program to reach out especially to Mexican and to other Hispanic groups. In short, it would appear that the most organized minorities who were more vocally critical of the IRCA bill were precisely the ones who most benefited from the amnesty program's implementation efforts and from the compromise provisions of the new law (e.g., the SAW legalization program). The data in Table 5.3 clearly seem to be a case of the "squeaky wheel gets the grease."

The Rand Corporation/Urban Institute study concluded the legalization program was successful (Baker 1990, 194–195). It noted:

> In the end, the basic lesson of legalization is quite simple: Change in the U.S. immigration system can be effected as much by reform of the benefits side as by modifying immigration law enforcement. We have seen legalization portrayed (not inaccurately) to Congress and to the public as part of a trade-off for a more rigorous enforcement package. However, over time legalization proved, in its own right, to be an effective step toward easing the imbalance between immigrant supply and demand that has plagued the United States throughout its history. Clearly, statutory and regulatory standards, the cooperation of many agencies, and the adoption of a generous spirit in implementation combined to enhance the effectiveness of such benefits-based strategies. (ibid., 194)

IMPROVING THE INS AND THE BORDER PATROL

IRCA also involved increased spending to improve enforcement capabilities of the Border Patrol and the INS, and additional allocations to carry out the added duties for the INS that were imposed by the law. A 50 percent expansion of the Border Patrol was mandated in the Moorhead Amendment of IRCA. The INS planned a multi-year period for that expansion in view of the size of the undertaking to recruit, train, acquire new equipment, and expand their facilities. In 1987, nine classes of new agents were hired and trained at the Border Patrol Academy and fourteen classes were conducted in 1988. The Border Patrol Academy staff worked with the Federal Law Enforcement Training Center to institute a number of modifications of facilities and class scheduling in order to ensure a high standard of training with the increased number of trainees. Since passage of IRCA, a total of 1,100 new Border Patrol agents have been hired and trained, but that total still falls short of the intended strength of force called for by IRCA. As we have seen, moreover, their increased responsibilities meant that even with the expansion of personnel, actual "line-watch hours" are only slightly above pre-IRCA levels (Bean, Vernez, and Keely 1989, 44–45; Immigration and Naturalization Service, *INS Reporter,* January 1988, 21–22).

The INS itself has also been greatly impacted by IRCA. Its budget and staff have increased, as well as its responsibilities, as we have seen. Has IRCA led to an improvement of the INS in its efficiency or attitude? Certainly, the computerization of INS record-keeping has vastly expanded as a result of IRCA. While that process had been under way, it can be safely said that IRCA increased the rate at which the INS computerized its operations (field interviews: INS staff in Arizona and California).

Our survey questionnaire raised the issue of increased efficiency in the INS. Among the state officials who responded to this question, 51 percent felt that they could not answer because their direct contact with the INS was insufficient to do so (e.g., many of them dealt with DHHS via the SLIAG programs rather than the INS), or had insufficient pre-IRCA dealings with the INS to assess any improvement or lack thereof in its operations. Of those who did answer, 21 percent noted some increase in INS efficiency, while 28 percent noted no improvement. The QDE agency personnel had, of course, many more direct dealings with the INS in assisting the implementation of the legalization program, and many had pre-IRCA experience with the INS. Thus, only 7 percent of the QDE respondents felt unable to answer that question. Among those who did respond, 38 percent acknowledged some improvement in the efficiency of the INS since passage of IRCA, while 55 percent said there was no improvement based on their experiences with the INS. These data are shown and compared in Table 5.4.

A related concern is that of the attitude of the INS toward clients. Did the change in responsibility of the INS, from one primarily of enforcement to one with at least some concern to reach out and legalize the undocumented aliens, impact on the INS to bring about an improvement in the attitude of INS personnel? Certainly evidence of such was strongly indicated in our field interviews, often frankly acknowledged by those being interviewed for this study. Many of the QDE agency staff interviewed, however, felt that INS attitudes were bad and did not improve much over time.

The responses to our mailed questionnaire provided a likewise varied picture: Among state officials who responded, a majority (51 percent) felt unable to assess a change, either because of insufficient direct dealing with the INS or because they had no prior dealings with the INS prior to IRCA's enactment. Of those who did respond, 18 percent noted an improvement in INS staff attitudes, while 30 percent claimed no such improvement. A state

Table 5.4
Improvement in INS Efficiency as a Result of IRCA, by State Officials/QDEs

Change in INS Efficiency	State Officials	QDEs	Total
Increased in INS Efficiency Noted	16 (21%)	21 (38%)	37
No Increase in Efficiency of INS Noted Post-IRCA	22 (28%)	30 (55%)	52
Not Able to Answer	39 (51%)	4 (7%)	43
Total	77 (100%)	55 (100%)	132

Chi Square = 27.52; df = 2; .001 level of significance

official's response to that item reflects those negative assessments: "No. In the early phases of IRCA, legalization and employer sanctions alike, INS made concerted efforts to bring meaning to the word 'service' in INS. However, as IRCA progressed, INS made it clear that its principal responsibility was that of policing and enforcing for immigration compliance and returned to that mode of operation."

QDE agency respondents, again, had many more direct dealings with the INS while implementing IRCA. Thus, only 7 percent of the respondents felt unable to answer that question. Among those who did reply, 22 percent noted some improvement in INS staff attitudes, usually mentioning upper-level management in particular, and generally more often the legalization offices, as opposed to the district INS offices as well. The following quote is typical of such responses.

> Our relationship with the INS has been wonderful. They are cooperative and have provided us with an economic incentive. Through our mutual relationship, we have sensitized an awareness between the community and the INS. The legalization offices facilitate us with the opportunity to have a mutual relationship in terms of helping clients in the Amnesty Program, but there is a difference when it comes to the attitude of local regional immigration offices due to the unfamiliarity with staff personnel.

A majority (53 percent) of respondents, however, felt that there was no improvement in INS staff attitudes. The following response reflects those typical comments well.

> The INS has implemented IRCA in a haphazard, rushed and poorly planned manner. Regulations were consistently late in coming. Many changes and inconsistencies

in the practices of the Baltimore and the Arlington offices resulted in confusion and delay. The INS staff (examiners) were sometimes unnecessarily harsh and rude at Baltimore. Over 200 of our cases are still pending adjudication. Staff at the Baltimore office were extremely demanding in the burden of proof. INS interpreted the regulations narrowly, and continue to do so in contrast to the liberal intent of the Congress.

These data are shown and compared in Table 5.5.

UNANTICIPATED CONSEQUENCES

As with any major policy change, IRCA also produced some consequences unanticipated by its Congressional decision makers. A few of those will be highlighted briefly in this section.

Congress apparently assumed that the INS's implementation of IRCA would be uniform across the country. That has not been the case. The INS has historically been a highly decentralized agency, with individual regions, Border Patrol sectors, and district offices having considerable discretion. While the assumption of uniform administration of federal legislation is common, Congress clearly did not anticipate the wide variation the INS has shown in implementing IRCA. Differences in implementation have been very significant in both employer-sanctions and legalization programs. Those differences were among the most striking findings of one Rand Corporation/Urban Institute study (McDonnell and Hill 1989, 33). They were also clearly evident throughout our field interviews.

The degree of variation in the enforcement strategies across INS regions and between the Border Patrol and the investigations staff manifested itself in different targeting strategies (for instance, broad coverage versus focus

Table 5.5
Change in INS Personnel Attitude as a Result of IRCA, by State Officials/QDEs

Change in INS Staff's Attitudes	State Officials	QDEs	Total
Noted Improved Attitudes in INS	14 (18%)	22 (40%)	36
No Improved Attitudes in INS	24 (31%)	29 (53%)	53
No Answer	39 (51%)	4 (7%)	43
Total	77 (100%)	55 (100%)	132

Chi Square = 27.84; df = 2; .001 level of significance

upon particular types); operating philosophies (e.g., bringing companies into compliance versus apprehension of aliens); and investigation strategies. We have already noted the differences between Florida and New York in the manner in which the Haitian target group was treated, and the differences between legalization investigators seeking fraud and those processing the applications.

Moreover, our field interviews with state agency, district INS, and QDE staff all indicated considerable variation among regions and district offices and among local legalization offices within regions and districts.

Our survey questionnaire responses also indicated considerable differences. Again, state official respondents often did not deal directly enough with the INS offices (rather dealing instead with DHHS), or did not deal with more than one INS office, and therefore 55 percent of them were unable to answer that question. Among state officials who did respond, 18 percent noted differences among INS offices in the implementation of IRCA's legalization and employer-sanctions programs. The following quote from two state agencies, one from the East and one from the West, reflect those responses.

> Yes. Many provisions of IRCA leave many policy considerations to the "discretion of the District Director." The District Director in our district has dealt with a number of issues falling into his discretion in a manner totally inconsistent with the manner in which the same situation is being handled by other District Directors. However, we would not attribute any of the rigid treatment that our District Director showed to racial biases. His attitudes are merely his best effort to run his office by the letter of the regulations. The District Director feels that his discretion is to be used only in very limited instances.

> Yes. Each office operates differently while each region is relatively autonomous. I think that the Western Region has shown a sensitivity to the clients that we serve and has worked hard at creating a working partnership with both the clients and our agencies.

Yet, 27 percent of state agency responses did not experience differences among local offices in their dealings with the INS.

Our QDE agency respondents, again, had many more direct dealings with the INS. Among those responses, 18 percent felt unable to answer the question, mostly because they dealt only with one office and thus felt unable to judge. Of those who did make an assessment, 55 percent experienced differences between INS offices in the implementation of the legalization programs, and 27 percent said they did not experience differences. These data are shown and compared in Table 5.6.

Differences in the implementation of employer sanctions are significant because they are likely to result in corresponding variations in the percep-

Table 5.6
Differences in IRCA Implementation, by State Officials/QDEs

INS Implementation	State Officials	QDEs	Total
Saw Differences in Implementation	14 (18%)	30 (55%)	44
No Differences Noted in Implementation	21 (27%)	15 (27%)	36
No Answer to Item	42 (55%)	10 (18%)	52
Total	77 (100%)	55 (100%)	132

Chi Square = 25.55; df = 2; .001 level of significance

tion among businesses as to the likelihood of enforcement and hence, in the businesses' decisions about whether to comply with IRCA (McDonnell and Hill 1989, 33).

Likewise, variation occurred in the implementation of legalization. One such example is in the number of applicants. In New York only 118,000 applied, while in Los Angeles 800,000 did so. In part, these differences may reflect variations in the composition of eligible immigrant populations. In Los Angeles there were greater proportions of the immigrant population who were eligible, and their ethnic homogeneity made it easier to reach them with information about the amnesty program. Nevertheless, even when those factors are controlled for, differences in INS implementation in the two cities (e.g., in the amount and type of outreach, location of legalization offices, and the like) were still significant (ibid., 34).

Similarly, variation in the denial rate of adjudication was noted in another Rand Corporation/Urban Institute study of IRCA. Overall, it found a low rate of denial as a product of the leveling effect of the regional processing facilities, and that general legalization adjudications were overwhelmingly positive. It also noted, however, variation among the legalization offices. The average rate of adjudications denied was 3.7 percent, the range was from 0.5 percent in East Los Angeles to 12.2 percent in El Paso (Baker 1990, 159).

Another unanticipated consequence was the degree to which other enforcement priorities would compete with employer sanctions. The apprehension of criminal aliens, discovery of marriage fraud, and especially the drug interdiction efforts competed greatly with the employer-sanctions enforcement efforts. To cite one Rand Corporation/Urban Institute study of IRCA on this point:

> Our fieldwork indicates that employer sanctions is still "first among equals" in the ranking of enforcement priorities, but that position is becoming increasingly difficult to maintain, particularly as drug interdiction and criminal aliens receive greater visibility. Because they did not adequately take into account how IRCA would compete with other INS functions, its Congressional supporters may find that employer sanctions may be implemented at a much lower level of staff time and attention than was assumed necessary for the policy to be effective. (McDonnell and Hill 1989, 34)

Finally, perhaps the most significant unanticipated consequence of IRCA has emerged from its intergovernmental complexities, particularly regarding the SLIAG program. By dividing and decentralizing its implementation among the various federal, state, and local agencies, IRCA's enactment has profound import for those various bureaucracies that deal with one another. In that regard, perhaps in the long run the most significant impact of IRCA, and one clearly unanticipated by its supporters, will be its effect on other federal grant-in-aid programs. The decision to have the DHHS refund the state and local agencies through the SLIAG grant programs turns the usual approach to federal grants around by 180 degrees. That approach may well have profound implications for future federal grant programs. The management control afforded the DHHS in implementing the SLIAG program has been a nightmare for state and local officials who have had to deal with the program. But in a time of increasingly extreme federal budget constraints, such an approach may prove exceptionally attractive to the federal administration and may well spill over into other health and welfare programs, and even into other federal departments (HUD and the Department of Education being the most likely).

It remains to be seen to what extent the legalization program's Phase II will be troubled by related unanticipated problems in the outreach programs to keep those who have successfully completed Phase I, to continue to progress through Phase II. In regard to this, the difficulties in administering SLIAG alluded to previously may result in state and local governments being unable to provide sufficient numbers or distributions of civics and language classes to enable ELAs to complete their requirements in the 18-month period during which they must move through Phase II of the legalization program. Thus, there may very well be the unanticipated consequence of significant numbers of legalizing aliens failing to become permanent residents and ultimately naturalized citizens.

Likewise, it is simply too early to assess IRCA's long-term impact on other issues for which research has just begun. The long-term effect of the SAW, and possibly the RAW, programs on agriculture and on the U.S. economy more generally remains to be assessed. Nor can we yet tell to what extent IRCA has caused those undocumented aliens already here who either could not or who chose not to legalize to return to their country of origin. Likewise, we cannot yet adequately assess IRCA's likely significant effect on U.S. international relations, especially with such bordering nations as Mexico and Canada, but also with Central American and Caribbean nations like Guatemala, El Salvador, and the Dominican Republic; as well as with Asian countries such as China, the Philippines, and Korea.

This initial assessment of the impact of IRCA clearly demonstrates the need for more research and better data upon which to measure impact—both anticipated and unanticipated effects. Wage and worker-condition data need to be gathered by the DOL to view IRCA's long-term impact. Better data on the number of illegal aliens who may still be entering are needed, as is a more precise measure of the increased incidence of the use of phony documents. To date, anecdotal indications are such that illegal aliens continue to enter at roughly the pre-IRCA levels. Popular journalistic accounts point to a marked increase in the use of phony documents. But we have no firm data on either of these aspects. Some more reliable data on the number of visa overstayers who are still able to circumvent IRCA's employer-sanctions provisions need to be gathered and assessed in a more rigorous manner. Certainly, the evidence from the GAO survey and from comments from relevent nongovernment agencies suggests that there is significant under-reporting of alleged discrimination practices. Some means to more accurately measure such under-reported data would be highly desirable for future social science research and for government study of this important area of policy research.

It is to those future policy needs and trends and to the corresponding research needs that we turn our attention in the final chapter. That chapter will also highlight some lessons to be learned about the policy process from a study of the IRCA case, and will briefly discuss the effort to reform legal immigration as enacted in the 1990 law.

NOTES

1. For a discussion of some of the problems of doing so, see *National Journal,* 7 March 1987, p. 390; General Accounting Office 1987a, 5; Bean, Vernez, and Keely 1989, 66–67; Crane et al. 1990, viii).

2. See, for example, Ash and Crane 1989; Massey, Donato, and Liaing 1989; and Woodrow and Passel 1989.

3. White, Bean, and Espanshade 1989. This study is an exception to the general consensus among researchers about the limited effects of IRCA to date. It has been criticized on a couple of grounds, including (1) using 1986 as the base year, one which was atypical relative to the previous ten-year trend; (2) including some IRCA-related variables in their model but not others (e.g., they included SAWs but not LAWs); (3) making inferences based on statistically insignificant relationships (McDonnell and Hill 1989, 28). The second study is that of Crane et al. 1990. In this

author's opinion, it is the most thorough attempt to assess the decline in the illegal immigration flow directly attributable to the employer-sanctions provision.

4. Mark Miller, "The Times Poll: Despite New Laws U.S. Still a Lure in Mexico," *Los Angeles Times,* 21 August 1989, pp. 10–11. See also McDonnell and Hill 1989, 28; "Illegal Migration's Fact of Life, Study Concludes," *Washington Post,* 15 November 1987, p. 18; "Immigration Law Alone Can't Work," *Chicago Times/News,* 10 April 1987, p. 42; "Illegal Alien Influx: Illusion vs. Reality," *Washington Post,* 24 April 1988, A4; Douglas Massey 1987b, 1372–1403; and "Mexican Hearts, California Dreams," *Los Angeles Times Magazine,* 7 September 1987, pp. 7–28.

5. N.Y. Department of Social Services, *Report,* November 1988, 10. The Oregon and Arizona state reports likewise conclude IRCA has resulted in significant employer discrimination in their respective states.

6. For a review of the estimated number of illegal aliens during the 1970s, see Siegel, Passel, and Robinson (1980). For a review of more recent estimates, see the Panel on Immigration Statistics (1985).

7. Ibid. Hoefer, 1988.

CHAPTER 6

Immigration Policy for the 1990s

Public policy can usefully be defined as an intentive course of action followed by public officials or bodies in dealing with a perceived problem. Thus, immigration policy, as all public policy, is a dynamic, ongoing process. A specific *policy decision*—such as Congress's enactment of IRCA—is a discrete act by public officials, authoritative decision makers, that in some manner authorizes public policy. It is one step in attempting to carry out that intentive course of action. But specific policy decisions invariably must be implemented. That produces *policy outputs*—the tangible manifestations of public policies; or what governments actually do or consciously choose not to do in trying to implement the policy decision. Invariably, such policy outputs result in *policy outcomes*—the consequences for society, both intended and unanticipated, that flow from the action or selected inaction of government. Outcomes drive the policy process forward, generating new or continued demands for policy revision.

This final chapter focuses upon the dynamic process of immigration policy. Passage of IRCA, and even the degree of its successful implementation, is not the end of immigration policy making in the United States. It is but a phase in that ongoing process. Chapter 6, therefore, begins with a discussion of bills before Congress, culminating with the passage of a new law in 1990, intended to reform the *legal* immigration process.

That discussion is followed by a section that is more speculative. It discusses where IRCA and the 1990 law may lead. By observing ongoing trends in the immigration process, and by critically observing some of the unanticipated consequences of those laws, one can project the direction in which future policy initiatives are likely to proceed for the remainder of this decade.

Finally, this chapter closes with a brief discussion of some lessons to be learned about the policy process that the examination of immigration reform affords us. It highlights some insights into the policy process gleaned from that examination.

PROPOSED IMMIGRATION POLICY REFORMS

As we have discussed, IRCA stressed very heavily the *illegal alien influx* aspect of immigration problems. The law was enacted only after protracted struggle and only by incorporating several key compromises that resulted in divergent outcomes when implemented. Several proposals for continued immigration policy reform addressed aspects of the immigration problem simply not dealt with by IRCA.[1] Other proposals essentially were refinements of that approach when the need became apparent because of the difficulties that developed when implementing IRCA.

Senate Proposals

On March 15, 1988, the Senate passed S-2104, more commonly known as the Kennedy–Simpson bill, by a vote of 88 to 4. This proposal attempted to further reform current U.S. immigration law primarily by dealing with a number of aspects of *legal* immigration not dealt with by IRCA, although a few of its provisions were obvious attempts by its sponsors to legislate actions seen as problems or failures in the implementation of IRCA. Several aspects of the Kennedy–Simpson bill addressed recommendations for revision of legal immigration that were made in the SCIRP report.

A major concern of the Select Commission report concerned the question of total legal immigration that should be allowed annually and the balance within and among the family reunification categories, and what changes, if any, should be made in the categories of nonfamily or independent immigrants. The commission staff presented a model with a cap of 750,000 and invited the commissioners and their staffs to present models of their own. It also presented the idea of separate tracks based on specified goals of immigration policy: (1) family reunification; (2) independent immigrants; and (3) refugees. The commission, however, by a vote of 15 to 1, rejected a specified cap (Tomasi 1989, 56).

The Kennedy–Simpson bill followed the SCIRP recommendations in identifying separate tracks for family and nonfamily immigrants, by calling for increased total legal immigration, and by slightly tipping the ratio of independent to family-related immigrants. It likewise separated refugees from family-related immigrants. It followed the Select Commission's recommendations for a substantial number of visas set aside for "second preference" family reunification by doubling the numbers for this preference, but narrowed the category to include only spouses and unmarried children of permanent residents under the age of 26.

An important difference in S-2104 from what the SCIRP suggested was that S-2104 retained per-country ceilings for spouses and minor unmarried children of permanent resident aliens under the age of 26. It continued to give great weight to family reunification by reserving 470,000 visas for that category. S-2104 also allocated 120,000 visas for independent immigrants, a level more generous than that recommended by SCIRP. It further provided for 55,000 independent immigrants to be admitted according to a point system, a method of selection rejected by SCIRP.

The Kennedy–Simpson bill also called for establishing an eligibility for entrepreneurs who create at least ten jobs, setting a minimum investment of $1 million. It also provided for a study of the permanent labor certification process and proposed changes in immigration and naturalization rules that would benefit U.S. workers, employers, and taxpayers (Tomasi 1989, 81–82).

The Kennedy–Simpson bill tried to alter the trends of the past two decades by using its "two-track" preference system—the one for family reunification and the other for independent immigrants. The bill created separate avenues of entrance for immigrants with needed job skills and more than doubled the number of such visas from 54,000 to 150,000. It allowed any unused visas in one preference to be allocated to the next preference.[2]

The bill sought to modify existing legal immigration in several ways. There were no limits on the number of visas for immediate relatives of U.S. citizens. While the bill sought to keep the number of such visas unlimited, it based the number of available family preference visas on the level of immediate relative immigration. The number admitted under family preference categories was to be capped at 480,000 *minus* the number of relatives of U.S. citizens admitted during the previous fiscal year. Thus, any increase in the number of immediate relatives would reduce correspondingly the number available for the family preference track.

The bill was amended on the Senate floor to guarantee a minimum number of 216,000 for family preference visas (the number admitted during 1988) regardless of how many immediate relatives of U.S. citizens had entered during the previous year. In the words of Senator Simpson, "The ceiling has a hole in it" (Bean, Vernez, and Keely 1989, 105).

Prior law had no age limit on eligible unmarried children, but the proposal would have set a limit for unmarried children to be under age 26. Critics of the bill argued this would, over time, decrease the availability of second preference visas.

The Kennedy–Simpson bill allocated up to 150,000 independent visas. They were aimed at drawing better educated and skilled workers.

The Kennedy–Simpson–Simon bill was a slightly modified version of one passed by the Senate in 1988, but not voted on in the House. That version had changes made as a compromise to a bill sponsored by Sen. Paul Simon (D., Ill.). In an obvious attempt to address some problems associated with the implementation of IRCA, it also contained an amendment to end direct federal benefits to undocumented immigrants and a provision to grant stays of deportation to immediate relatives of people in the process of legalizing under IRCA. In response to the repression of the pro-democracy movement in mainland China, it allowed for an increase in the annual immigration level from Hong Kong from 2 percent to 3.5 percent of the worldwide total. It also let Chinese students already in the United States remain for four years, and to qualify for legal residency (Bean, Vernez, and Keely 1989, 106–107).

Sen. Dennis DeConcini (D., Ariz.) sponsored a bill (S-332) several times that would temporarily halt the deportation of Salvadorans and Nicaraguans from the United States (a companion bill in the House was sponsored by Rep. Joseph Moakley (D., Mass.). Despite the 1983 Sense-of-Congress Resolution, the Reagan and the Bush administrations opposed granting Emergency Voluntary Departure (EVD) status to Salvadorans. Representative Moakley and Senator DeConcini first launched their antideportation bills during the pre-IRCA debate on immigration reform, and the Moakley amendment, as we discussed in Chapter 3, was passed by the House and was considered as part of IRCA, but was deleted in the compromises of the conference committee. The enactment of IRCA aggravated the problems of many Salvadorans and Nicaraguans and led Senator DeConcini to sponsor the new Senate bill to deal with the situation (Church World Service 1987, 131–132).

The Senate bills had companion bills in the House of Representatives. It is on those House bills we focus our attention next.

House Proposals

The companion bill to the Senate's Kennedy–Simpson–Simon bill was sponsored by Rep. Howard Berman (D., Calif.), HR-672. It was similar to the pre-compromise Simon bill in that it contained no overall cap on total immigration. The Berman bill also exempted immediate relatives of permanent residents from the current family preference limit. Under the 1965 law, the maximum per-country visa allotment was 20,000. The Senate version set that at 7 percent of the total, and the Berman bill set it at 22,000 (Table 7.3 in Bean, Vernez, and Keely 1989, 102).

The House also considered the Moakley bill (HR-618), the companion bill to Senator DeConcini's measure against deportation of Salvadorans and Nicaraguans.

The major House proposal to reform legal immigration law was a bill cosponsored by Chairman Rodino and Representative Mazzoli, HR-5115. It differed from the Kennedy–Simpson–Simon bill in the Senate by imposing neither a ceiling on annual admissions of immediate relatives of U.S. citizens nor by offsetting such against other family-sponsored immigration. The Rodino–Mazzoli bill, like the Senate's compromise version, raised third and sixth preference-sponsored immigrant preference limits from 54,000 visas to 150,000 (Tomasi 1989, 75).

Like the Senate version of these proposed revisions of legal immigration, the Rodino–Mazzoli bill provided for three new independent immigrant classifications (replacing but building upon the 1965 law's third and sixth preference categories). Under the bill, each of the three classifications would receive one-third of the total admissions for that category—that is, 50,000 visas per year.

The Rodino–Mazzoli bill likewise reallocated worldwide admissions between the family-sponsored and the employer-sponsored immigrant categories. It provided that in the case where one country reached the 20,000 limit, its visas were to be allocated between family-sponsored and "independent" immigrants at a ratio of 1.44 to 1; that is, the same ratio of the overall family preferences (216,000) to "independents" (150,000). This formula was intended to impact particularly upon the most recently "oversubscribed" countries—China, the Dominican Republic, India, Korea, Mexico, and the Philippines (ibid., 79).

Like the Senate bill, the House bill would have permitted spouses and minor children of legalized aliens to remain with or join their immediate family members in the United States, and these additional visas would not be subject to any per-country limitations. That provision attempted to rectify the most severe problem of IRCA's legalization program implementation that split the families of many legalizing aliens.

Finally, the bill extended a section of IRCA that permitted nationals of certain countries determined to have been adversely affected by the abolition of the national-origins quota law to compete for 10,000 unrestricted visas. The Rodino–Mazzoli bill called for an additional 10,000 visas to be made available in each of the fiscal years 1989–1993 for those who submitted applications under Section 314 of IRCA (ibid., 80–81).

Another reform proposal generated by problems associated with implementing IRCA concerned the use of phony documents. Many have called for the development of a relatively tamper-proof Social Security card that could then be used as the sole document to certify work authorization (see, for example, GAO 1988a). Others have opposed such an idea as being too close to some sort of national ID card. Many European nations using the employer-sanctions approach have adopted a card to more effectively control and monitor work authorization. A step in that direction was proposed in a bill sponsored by Rep. Bruce Morrison (D., Conn.). That bill set up use of a new tamper-proof Social Security card on a voluntary basis among recipients of federal welfare benefit programs. Such new tamper-proof Social Security cards could then be used for all identification purposes—including, of course, authorization to work.[3]

Of great concern to those advocating or opposing modifications of the 1965 law's fifth preference was what has been called "the multiplier effect." When the 1965 law was enacted, Congress was so focused upon elimination of the origins system that it paid little attention to the fifth preference allocation, sometimes referred to as the "brothers and sisters act" (Reimers 1985). Congress expected continued reform, but in fact, the 1965 act went on virtually unrevised until IRCA, some 21 years later. Total legal immigration increased steadily because of the largely unanticipated consequences of the 1965 act, the unforeseen increases in the number of immediate relatives.

The staff of SCIRP, and many in Congress as well, felt that allowing the "brothers and sisters" provision was what accounted for the heavy increases in post–1965 immigration because of a multiplier effect:

> Further, the staff found that the inclusion of a preference for all brothers and sisters of adult U.S. citizens creates exponential visa demand. Married siblings—which account for about half of those entering—bring spouses who, upon naturalization, can then petition to bring their parents and siblings, along with their families. And so the chain continues. (U.S. President's SCIRP 1981a, 362–363)

Several studies conducted since IRCA, however, have proven such fears to be illusory. One 1986 study found the multiplier effect in the first ten years to be one, with the highest rates of sponsorship for those entering under labor visas. Another study of 2,000 prospective Korean and Filipino immigrants found that although each had up to 25 potentially eligible relatives, only 20 percent to 25 percent of those were actually likely to emigrate, and that those fell off over time. A 1988 GAO study found little evidence of any multiplier effect except for Asian countries, but even in those cases, the long backlogs made the average time between the arrival of the petitioner and his or her relatives over 12 years (Tomasi 1989, 89).

Congress has passed several acts in the years since IRCA that modified very slightly the fringes of existing legal immigration policy. In 1987, it passed the Amerasian Homecoming Act (101 Statutes-at-Large 1329), which was an appropriations law providing for admission of children born in Vietnam between specified dates to Vietnamese mothers and American fathers, together with their immediate relatives. Though admitted as nonquota immigrants, they did receive refugee program benefits.

In 1988, as part of the U.S.–Canada Free Trade Agreement Implementation Act (102 Statutes-at-Large 1876), Congress facilitated temporary entry on a reciprocal basis between the United States and Canada. That same year, in the act of November 15, 1988 (102 Statutes-at-Large 3908), Congress amended the Immigration and Nationality Act of 1952 by providing for the extension of stay for certain nonimmigrant H-1 nurses. In the Foreign Operations Act of 1989 (103 Statutes-at-Large 3908), in an appropriations bill, Congress adjusted to permanent residence status certain Soviet and Indochinese nationals who were paroled into the United States between certain dates after denial of refugee status.

Finally, in December 1989, Congress amended the Immigration and Nationality Act of 1952 (Statutes-at-Large 2099) as the Immigration Nursing Relief Act of 1989, wherein it adjusted to permanent residence status without numerical limitations certain nonimmigrants employed as Registered

Nurses for at least three years and who met established certification standards. The really extensive reform of legal immigration came with the enactment of the Immigration Act of November 29, 1990 (104 Statutes-at-Large 4978).

THE IMMIGRATION ACT OF 1990

The Immigration Act of 1990 extensively reformed legal immigration. It culminated the effort of reform begun with SCIRP in 1979 and contained elements of virtually all the ideas and bills already discussed. It constituted a major overhaul of the 1965 act. Its major provisions are listed here:

Increased total immigration under an overall flexible "cap" of 675,000 immigrants beginning in fiscal year 1995, preceded by a 700,000 level during the fiscal years 1992 through 1994. The 675,000 level consisted of: 480,000 family-sponsored immigrants; 140,000 employment-based immigrants; and 55,000 "diversity immigrants."

Revised all grounds for exclusion and deportation, significantly rewriting the political and ideological grounds. For example, it repealed the bar against the admission of communists as nonimmigrants and limited the exclusion of aliens on foreign policy grounds.

It authorized the Attorney General to grant temporary protected status to undocumented alien nationals of designated countries subject to armed conflict or natural disasters.

It revised and established new nonimmigrant admission categories by:

1. Redefining the H-1(b) temporary worker category and limited admissions to 65,000 annually; and
2. Creating new temporary worker admission categories, some with annual caps on the number of admissions.

It revised and extended through fiscal year 1994 the Visa Waiver Pilot Program.

It revised naturalization authority and requirements by:

1. Transferring the exclusive jurisdiction to naturalize aliens from the Federal and State courts to the Attorney General; and
2. Amending the substantive requirements for naturalization: State residency requirements revised and reduced to 3 months added another ground for waiving the English language requirement; lifted the permanent bar to naturalization for aliens who applied to be relieved from U.S. military service on the grounds of alienage who previously served in the service of the country of the alien's nationality.

It revised enforcement activities in several ways:

1. Broadened the definition of "aggravated felony" and imposed new legal disabilities on aliens convicted of such crimes
2. Revised employer-sanctions provisions of the Immigration Reform and Control Act of 1986
3. Authorized funds for the increase by 1,000 of the personnel level of the Border Patrol

4. Revised criminal and deportation provisions

It recodified the 32 grounds for exclusion into 9 categories, including revising and repealing some of the grounds (especially health grounds). (*Congressional Record—House,* 26 October 1990, H-13203–H-13240)

It was enacted with the support of, or over the opposition of, many of the same groups and Congressional voting coalitions as were involved in the passage of IRCA. Its major authors in the Senate were Kennedy, Simpson, and Simon. In the House, its chief author was Rep. Bruce Morrison.

The bill passed on the last day of the session, and then only after a last-minute flap that nearly killed the bill as patched together in the conference committee. That last-minute flap was engineered by the Hispanic Caucus members. They held up consideration of the conference report on October 26. They opposed a small pilot program included in the conference committee's bill to establish a forgery-proof driver's license that could be used by employers to screen out illegal workers. They argued the program was the first step toward a national identification card. California Democrats Edward Roybal and Esteban Torress, and other Hispanic Caucus members worked the House floor to persuade their colleagues to vote against the provision on civil rights grounds, arguing the program was a threat to privacy and individual liberties.

They won over black members, many of whom had significant Hispanic populations in their districts, and who were frustrated with President Bush's veto of a Civil Rights bill. They also won over liberal Democrats who opposed it on civil rights grounds and some GOP members who were against the overall bill. The vote on the rule was 186 to 235.

Proponents then came up with the idea of a concurrent resolution to strip out the license provision from the conference report. By a voice vote, both chambers agreed to strip the license proposal, allowing the House vote to adopt the conference report 264 to 118 (*Congressional Quarterly Weekly Report,* 3 November 1990, 3753). That vote is detailed in Appendix C.

Surprisingly, Sen. Alan Simpson (R., Wyo.), who earlier had held up the bill in conference until he got a deal that included the driver's license project, dropped it without a fight. Also somewhat surprisingly, Representative Moakley (D., Mass.) had won from House–Senate conferees a stay of deportation for Salvadorans living here illegally. He had worked for the deportation stay for seven years and had not expected Senate proponents of the bill serving on the conference committee to include it in the conference report.

Even with the dropping of the pilot program for a tamper-proof license, the conference report bill faced some opposition, of course, in both chambers of the Congress. For example, Representative Bryant (D., Tex.) opposed it because: "the simple fact that today in the United States of America we admit 530,000 legal immigrants to this country every year, more than all the other countries of the world combined admit to their countries, at a time in which we are unable to meet the basic needs of our own citizens and unable even to pay the bills of our country" (*Congressional Record—House,* 27 October 1990, H-12359).

Rep. Tom J. Campbell (R., Calif.) objected to the provision allowing investors to immigrate, which he argued was forced into the conference report version of the bill by three senators who lacked the power to get the provision included during the two-year session's deliberations, but were able—he argued—to get it included by reason of the desperately late hour in the Congress, putting the three senators in a position to insist on their way. He stated, "Standing alone, a provision in immigration law that favors those with wealth would fail because the overwhelming majority of the people's representatives would oppose such a stark departure from what we think of America. We must not let the shortness of time stampede us into a fundamental breach of faith" (ibid., H-12362).

Representative Lewis (R., Fla.) objected to the bill on the grounds that it had no compensation for the increased costs to state and local governments in states that received the bulk of the immigrants entering the country. In his words:

> Well, Mr. Speaker, here we are again, increasing the numbers. I would like my colleagues who live in the states who are not affected by this type of immigration in southern California and Texas, on the Rio Grande and in southern Florida, to go back and explain to their people that we did you a favor, that we let the people of southern California, we let the people of southern Texas, and we let the people of southern Florida foot the bill for this particular amendment to the Immigration Act. I think this is wrong. (ibid., H-12363)

In the U.S. Senate debate on the conference report, strong opposition was voiced by several senators. Sen. Nancy Kassebaum (R., Kans.) objected to a provision that expanded the secretary of state's authority to exclude any alien if the admission would compromise a compeling U.S. foreign policy interest. As she stated it:

> I am concerned about the procedure used to adopt this proposal. It was not debated or discussed by either body or by the committees of jurisdiction. Yet we are presented with a fait accompli—as part of a back-room deal we are making significant changes in U.S. immigration policy. . . . This is an issue of great concern to me, and next session I intend to promptly revisit this issue. (*Congressional Record—Senate,* 26 October 1990, S-17114)

Her objection to the bill was echoed by Senators Daniel Moynihan (D., N.Y.), Bob Kerry (D., Nebr.), Alan Cranston (D., Calif.), Terry Sanford (D., N.C.), and Paul Sarbanes (D., Md.).

Sen. Robert Byrd (D., W.Va.) opposed the bill largely on financial grounds, arguing that it further eroded and drained already limited resources for U.S. citizens (ibid., S-17117).

Proponents of the conference report argued equally strenuously, and ultimately more persuasively, for its passage. The chair of the conference committee and primary mover of the bill in the House was Rep. Bruce Morrison (D., Conn.). He characterized and summarized the bill as follows:

> This legislation is historic legislation. It reforms our immigration system in ways more extensive and more broad than any legislation this Congress has ever considered before. . . . First, it is strong on the improvement of family unification. This is pro-family legislation. . . . Second, this legislation protects American jobs. . . . Third, this legislation reopens the door of immigration to countries which have had that door closed since 1965, countries such as Ireland, Italy, Poland, countries that have been part of the basic source of immigration to this nation. . . . We also in this legislation streamline the process by which people become citizens, implementing a long recommended provision regarding administrative naturalization, so there will not be the long waits there are today for those who seek to become citizens. . . . It rightly furthers America's reputation for generosity. In fact, we are a country that will continue to accept as many newcomers as the rest of the world combined. . . . The conference committee bill, while maintaining family reunification as the cornerstone of U.S. immigration policy, places a greater emphasis on skilled immigrants. This improvement puts America's interests first by recognizing the talents skilled immigrants have to offer. (*Congressional Record—House,* 27 October 1990, H-12360)

He went on to stress the bill's increased support of the INS and its provisions for more stringent measures against illegal alien smugglers, noting that after a few years of declining arrests at the borders, apprehensions of illegal aliens in 1990 topped 1 million. The conference report measure increased penalties for "coyotes" along the border who prey on scared aliens and reduce people to cargo. He stressed its provisions to increase INS citizen's arrest powers for people or drug smugglers, and its provision to authorize hiring an additional 1,000 Border Patrol personnel (ibid., H-12361).

Representatives Lamar Smith (R., Tex.) and William McCollum (R., Fla.) both spoke in favor of its provisions to increase job-skills related immigration. In McCollum's words:

> Under what is being adopted here tonight, we will be able to have 55,000 seed immigrants in the diversity category who have not been able to come here before who will have educational skills, and so forth, that do not have family connections, and we will be able to have 140,000 new skilled workers able to come here who do not have the family connections. I think it is very important that we have these skilled immigrants. (ibid., H-12362)

Representatives Howard Berman (D., Calif.) and John Moakley (D., Mass.) both heavily emphasized the provision regarding refugees from El Salvador. In Berman's words:

Mr. Speaker, we have increased country ceilings effectively from 20,000 to approximately 25,000. We have included in this bill a provision which we were neglectful of including when we passed the Immigration Reform and Control Act, which finally provides codified stays of deportation and work authorization for spouses and minor children of newly legalized aliens, not to mention the eight-year effort of the chairman of the Rules Committee to provide EVD status, temporary protected status for the Salvadorans, and a massive reform of the horrible McCarran–Walter immigration legislation of many years ago. (ibid., H-12363)

Rep. John Porter (R., Ill.) emphasized the bill's provisions for the investment category of new immigrants in the following manner:

The legislation contains many important provisions, and three of them are on immigration from the Crown Colony of Hong Kong. Hong Kong, as many Members are well aware, is one of the world's great economic miracles, representing, perhaps, the most vibrant economy in the world, which will come under the control of Communist China in 1997. With Tienanmen Square and the ongoing abuses of human rights by the People's Republic of China, understandably the people of Hong Kong are extremely nervous about their future, and Mr. Speaker, they are voting with their feet and leaving Hong Kong in record numbers.

These are the entrepreneurs who know how to create jobs and make another economy equally vibrant. . . . The bill contains three provisions that are of great help. First, it raises the quota from 5,000 to 10,000. Second, it creates a special quota for Hong Kong employees of U.S. businesses of 12,000 a year. Third it creates an unprecedented type of visa, one that is exercisable at the holder's discretion over a long period of time, five years past the 1997 date. (ibid., H-12363)

As for Senate supporters of the bill, perhaps it is best to cite here the words of two of its major authors, Senators Kennedy (D., Mass.) and Simpson (R., Wyo.). Senator Kennedy described the bill as follows:

This bill, like all major legislation, represents many years of work, and many efforts at compromise. This measure is the culmination of a decade-long effort which began in 1979 with the Select Commission on Immigration and Refugee Policy. The commission's report laid the basis for the most comprehensive reforms of the nation's immigration laws in our history. This effort has been a two-step process. In 1986 we enacted a far-reaching measure to deal with illegal immigration. In this bill, an equally far-reaching reform of legal immigration will be achieved. . . . Our goal has been to reform the current immigration system – which has not changed in 25 years – so that it will more faithfully serve the national interest, and be more flexible and open to immigrants from nations which are so short-changed by current law. . . . This compromise creates two separate preference systems for immigration visas – one for close family members, another for independent immigration. This two-track system was first recommended by the Select Commission. (*Congressional Record – Senate,* 26 October 1990, S-17106)

Senator Simpson stressed yet another aspect of the bill:

But the bill provides, for the very first time, a mechanism through which the national level of immigration in the United States will be reviewed by the President and by the Congress every 3 years. So never again will we go 25 to 30 years without carefully reviewing immigration levels, how they should be adjusted to bring our immigration policy more into line with our national interests. (ibid., S-17109)

Finally, Sen. John Chafee (R., R.I.) strongly advocated passage of the bill by stressing its provision to rectify a problem from IRCA, the question of EVD status (ibid., S-17116).

As stated, when the measure finally came to a vote, it passed in the House by a vote of 264 in favor to 118 against, with 50 not voting. In the Senate, the measure was adopted even more comfortably, by a vote of 89 to 8, with 3 not voting. The Immigration Act of 1990 split voting blocs much like IRCA did, but with more unanimity among some of the caucus blocs.

In terms of political party alignments, in the House, Democrats voted 168 in favor of the bill to 55 against it. Also in the House vote, Republicans supported the measure by a vote of 92 in favor to 63 against it. Among the fifty members not voting on the issue, thirty-four were Democrats and sixteen were Republicans.

In the Senate, Democrats supported the more liberal (than IRCA) reform of legal immigration by a margin of 50 in favor to 3 opposed, with 1 not voting. Republican Senators favored the measure by 39 for to 5 against, with 2 not voting. These data are summarized and analyzed as to their statistical significance in Table 6.1.

Similarly, the Hispanic and Black Congressional Caucus votes are examined in Table 6.2. Clearly, the vote for reforming legal immigration did not split these voting blocs anywhere nearly as dramatically as did the vote for IRCA. The following presents how the state delegations of the six most immigrant-populous states split their votes on the 1990 act.

Arizona (7 total)—6 for, 1 against; Democrats: 2 for, 0 against; Republicans: 4 for, 1 against

California (50 total)—29 for, 15 against, 5 NV, 1 Absent; Democrats: 24 for, 2 against; Republicans: 5 for, 13 against

Florida (21 total)—10 for, 9 against, 2 NV; Democrats: 5 for, 2 against; Republicans: 5 for, 7 against

Illinois (21 total)—15 for, 2 against, 4 NV; Democrats: 10 for, 1 against; Republicans: 5 for, 1 against

New York (36 total)—30 for, 0 against, 4 NV, 2 Absent; Democrats: 18 for, 0 against; Republicans: 12 for, 0 against

Texas (31 total)—19 for, 11 against, 1 NV; Democrats: 12 for, 8 against; Republicans: 7 for, 3 against

Table 6.1
Roll Call Vote, Immigration Reform Act of 1990, by Political Party Affiliation, U.S. Congress

Party	Favored	Opposed	Not Voting	Total
Democrats	218 (62%)	58 (46%)	35 (66%)	311
Republicans	131 (38%)	68 (54%)	18 (34%)	217
Total	349 (100%)	126 (100%)	53 (100%)	528

Chi Square = 9.206; .01 level of significance

Table 6.2
Selected Caucus Votes on Immigration Act of 1990 (House Roll Call Vote #530)

Total Vote: 264 Yes, 118 No, 50 Not Voting

Hispanic Caucus Members

Favored	Opposed
Bustamente, D, Tex. +	
de la Garza, D, Tex. -	
Edwards, D, Calif. -	
Gonzales, D, Tex. -	
Martinez, D, Calif. -	
Ortiz, D, Tex. +	
Richardson, D, N.M. +	
Roybal, D, Calif. -	
Torress, D, Calif. +	

Black Congression Caucus

Favored	Opposed	Not Voting
Clay, D, Mo. +	Savage, D, Ill. +	Hawkins, D, Calif. -
Collins, D, Ill. +		Fauntroy, D, D.C. +
Conyers, D, Mich. -		
Dellums, D, Calif. -		
Dixon, D, Calif. +		
Dymally, D, Calif. -		
Ford, D, Tenn. +		
Gray, D, Pa. +		
Hayes, D, Ill. -		
Owens, D, N.Y. +		
Rangel, D, N.Y. +		
Stokes, D, Ohio +		
Towns, D, N.Y. -		

Notes: +, voted same way on IRCA; −, voted differently on IRCA.

IMPLICATIONS FOR FUTURE POLICY ACTION

What does this analysis of the immigration reform efforts of the 1980s, beginning with IRCA and culminating with the enactment of the Immigration Act of 1990, suggest as to future policy action by Congress with respect to the issues discussed herein? Clearly, the historical record of past immigration policy demonstrates that each major modification of immigration policy contained within the new approach the very "seeds" that led to demand for a subsequent cycle of revisions (LeMay 1987). Equally clear, the immigration issue is one that has not been totally resolved. It is a topic that remains on the front burner of political concern.

Where might the immigration reforms already discussed lead in terms of pressures and resulting proposals for future revision? This section will briefly highlight several that are suggested by the reforms to date.

Employer sanctions was among the most controversial aspects of IRCA during the debate over its enactment. Its implementation has only engendered more conflict. Clearly the employer-sanctions approach, as implemented to date, has not led to the sustained reduction in illegal immigration for which its sponsors had hoped. There remains in the country a clear feeling that we still have lost control over our borders.

The finding by the GAO that sanctions have increased discrimination will fuel efforts to end employer sanctions. Others will respond to such pressures with efforts to revise the approach by continuing to tighten enforcement efforts through more tamper-proof documentation, increased efforts to beef up the Border Patrol, and further education efforts on the part of the INS with respect to the nation's employers. While in the immediate future it is unlikely that Congress will end employer sanctions, continued efforts to revise the approach are highly likely. One such reform to improve the sanctions provisions of IRCA centers on the verification process and the simplification of documents used to show worker eligibility.

By the mid-1990s, the INS plans to reduce the number of work eligibility cards it issues from ten to two, and to make those cards much more difficult to counterfeit. It also plans to replace over 30 million old INS cards with new ones. This schedule, however, depends upon Congressional approval of additional funding and personnel. In its 1990 report, the GAO concluded that unless this process were expedited, little would be done in the near term to reduce employer confusion and uncertainty about the work eligibility status of aliens, and the resulting discrimination already noted (GAO 1990, 7).

The Systematic Alien Verification for Entitlements (SAVE) provision of IRCA has raised considerable concern as to its cost-effectiveness. Studies currently under way in a number of states will likely demonstrate that the program is not, in fact, cost-effective. It is likely that proposals to end the SAVE program will be forthcoming during the next few years, given its lack of popularity among state and local government officials.

In the 1990 act, congressional rejection of some sort of voluntary system to develop a tamper-proof driver's license has shown how difficult it will be for such an evolutionary progression in the direction of developing such a tamper-proof card. It is equally clear, however, that the technology to produce it has already been developed. European experience with the employer-sanctions approach demonstrates the need for such a document to effectively enforce sanctions. Should the employer-sanctions approach be abandoned, however, then projections for some sort of tamper-proof work authorization card would be unlikely. While movement in the policy direction of developing such a card is likely if the United States maintains an employer-sanctions approach to immigration policy, the highly political controversial nature of that policy direction means the progression will be slow, tortuous, and probably piecemeal.

Moreover, as of 1989, the INS still relies upon manual compilations of district and sector reports on their employer-sanctions activities. The GAO 1990 report noted the inadequacy of that system and strongly recommended that the INS needed to implement a service-wide automated employer-sanctions information system (ibid., 97).

The 1990 act's expansion of the Attorney General's authority was a controversial provision that was included in the conference committee's deliberations over the two chambers' bills. It will carefully be watched by various Senate members concerned about the issue, and well may generate future proposals to revise the new law.

The SLIAG program of IRCA offers the federal government maximum administrative control over grants-in-aid programs. Given the high probability for increased budgetary deficit pressures throughout the 1990s, it will be likely that proposals to adopt this new approach to federal grants will spread from IRCA's SLIAG to other federal grant programs. A logical progression for such future policy development, given our understanding of how policy innovations spread, is for the DHHS to first begin advocating use of this type of approach in other welfare grant programs that it administers. If that happens, then the expansion is likely to flow to related federal department grant programs—such as those administered by the Department of Education or the Department of Housing and Urban Development.

The refund approach to such grants both delays the expenditure outlays and likely discourages state and local governments from becoming involved. They probably also have to absorb more of the costs of such programs than they would otherwise have to do if the grant program were not on such a refund basis. Given the current federal deficit posture, such aspects of SLIAG are likely to prove to be highly alluring.

The costs of dealing with immigrants (legal, legalizing, and illegals) and refugees have been significant and to a great extent borne by state and local governments. For example, in the 1980s, the state of California absorbed an estimated 3 million legal and illegal immigrants, and an additional 3 million are expected during the 1990s. During fiscal year 1992, California spent roughly $1.7 billion on services to the immigrant population. As noted, although IRCA included $4 billion to assist the state and local governments through 1994, each year the money set aside for that aid has been raided by Congress. California, which has over 61 percent of the immigrants legalized by IRCA, has had to pay most of the costs for housing, education, and health care (Canlen 1993, 49). Certainly, the costs of continued immigration will be a topic before the Congress, as will bills to address which level of government will bear those costs.

To the extent that future research and studies already mandated demonstrate that employer sanctions are proven to be of limited effectiveness in reducing the flow of undocumented aliens into the United States or of effectively forcing those already in the United States to leave, then the greater the pressure will be for future policy revision to move in the direction of action to establish bilateral or even international agreements to reduce pressure from sending nations. The mandatory studies by the GAO and the DOL already under way because of IRCA will likely provide increased evidence of the importance of push variables. The new 1990 act provides for regular and continued study of the immigration process.

It is very probable that such studies will further document the push side of the immigration flow. Future legislative action on the drug problem involving bilateral or even multilateral agreements with producing nations of the drug influx may well provide additional precedent and pressure to move U.S. immigration policy in the direction of a multinational approach. Such direction seems clearly compatible with the new Clinton administration's approach to foreign policy matters generally.

Indeed, the recent passage of the North American Free Trade Agreement (NAFTA) clearly is seen as a step in that direction. Proponents of the treaty argued strenuously that its benefits to the Mexican economy would have a beneficial impact on illegal immigration pressures. To the extent that the Mexican economy is expanded, jobs are created, and the standard of living rises, there will be a corresponding reduction in pressure to emigrate north. Even opponents of the agreement, arguing that the treaty's enactment would cause up to 500,000 jobs to drain south of the border, were conceding that point.

NAFTA's impact is not likely to be that dramatic on either the Mexican or the U.S. economy. But it should reduce the flow of illegal aliens to the extent that it does create opportunity in Mexico. It represents a multinational approach favored by the Clinton administration. It attacks the problem by impacting on the push factors leading to illegal immigration.

The lack of firm data with which to measure many of the effects of IRCA has often been mentioned herein. Clearly, the IRCA case has demonstrated the need for gathering more basic data and research evidence on the entire immigration process. IRCA mandated several such studies. The 1990 act expands such efforts and research. That trend is one that can easily be seen as continuing. As two prominent immigration scholars noted: "Without a well-funded and effective immigration data management system, the controversy surrounding 'numbers' will continue well beyond the end of the [IRCA] legalization program" (Meissner and Papademetriou 1988, 104).

Unfortunately, during the past four fiscal years, the INS Statistical Division has been budgeted at only $1 million per year to cover staffing and contract research costs. Despite the fact that Congress has substantially expanded its reporting and research requirements, it has not received a commensurate increase in staffing or budgeting. Developments in research technology and capabilities offer the clear potential to develop "an effective immigration data-management system," and pressure on Congress to pursue further research is very probable. While Congress, in the 1990 act, indicated a willingness to authorize the expansion of INS personnel, it has yet to increase as substantially the actual funding.

In 1993, the Clinton administration proposed substantial increases in the budget, but whether increased funding survives the latest budget crisis and efforts at deficit reduction remains to be seen. Past support and the INS's image as an inefficient and often troubled bureaucracy would argue against much optimism in that regard.

Indeed, stepped-up law enforcement and adding more federal agents alone won't solve the illegal alien problem. The Border Patrol suffers from high turnover, poor training, little supervision, and a fortress mentality. The INS, which fills many of its upper-level positions from the ranks of the Border Patrol, has often been under fire for allegations of discrimination, mismanagement, and misconduct. Both the INS and its Border Patrol division have been viewed as in need of a significant overhaul. The Justice Department, under the new Attorney General Janet Reno, has proposed significant reorganization of the INS. The Clinton administration is on record to restructure the agency, and Congress has also been considering it.

> U.S. Senator Dianne Feinstein (D-California) wants to increase funding to the border patrol by imposing a controversial $1-per-person border-crossing fee. State Senator Art Torres (D-Los Angeles) has proposed the formation of an office of immigrant affairs to coordinate services. Another idea, proposed by a congressional committee in 1990, is to merge the INS, the border patrol, U.S. Customs, and certain divisions of the Treasury, Labor, and Health and Human Services departments into one federal agency responsible for admitting, processing and resettling immigrants. (Canlen 1993, 49)

A problem related to IRCA is the entire question of reforming U.S. refugee programs. While the 1990 act revised aspects of U.S. refugee policy, worldwide pressures are leading to increased momentum for still more revisions of refugee policy.

For example, events in eastern Europe increase pressure or simply enable greater migration from eastern to western Europe, and pressure to allow for greater revision in refugee policy is likely.

Current refugee policy determines that the President, at the beginning of each fiscal year, reviews the worldwide refugee situation and authorizes the number of admissions for the next year. For 1991, the admission ceiling was set at 131,000 (Immigration and Naturalization Service 1992, 74). An unfunded reserve of 10,000 was established in 1987 so that refugees could be admitted with private sector funding. Under the Refugee Act of 1980, refugees are eligible to adjust to lawful permanent resident status after one year and are exempt from the worldwide annual limitation of 270,000 immigrants.

Another area of immigration policy sure to be revised is that of political asylum. The Refugee Act of 1980 regulates U.S. asylum policy as well as refugee policy. A key aspect of the asylum policy hinges on the location of the person upon application. The 1980 Refugee Act established a statutory basis for granting asylum in the United States consistent with the 1967 United Nations Protocol on Refugees. The law's definition of a person seeking asylum conforms to the same criteria and categories of persecution as a refugee. The refugee is outside the United States at the time of application; the person seeking asylum is at a port of entry or is in the United States. An alien physically present in the country or at a port of entry may request asylum.

Asylum procedures require that an INS officer interview each applicant and consult with the Bureau of Human Rights and Humanitarian Affairs of the Department of State for an advisory opinion on every asylum case. There are no limits set by law on the number of individuals who may be granted asylum in a fiscal year. An alien denied asylum by the INS may renew the asylum request with an immigration judge during a deportation or exclusion hearing—so simply requesting asylum is virtually tantamount to being able to stay in the United States for several years (ibid., 77).

The INS began implementing new asylum regulations in 1991 based on ones published in the *Federal Register* in July 1990. These established a corps of asylum officers within the INS, shifted decision authority from district directors to the Asylum Officer Corps, and set up a resource documentation center to provide information on human rights conditions throughout the world. Roughly 62,000 asylum applications were filed during 1991, down from the 73,637 filed in 1990. There was a backlog of 97,288 unresolved claims at the beginning of 1991, which grew to 141,000 by the end of the year. Central Americans continued to dominate the requests-for-asylum caseload. As of 1991, the top three nationalities were Salvadorans (34,970), Nicaraguans (23,867), and Guatemalans (15,146). Roughly 2,400 claims were granted in 1991.

Since the 1980 act was passed, 67,400 individuals have been granted asylum by the INS, of whom 66,300 persons seeking asylum have adjusted to permanent resident status. The tremendous rise in asylum cases had been unforeseen by the Select Commission. In the words of Lawrence Fuchs, "We didn't expect the asylum problem. We thought of it as a ballerina in the tutu saying, 'I defect, I defect'" (*Newsweek,* 9 August 1993, 22).

The asylum problem was publicly highlighted in 1993 when several boatloads of Chinese attempted to enter the United States illegally, both off the shores of New York and California. In the latter case, the government prevented them from landing so that they could not request asylum. The Bush administration had set a precedent that Chinese from the mainland who were of childbearing age qualified for such status given the Chinese government's policy of limiting children to one per family. The Clinton administration persuaded the Mexican government to accept the boatload so that the Chinese aboard could be immediately flown back to China (see for example, *Time,* 21 June 1993, 26; and *Newsweek,* 21 June 1993, 34–41).

The renewed influx of illegal immigrants and the highly publicized incidents of asylum cases or attempts to smuggle them in for that purpose have helped to fuel public opposition to immigration. A 1993 poll conducted by *Newsweek* found that 60 percent of all Americans think that the current levels of immigration are bad. Fifty-nine percent also said that many immigrants wind up on welfare, and only 20 percent think of the country as a "melting pot" (*Newsweek,* 9 August 1993, 18). Asylum policy is clearly a topic that the Congress will be forced to revise.

The public sentiment against immigration has given rise to calls for legislation that would end automatic granting of U.S. citizenship to any child born of an illegal alien (Senate Spending Bill Targets Immigrants, 30 July 1993, A2).

Primarily in response to such rising political sentiment, the Clinton administration in 1993 requested Congress approve new spending and new measures to tighten defenses against undocumented aliens. The administration announced a $172.5 million immigration reform package that included proposals for quick settlement of asylum claims, a beefed-up Border Patrol, and prosecution of alien smuggling rings under the nation's racketeering laws. The proposal would increase the INS's visibility and stature within the Justice Department, placing it on a par with the FBI. Stating that the country's borders "leak like a sieve," the President said that the measure would double prison sentences for convicted smugglers, authorize the INS use of wiretaps in alien smuggling investigations, and expand INS authority to seize assets of smugglers. The proposal would be funded by raising from $5 to $6 the international airport inspection fee and by increasing fees for various benefits such as naturalization adjustment of immigrant status. Its major provisions are highlighted here:

- $45 million to hire, train, and equip up to 600 more Border Patrol agents and to purchase high-tech equipment such as sensors and low-light televisions.
- $45 million for the state department to improve and expand its ability to issue fraud-proof visas and passports.

- $12.7 million to expand preinspection of passengers at overseas airports before they get on U.S.-bound planes.
- $31.2 million for quick asylum ajudication by specially trained officers for aliens arriving at airports without documents.
- $11 million to expand the INS program for deportation hearings for jailed alien felons while they are in prison. (ibid., A1)

As part of the $23.6 billion spending bill approved by the Senate in July 1993, the 87 to 13 vote on the appropriations bill for the departments of Commerce, Justice, and State included $131 million for a new border-control initiative, $39 million to hire 600 new Border Patrol agents, $11 million for 254 other INS positions, $75 million for INS processing centers and alien detention facilities, and $6 million to restore 93 Border Patrol positions eliminated in the administration's original budget request. The Senate also sanctioned $10 million to modernize the visa processing system overseas to better prevent the entry of terrorists into the country. In total, the Senate appropriations were $1.3 billion less than what the administration had wanted, but some $2.7 billion more than what the House approved earlier in July 1993. As of this writing, the two chambers will hold talks to work out their differences (ibid., A2).

INSIGHTS INTO THE POLICY PROCESS

This final section highlights some lessons to be drawn from the case study of immigration reform about the nature of the public policy process. The study of the Immigration Reform and Control Act of 1986 and the Immigration Act of 1990 provides useful insights into the policy process.

The first such lesson one can draw from this examination of the IRCA case reflects on the nature of how perception of a problem so strongly shapes the proposed solutions to such a problem as embodied in a particular public policy decision. As the earlier chapters of this study demonstrated, the proponents of IRCA focused greatly on the illegal alien aspect of current immigration problems. That focus, in turn, underscored the proponents' assumptions as to the nature of the undocumented alien influx.

The perception of the illegal alien flow shared by those pushing for the adoption of IRCA was that the illegal aliens constituted the most severe aspect of the immigration influx, and that the nation first had to seize control of its borders by controlling the illegal alien flow before any other immigration reforms were possible. That view dictated the adoption of the controversial and somewhat radical new approach to immigration policy embodied in the employer-sanctions provisions. The nature of the *perceived* policy problem largely dictates the proposed solutions. So, too, the SCIRP report largely set the guidelines and the approach for the reform of legal immigration policy as enacted in the Immigration Act of 1990. The broad guidelines and two-track approach to the preference system reforms were all set by the commission's perspective of the nature of the problems of the legal immigration system.

Another lesson the IRCA case so richly illustrates is the critical role played in the policy process by faction *mediators*. Key legislative actors, caucus leaders, political party leaders, and interest group leaders sometimes work to achieve policy conflict resolution using integrative solutions to craft compromises in the policy debate rather than always attempting to resolve such conflict by competition. Integrative solutions are only possible when the policy conflict involves the right mix of preconditions making such integrative solutions potentially rewarding, and when sufficient factional leaders opt to play the role of mediators.

Another lesson about the policy process exemplified by the IRCA case concerns the key compromises needed to get a new policy decision enacted. Such compromises may achieve a solution that finally allows a majority of legislators to vote enactment, but such compromises inherently involve problems for the implementation process. Conflicting values or goals embodied in compromises enable legislators to vote for a bill. But a particular bureaucracy must be selected to implement the law. When it develops its very specific rules and regulations to implement such conflicting goals, it inevitably faces severe implementation problems.

And when policy is implemented in a way that involves complex intergovernmental relationships, as was IRCA, even more implementation problems result. Policy decisions that divide responsibilities for implementation of a policy between several federal agencies and departments, and several levels of governments, will by their very nature create enormously complex program implementation problems. The various bureaucracies will have to develop new relationships with one another. That process means delays, confusion, and at times, conflicting rules and regulations. Different agencies employ different languages, work under different traditions and emphases, and assume a different bureaucratic view of the relevant policy world. Those differences may not impose insurmountable problems, but they surely will pose problems for the implementation process.

Such policy compromise and intergovernmental complexities not only generate implementation problems, they are among the primary sources of unanticipated consequences. In order to get a law passed, legislative policymakers frequently "paper over" inherent conflicts that emerge when the bureaucrats need to develop their respective rules and regulations, and hire and train their staffs to implement the policy decision. Such implementation invariably will lead to some consequences that the legislators either intentionally overlooked or simply did not foresee.

In the case of the 1990 Immigration Act, the unforeseen problems that clearly remain and will necessitate renewed action by Congress are mostly centered on refugee and asylum aspects wherein worldwide developments have quickly and simply overwhelmed the system designed by the legislators to cope with those vexing problems. The very nature of asylum is being modified dramatically by world events simply unforeseen earlier. The huge waves of refugees were also somewhat unanticipated, and clearly are outstripping our policy to deal with them.

Another primary source of such unanticipated consequences is well illustrated by the IRCA case study. Design flaws in the legislative strategy, or invalid assumptions upon which that strategy was based, are also likely to produce unanticipated consequences. Congressional proponents of IRCA, for instance, assumed that pull factors were primary in the immigration flow. To the degree that such an assumption is incorrect, employer sanctions will correspondingly fail to stem the flow of undocumented aliens. Congress further assumed a *uniform* administration of sanctions. But by giving the highly decentralized INS the primary responsibility for implementing enforcement of sanctions, such uniform implementation was frustrated. But as shown earlier, diversity among regional, district, and even local INS offices in implementing sanctions meant that employers developed different assessments as to the costs of complying with or avoiding full or even partial compliance with the sanctions provisions of IRCA. The decision to fund state and local expenses through the DHHS's implementation of SLIAG resulted in unanticipated difficulties in that program. It may well lead to this new approach to federal grant programs spilling over into other programs and agencies.

Another source of unanticipated consequences, and another lesson afforded by the IRCA case, flows from the radically new approach to policy. When a policy decision, such as IRCA, alters prior public policy into a substantially new direction, it invariably results in some unanticipated consequences. Slow, evolutionary, or incremental changes in policy seldom generate such surprise developments precisely because they follow paths and employ implementation rules (the typical "standard operating procedures" [SOPs] associated with a given bureaucratic agency) that are considered to be tried and true and that offer few surprises.

New policy approaches tend to be based on new assumptions about the environment of the policy. New approaches, by necessity, mean that the implementing bureaucracy must develop new or radically different rules and regulations. But such agencies generally tend to resist changes in their SOPs. More often than not, they will bend the policy to fit their SOPs rather than change their SOPs to fit new policy. But even if they willingly try to comply with the new spirit and approach to a policy, the intergovernmental relations that need to be developed can often result in unanticipated consequences, sometimes flowing from the simple fact that they employ different languages.

Immigration reform, both for legal and illegal immigration, also illustrates the inherent political nature of the policy process. It is impossible to separate politics from administration, and often foreign from domestic aspects of policy. As stated previously, public policy is a course of action to deal with a problem. But problem resolution invariably involves or produces conflict among relevant interest groups, various government agencies, and the elected (executive or legislative branch) officials who comprise the related policy faction. Conflict resolution among factions is what the political process is all about—an unending search for a balance among conflicting values. Politics is an orderly means for peacefully achieving conflict resolution. Therefore, the public policy process is inherently a political process.

Finally, the study of immigration policy reform provides us with useful insight into the nature of the policy process as a "flow." The policy process is a dynamic, ongoing, flowing search for an appropriate course of action to cope with problems. As these immigration reform cases show so well, when the nature of the problem being dealt with is very complex, the policy process itself becomes complicated. Just as the immigration process is so complex and difficult to fully understand and grasp, so too is any policy process designed by legislators to cope with the complexities of that migration flow.

How IRCA came to be enacted at the time and in the manner that it was finally adopted is a difficult process to understand because it was so complex. So too, the implementation of IRCA has been shown to be complicated and as yet not clear in its impacts upon the environment. And as our own meager efforts to evaluate IRCA have illustrated, the assessment of public policy is a difficult and complex job because the focus of our analysis is such a rich, complicated, and diverse process.

This chapter closes in the hope that the study of immigration reform has proven to be worth the effort. Surely, complexity results not only in difficulty, but also in a rich view of human political behavior that is all the more interesting because of its very complexity. We trust the effort has been rewarding to the reader.

NOTES

1. For a thorough discussion of the various major bills concerning legal immigration reform considered by Congress, see Bean, Vernez, and Keely 1989, 101–108; Tomasi 1989, 55–102; Church World Service 1987, 129–132.

2. Conflict over the "fifth category" revisions has been especially intense with proponents and antagonists alike focusing on those "backlog" problems in their various proposals to amend current legal immigration. Besides those discussed herein, the INS has drafted its own version of a Legal Immigration Reform Plan (see discussion in Tomasi 1989, 85–87).

3. GAO 1988a.

APPENDIX A

List of Interviewees

Adams, Mr. Lawrence-Legislative Assistant, Rep. Charles Pashayan (R., CA.), Hon. Member, Hispanic Caucus, D.C.

Allan, Yanik-South Dade Immigration Association, QDE, Homestead, Florida

Almanza, Norma Plascencia-National Immigration, Refugee and Citizenship Forum, Austin, Texas

Austin, Phillip-Chief Counsel, Civil Rights Division, Office of the Attorney General, Phoenix, Arizona

Barnes, Walter-Chief, Office of Refugee Services, Department of Social Services, Sacramento, California

Berman, Michael-IRCA Unit, Illinois Department of Public Aid, Chicago, Illinois

Blakeway, Lisa-Catholic Community Services, QDE, Sacramento, California

Borg, Ron-SLIAG Coordinator, Texas Department of Human Services, Austin, Texas

Brechtel, John-Assistant Director of Investigations, INS District Office, Los Angeles, California

Brown, Suzanne-Immigration Project Coordinator, Illinois Conference of Churches, QDE, Springfield, Illinois

Cardenas, Richard-Catholic Charities (QDE), Los Angeles, CA.

Chambers, Billie-Adult Education Director, Austin Community College, Austin, Texas

Dembrosky, Henry-SLIAG Coordinator, Austin Community College, Austin, Texas

Dunn, Janice-Project Coordinator, Department of Commerce, Phoenix, Arizona

Epstein, Richard-Department of Health and Welfare, Sacramento, CA

Evans, Karl-Wesley Community Center, QDE, Phoenix, Arizona

Flores, Alicia-Migrant Farm Workers Project, QDE, Sacramento, CA.

Gabriel, Roy-Alien Legalization for Agriculture, QDE, Sacramento, California

Gilbert, Paul-Deputy Director, INS, Los Angeles, California

Griffin, Donald-Executive Director, Commission of Human Relations Tallahasee, Florida

Harman, Wendy-Department of Administration, Phoenix, Arizona

Helmar, Mark-Assistant Secretary for Program and Fiscal Affairs, Department of Health and Welfare, Sacramento, CA.

Henry, Neil-INS, Director of Enforcement, Los Angeles, CA.

Houza, Marguerite Rivera-Project Coordinator, SLIAG, Texas Health and Human Services Coordinating Council, Austin, Texas

Hudson, Lynne-SLIAG Coordinator, Texas Department of Health, Austin, Texas

Kurzban, Ira-Kurzban, Kurzban and Weinger, PA (Immigration Lawyer), Miami, Florida

Kohler, Greg-Refugee Programs Administration, Department of Health and Rehabilitative Services, Tallahassee, Florida

Little, Sherill-Haitian Refugee Center, QDE, Miami, Florida

Marzahl, David-Coordinator, Chicago Committee on Immigration Protection, Travelers and Immigrants Aid, QDE, Chicago, Illinois

May, Eliza-Legalization Coordinator, National Association of Latino Elected Officials, San Antonio, Texas

McFarland, Karen-Intergovernmental Coordination Office, Office of Planning and Budgeting, Executive Office of the Governor, Tallahassee, Florida

Myers, Ruth Anne-District Director, INS, Phoenix, Arizona

Noone, Kevin-Executive Director, Commission on Intergovernmental Cooperation, Springfield, Illinois

O'Day, Trish-Program Analyst, Texas Department of Health, Austin, Texas

Olivarez, Laura-California Human Development Corporation, QDE, Sacramento, California

Perry, Richard-Deputy District Director, INS, Phoenix, Arizona

Roberts, Robin-Program Analyst, Texas Employment Commission, Austin, Texas

Rosenfeld, Jose-Legislative Assistant, Representative Albert Bustamante (D., TX.)

Roussos, Pavlos-SLIAG Coordinator, Adult Education, Texas Education Agency, Austin, Texas

Ruiz, Terresa-Illinois State Board of Education, Chicago, Ill.

Samulski-Korzeniowski, Therese-IRCA Unit, Illinois Department of Public Aid, Chicago, Illinois

Sanchez, Nancy-Catholic Charities, QDE, Los Angeles, California

Shaw, Larry-Office of the Speaker, Texas State Legislature, Austin, Texas

Silverman, Edwin-Naturalization Service Section, Illinois Department of Public Aid, Chicago, Illinois

Spinthourakis, Dr. Julia-OMC Manager for Policy, Office of the Secretary, Refugee Administration, Department of Health and Rehabilitative Service, Tallahassee, Florida

Thompson, Nancy-California Human Development Corporation, QDE, Sacramento, California

Tucker, Ann Dee-Program Analyst, Texas Department of Health, Austin, Texas

Voss, Steve-Catholic Charities, QDE, Los Angeles, California

White, Chloe-Illinois State Board of Education, Chicago, Illinois

Wittenberg, Nancy--Refugee Programs Administration, Department of Health and Rehabilitative Services, Tallahassee, Florida

APPENDIX B

The Roll Call Votes Enacting IRCA

The House Roll Call Vote, #469, Enacting IRCA:

Voting for Enactment (238)

Abercrombie, D., Hawaii
Ackerman, D., N.Y.
Alexander, D., Ark.
Anderson, D., Calif.
Annunzio, D., Ill.
Anthony, D., Ark.
Aspin, D., Wis.
Atkins, D., Miss.
AuCoin, D., Oreg.
Barnes, D., Md.
Bates, D., Calif.
Bedell, D., Iowa
Beilenson, D., Calif.
Bennett, D., Fla.
Bereuter, R., Nebr.
Berman, D., Calif.
Boehlert, R., N.Y.
Boland, D., Mass.
Bonior, D., Mich.
Bonker, D., Wash.
Borski, D., Pa.
Bosco, D., Calif.
Boucher, D., Va.
Brown, D., Calif.
Bruce, D., Ill.
Bryant, D., Tex.
Bustamante, D., Tex.
Byron, D., Md.
Carper, D., Del.
Chandler, R., Wash.
Chaney, R., Wyo.
Clay, D., Mo.
Clinger, R., Pa.
Coelho, D., Calif.
Coleman, R., Mo.
Collins, D., Ill.
Conte, R., Mass.
Cooper, D., Tenn.
Coughlin, R., Pa.
Coyne, D., Pa.
Dennemeyer, R., Calif.
Darden, D., Ga.
Dashle, D., S.D.
Davis, R., Mich.
Derrick, D., S.C.
DeWine, R., Ohio
Dicks, D., Mich.
Dingle, D., Mich.
DioGuardi, R., N.Y.
Dixon, D., Calif.
Donnelly, D., Mass.
Dorgan, D., N.D.
Dornan, R. Calif.
Dowdy, D., N. Y.
Downey, D., N.Y.
Durbin, D., Ill.
Dwyer, D., N.J.
Early, D., Mass.
Eckart, R., N.Y.
Edgar, D., Pa.
Evans, R., Iowa
Fascell, D., Fla.
Fazio, D., Calif.
Feighan, D., Ohio
Fish, R., N.Y.
Florio, D., N.J.
Foglietta, D., Pa.
Foley, D., Wash.
Ford, D., Mich.
Ford, D., Tenn.
Frank, D., Mass.
Franzel, R., Minn.
Fugua, D., Fla.
Gejdenson, D., Conn.
Gephardt, D., Mo.
Gibbons, D. Fla.
Gilman, R., N.Y.
Gingrich, R., Ga.
Glickman, D., Kan.
Goodling, R., Pa.
Gray, D., Ill.
Gray, D., Pa.
Green, R., N.Y.
Gunderson, R., Wis.
Hamilton, D., Ind.
Hatcher, D., Ga.
Hefner, D., N.C.
Henry, R., Mich.
Hillis, R., Ind.
Howard, D., N.J.
Hoyer, D., Md.
Huchaby, D., La.
Hutto, D., Fla.
Ireland, R., Fla.
Jeffords, R., Vt.
Johnson, R., Conn.
Kanjorski, D., Pa.
Kasich, R., Ohio
Kastenmeier, D., Wis.
Kennelly, D., Conn.
Kildee, D., Mich.
Kostmayer, D., Pa.
LaFalce, D., N.Y.
LaGomarsino, R., Calif.
Lantos, D., Calif.
Leach, R., Iowa
Lehman, D., Calif.
Lehman, D., Fla.
Levin, D., Mich.
Levine, D., Calif.
Lewis, R., Calif.
Lightfoot, R., Iowa
Lipinski, D., Ill.
Livingston, R., La.
Lott, R., Miss.
Lowery, R., Calif.
Luken, D., Ohio
Lungren, R., Calif.
MacKay, D., Fla.
Manton, D., N.Y.

Voting for Enactment (238)

Markey, D., Mass.
Martin, R., Ill.
Matsui, D., Calif.
Mavroules, D., Mass.
Mazzoli, D., Ken.
McCandless, R., Calif.
McCloskey, D., Ind.
McCollum, R., Fla.
McCurdey, D., Okla.
McDade, R., Pa.
McHugh, D., N.Y.
McKernan, R., Me.
McKinney, R., Conn.
McMillan, R., N.C.
Mica, D., Fla.
Michel, R., Ill.
Mikulski, D., Md.
Miller, R., Wash.
Miller, D., Calif.
Mitchell, D., Md.
Moakley, D., Mass.
Mollohan, D., W.V.
Monson, R., Utah
Montgomery, D., Miss.
Moody, D., Wis.
Moorhead, R., Calif.
Morrison, D., Conn.
Morrison, R., Wash.
Mrazek, D., N.Y.
Murtha, D., Pa.
Natcher, D., Kenn.
Nelson, D., Fla.
Nielson, R., Utah
Nowak, D., N.Y.
Oberstar, D., Minn.
Obey, D., Wis.
Ortiz, D., Tex.
Owens, D., N.Y.
Oxley, R., Ohio
Packard, R., Calif.
Panetta, D., Calif.
Pashayan, R., Calif.
Pease, D., Ohio
Penny, D., Minn.
Pepper, D., Fla.
Perkins, D., Ken.
Pickle, D., Tex.
Price, D., Ill.
Quillen, R., Tenn.
Rahall, D., W.V.
Richardson, D., N.M.
Ridge, R., Pa.
Rodino, D., N.J.
Roe, D., N.J.
Rogers, R., Ken.
Rose, D., N.C.
Rostenkowski, D., Ill.
Roth, R., Wis.
Rowland, R., Conn.
Sabo, D., Minn.
Schaefeer, R., Col.
Schever, D., N.Y.
Schneider, R., R.I.
Schulze, R., Pa.
Schumer, D., N.Y.
Seiberling, D., Ohio
Sharp, D., Ind.
Shaw, R., Fla.
Shumway, R., Calif.
Sikorski, D., Minn.
Sisisky, D., Va.
Slattery, D., Kan.
Smith, D., Fla.
Smith, R., Nebr.
Smith, R., N.J.
Snowe, R., Me.
Solarz, D., N.Y.
Spratt, D., S.C.
Stallings, D., Ind.
Strangeland, R., Minn.
Stark, D., Calif.
Stokes, D., Ohio
Strang, R., Col.
Studds, D., Mass.
Swift, D., Wash.
Synar, D., Okla.
Tauke, D., Iowa
Thomas, R., Calif.
Thomas, D., Ga.
Torres, D., Calif.
Torricelli, D., N.J.
Traxler, D., Mich.
Udall, D., Az.
Vento, D., Minn.
Volkemer, D., Mo.
Vucanovich, R., Nev.
Waldon, D., N.Y.
Walgren, D., Pa.
Walker, R., Pa.
Waxman, D., Calif.
Weber, R., Minn.
Wheat, D., Mo.
Whitehurst, R., Va.
Williams, D., Mont.
Wilson, D., Tex.
Wolf, R., Va.
Wolpe, D., Mich.
Wortley, R., N.Y.
Wright, D., Tex.
Wyden, D., Oreg.
Wylie, R., Ohio
Yates, D., Ill.
Young, D., Mo.
Zschau, R., Calif.

House Voting against IRCA (173)

Akaka, D., Hawaii
Andrews, D., Tex.
Applegate, D., Ohio
Archer, R., Tex.
Armey, R., Tex.
Barnard, D., Ga.
Bartlett, R., Tex.
Barton, R., Tex.
Bateman, R., Va.
Bentley, R., Md.
Bevill, D., Alab.
Biaggi, D., N.Y.
Bilirakis, R., Fla.
Bliley, R., Va.
Boggs, D., La.
Boner, D., Tenn.
Boulter, R., Tex.
Dymally, D., Calif.
Dyson, D., Mo.
Edwards, D., Calif.
Edwards, R., Okla.
Emerson, R., Mo.
English, D., Okla.
Erdreich, D., Alab.
Evans, D., Ill.
Fawell, R., Ill.
Fiedler, R., Calif.
Fields, R., Tex.
Flippo, D., Alab.
Franklin, R., Miss.
Frost, D., Tex.
Gallo, R. N.J.
Garcia, D., N.Y.
Gaydos, D., Pa.
Kolbe, R., Az.
Kolter, D., Fla.
Kramer, R., Col.
Leath, D., Tex.
Leland, D., Tex.
Lent, R., N.Y.
Lloyd, D., Tenn.
Loefler, R., Tex.
Lujan, R., N.M.
Mack, R., Fla.
Madigan, R., Ill.
Marlenee, R., Mont.
Martin, R., N.Y.
Martinez, D., Calif.
McCain, R., Az.
McGrath, R., N.Y.
Meyers, R., Calif.

House Voting against IRCA (173)

Boxer, D., Calif.
Broomfield, R., Mich.
Brown, R., Col.
Burton, D., Calif.
Burton, R., Ind.
Callahan, R., Alab.
Carney, R., N.Y.
Carr, D., Mich
Chapman, D., Tex.
Chappell, D., Fla.
Chappie, R., Calif.
Coats, R., Ind.
Cobey, R., N.C.
Coble, R., N.C.
Coleman, D., Tex.
Combest, R., Tex.
Courter, R., N.J.
Craig, R., Idaho
Crane, R., Ill.
Crockett, D., Mich.
Daniel, D., Va.
Daub, R., Nebr.
de la Garza, D., Tex.
DeLay, R., Tex.
Dellums, D., Calif.
Dickinson, R., Alab.
Dreier, R., Calif.
Duncan, R., Tenn.
Gekas, R., Pa.
Gonzales, D., Tex.
Gordon, D., Tenn.
Gradison, R., Ohio
Gregg, R., N.H.
Guarini, D., N.J.
Hall, D., Ohio
Hall, D., Tex.
Hammerschmidt, R., Ark.
Hawkins, D., Calif.
Hayes, D., Ill.
Hendon, R., N.C.
Hertel, D., Mich.
Hiler, R., Ind.
Holt, R., Md.
Hopkins, R., Ken.
Horton, R., N.Y.
Hubbard, D., Ken.
Hughes, D., N.J.
Hunter, R., Calif.
Hyde, R., Ill.
Jacobs, D., Ind.
Jenkins, D., Ga.
Jones, D., N.C.
Jones, D., Tenn.
Kaptur, D., Ohio
Kemp, R., N.Y.
Klerczka, D., Wis.
Miller, R., Ohio
Mineta, D., Calif.
Molinari, R., N.Y.
Murphy, D., Pa.
Myers, R., Ind.
Neal, D., N.C.
Oakar, D., Ohio
Olin, D., Va.
Parris, R., Va.
Petri, R., Wis.
Porter, R., Ill.
Pursell, R., Mich.
Rangel, D., N.Y.
Ray, D., Ga.
Regula, R., Ohio
Reid, D., Nev.
Rinaldo, R., N.J.
Ritter, R. Pa.
Roberts, D., Kan.
Robinson, D., Ark.
Roemer, D., La.
Roukema, R., N.J.
Rowland, D., Ga.
Roybal, D., Calif.
Russo, D., Ill.
Savage, D., Ill.
Saxton, R., N.J.
Schroeder, D., Col.

House Voting against IRCA

Schuette, R., Mich.
Sensenbrenner, R., Wis.
Sijander, R., Mich.
Skeen, R., N.M.
Skelton, D., Mo.
Slaughter, R., Va.
Smith, R., Okla.
Smith, R., N.H.
Snyder, R., Ken.
Solomon, R., N.Y.
Spence, R., S.C.
Staggers, D., W.V
Stenholm, D., Tex.
Stratton, D., N.Y.
Stump, R., Az.
Sundquist, R., Tenn.
Sweeney, R., Tex.
Swindall, R., Ga.
Tallon, D., S.C.
Tanzin, D., La.
Taylor, R., Mo.
Towns, D., N.Y.
Traficant, D., Ohio
Valentine, D., N.C.
VanderJagt, R., Mich.
Visclosky, D., Ind.
Watkins, D., Okla.
Whitley, D., N.C.
Whittaker, R., Kan.
Wirth, D., Col.
Yatron, D., Pa.
Young, R., Kan.
Young, R., Fla.

Not Voting(21)

Badham, R., Calif.
Braux, D., La.
Brooks, D., Tex.
Campbell, R., S.C.
Conyers, D., Mich.
Fowler, D., Ga.
Grotberg, R., Ill.
Hansen, R., Utah
Hartnett, R., S.C.
Jones, D., Okla.
Kindness, R., Ohio
Latta, R., Ohio
Long, D., La.
Lundine, D., N.Y.
McEwen, R., Ohio
Moore, R., La.
Nichols, D., Az.
Rudd, R., Az.
St. Germain, D., R.I.
Weaver, D., Oreg.
Weiss, D., N.Y.

The Senate Roll Call Vote # 357, Enacting IRCA

Voting For IRCA (63):

Andrews, R., N.D.
Baucus, D., Mont.
Bentsen, D., Tex.
Biden, D., Del.
Bingaman, D., N.M.
Boschwitz, R., Minn.
Bradley, D., N.J.
Burdick, D., N.D.
Gore, D., Tenn.
Grassley, R., Iowa
Harkin, D., Iowa
Hatfield, R., Oreg.
Hawkins, R., Fla.
Heinz, R., Pa.
Hollings, D., S.C.
Johnston, D., La.
Moynihan, D., N.Y.
Nunn, D., Ga.
Packwood, R., Oreg.
Pell, D., R.I.
Proxmire, D., Wis.
Pryor, D., Ark.
Quayle, R., Ind.
Rockefeller, D., W.V.

Voting For IRCA (63):

Byrd, D., W.V.	Kassebaum, R., Kan.	Roth, R., Del.
Chafee, R., R.I.	Kasten, R., Wis.	Sarbanes, D., Md.
Chiles, D., Fla.	Kerry, D., Mass.	Sasser, D., Ten.
Cranston, D., Calif.	Lautenberg, D., N.J.	Simon, D., Ill.
D'Amato, R., N.Y.	Levin, D., Mich.	Simpson, R., Wyo.
Danforth, R., Mo.	Long, D., La.	Specter, R., Pa.
Dixon, R., Ill.	Lugar, R., Ind.	Stafford, R., Vt.
Dodd, D., Conn.	Matsunaga, D., Hawaii	Stevens, R., Alab.
Dole, R., Kan.	Mattingly, R., Ga.	Thurmond, R., S.C.
Durenberger, R., Minn.	McConnell, R., Ken.	Trible, R., Va.
Eagleton, D., Mo.	Melcher, D., Mont.	Wallop, R. Wyo.
Exon, D., Nebr.	Metzenbaum, D., Ohio	Warner, R., Va.
		Weicker, R., Conn.
		Wilson, R., Calif.

Senate Vote against IRCA (24):

Abdnor, R., S.D.	Garn, R., Utah	Kennedy, D., Mass.
Armstrong, R., Col.	Gramm, R., Tex.	McClure, R., Idaho
Bumpers, D., Ark.	Hatch, R., Utah	Mitchell, D., Me.
Cochran, R., Miss.	Hecht, R., Nev.	Nickles, R., Okla.
Cohen, R., Me.	Heflin, D., Alask.	Pressler, R., S.D.
Denton, R., Alab.	Helms, R., N.C.	Riegle, D., Mich.
Damenici, R., N.M.	Humphrey, R., N.H.	Rudman, R., N.H.
Ford, D., Ken.	Inoye, D., Hawaii	Zorinsky, D., Nebr.

Not Voting (13):

Boren, D., Okla.	Glenn, D., Ohio	Leahy, D., Vt.
Broyhill, R., N.C.	Goldwater, R., Az.	Mathias, R., Md.
DeConcini, D., Az.	Gorton, R., Wash.	Murkowski, R., Alask.
Evans, D., Wash.	Laxalt, R., Nev.	Stennis, D., Miss.
		Symms, R., Idaho

Sources: Congressional Record—House, 15 October 1986, H10598-10599.
Congressional Record—Senate, 17 October 1986, S16915. State and party designation from *National Journal,* various issues.

APPENDIX C

Analysis of Hispanic Caucus Votes on IRCA

<u>Members Who Voted against IRCA</u>

Member/District	Characteristics of Member/District			
	Year Elected Congress	Minority Population	Presidential Vote	Liberalism Index
de la Garza, D, TX 15th District	1964	66%-Spanish 1%-Black 67%-Total	Reagan-46% Mondale-54%	ADA= 40 ACLU=58 COPE=57 Nat.Jrnl Econ=55 Soc.=52 FP =34 Av. =50
Edwards, D, CA 10th District	1962	24%-Spanish 19%-Asian 5%-Black 1%-Amer. Indian 40%-Total	Reagan-51% Mondale-48%	ADA= 100 ACLU=100 COPE= 93 Nat.Jrnl Econ= 86 Soc.= 84 FP = 87 Av. = 92
Garcia, D, NY 18th District	1978	49%-Spanish 44%-Black 1%-Asian 84%-Total	Reagan-19% Mondale-81%	ADA = 90 ACLU= 85 COPE= 95 Nat.Jrnl Econ= 86 Soc.= 84 FP. = 87 Av. = 88
Gonzales, D, TX 20th District	1961	56%-Spanish 9%-Black 1%-Asian 66%-Total	Reagan-41 Mondale-59	ADA = 95 ACLU=100 COPE= 90 Nat.Jrnl Econ= 84 Soc.= 70 FP. = 60 Av. = 83

Martinez, D, CA 30th District	1982	48%-Spanish 9%-Asian 1%-Black 1%-Amer. Indian 59%-Total	Reagan-55 Mondale-44	ADA = 95 ACLU= 80 COPE= 98 Nat.Jrnl Econ= 72 Soc.= 84 FP. = 84 Av. = 86
Roybal, D, CA 25th District	1962	57%-Spanish 10%-Black 8%-Asian 1%-Amer. Indian 76%-Total	Reagan-39 Mondale-60	ADA =100 ACLU= 93 COPE= 94 Nat.Jrnl Econ= 86 Soc.= 84 FP. = 87 Av. = 91
	Hispanic Caucus Members Who Voted for IRCA			
Bustamente, D, TX 23rd District	1984	51%-Spanish 4%-Black 1%-Asian 56%-Total	Reagan-59 Mondale-41	ADA = 70 ACLU= 81 COPE= 95 Nat.Jrnl Econ= 84 Soc.= 70 FP. = 60 Av. = 77
Coelho, D, CA 15th District	1978	20%-Spanish 2%-Black 1%-Asian 23%-Total	Reagan-59 Mondale-40	ADA = 80 ACLU= 85 COPE= 82 Nat.Jrnl Econ= 86 Soc.= 79 FP. = 69 Av. = 80
Ortiz, D, TX 27th District	1982	55%-Spanish 3%-Black 58%-Total	Reagan-53 Mondale-47	ADA = 60 ACLU= 60 COPE= 87 Nat.Jrnl Econ= 72 Soc.= 64 FP. = 38 Av. = 64
Richardson, D, NM 3rd District	1982	37%-Spanish 17%-Amer.Ind. 1%-Black 55%-Total	Reagan-53 Mondale-46	ADA = 85 ACLU= 80 COPE= 83 Nat.Jrnl Econ= 86 Soc.= 74 FP. = 66 Av. = 79
Torres, D, CA 34th District	1982	42%-Spanish 4%-Asian 2%-Black 1%-Amer. Ind. 49%-Total	Reagan-59 Mondale-40	ADA = 95 ACLU= 90 COPE=100 Nat.Jrnl Econ= 86 Soc.= 84 FP. = 81 Av. = 89

Source: Barone, Michael, and Grant Ujifusa, *The Almanac of American Politics, 1986, 1990* (Washington, D.C.: National Journal, 1985, 1989).

APPENDIX D

The Roll Call Votes Enacting the Immigration Act of 1990

House Roll Call Vote #530

Yeas = 264; Nays = 118; Not Voting = 50

Voting in Favor of the 1990 Act

Ackerman, D., N.Y. +
Alexander, D, Ark.+
Anderson, D, Calif. +
Annunzio, D, Ill. +
Anthony, D, Ark. +
Armey, R, Tex. (NA)
Atkins, D, Mass. +
AuCoin, D, Oreg. +
Baker, R, La. (NA)
Ballinger, R, N.C. (NA)
Bartlett, R, Tex. -
Barton, R, Tex. -
Bateman, R, Va. -
Bereuter, R, Nebr. +
Berman, D, Calif. +
Bilbray, D, N.M. (NA)
Bliley, R, Va. -
Boehlert, R, N.Y. +
Boggs, D, La. -
Bonior, D, Mich. +
Borski, D, Pa. +
Bosco, D, Calif. +
Brooks, D, Tex. -
Broomfield, R, Mich. -
Brown, D, Calif. +
Bruce, D, Ill. +
Buechner, R, Mo. (NA)
Bustamente, D,Tex. +
Campbell, D, Col. (NA)
Cardin, D, Md. (NA)
Carper, D, Del. +_
Carr, D, Mich. -
Chandler, R, Wash. +
Clarke, D, N.C. (NA)
Clay, D, Mo. +
Clinger, R, Pa. +
Coble, R, N.C. (NA)
Coleman, R, Mo. +
Coleman, D, Tex. -
Collins, D, Ill. +
Condit, D, Calif. (NA)
Conte, R, Mass. +
Conyers, D, Mich. -
Costello, D, Ill. (NA)
Coughlin, R, Pa. +
Courter, R, N.J. -
Coyne, D, Pa. +
Darden, D, Ga. +
de la Garza, D, Tex. -
DeFazio, D, Oreg. (NA)
DeLay, R, Tex. -
Dellums, D, Calif. -
DeWine, R, Ohio +
Dickinson, R, Alab. -
Dicks, R, Wash. +
Dixon, D, Calif. +
Donnelly, D, Mass. +
Dorgan, D, N.D. +
Douglas, R, N.H. (NA)
Downey, D, N.Y. +
Durbin, D, Ill. +
Dwyer, D, N.J. +
Dymally, D, Calif. -
Early, D, Mass. +
Edwards, D, Calif. -
Engel, D, N.Y. (NA)
Espy, D, Miss. (NA)
Evans, D, Ill. +

Voted for 1990 Act

Fascell, D, Fla. +
Fawell, R, Ill. -
Fazio, D, Calif. +
Feigham, D, Ohio +
Fish, R, N.Y. +
Flake, D, N.Y. (NA)
Foglietta, D, Pa. +
Ford, D, Mich. +
Ford, D, Tenn. +
Frank, D, Mass. +
Frenzel, R, Minn. +
Frost, D, Tex. -
Gallo, R, N.J. -
Gaydos, D, Pa. -
Gejdenson, D, Conn. +
Gekos, R, Pa. -
Gephardt, D, Mo. +
Gibbons, D, Fla. +
Gilmor, R, Ohio (NA)
Gilman, R, N.Y. +
Gonzales, D, Tex. -
Gradison, R, Ohio -
Grandy, R, Iowa (NA)
Grant, R, Fla. (NA)
Gray, D, Pa. (NA)
Green, R, N.Y. +
Guarini, D, N.J. -
Gunderson, R, Wis. +
Hall, D, Ohio -
Hamilton, D, Ind. +
Hatcher, D, Ga. +
Hayes, D, Ill. -
Hefner, D, N.C. +
Henry, R, Mich. +
Hiler, R, Ind. -
Hochbraechner, D, N.Y. (NA)
Horton, R, N.Y. -
Houghton, R, N.Y. (NA)
Hoyer, D, Md. +
Hughes, D, N.J. -
Hunter, R, Calif. -
Hyde, R, Ill. -
Ireland, R, Fla. +
Jacobs, D, Ind. -
Johnson, R, Conn. +
Johnson, D, S.D. (NA)
Jones, D, Ga. (NA)
Jones, D, N.C. -
Jontz, D, Ind. (NA)
Kanjorski, D, Pa. +
Kaptur, D, Ohio -
Kasich, R, Ohio +
Kastenmeier, D, Wis. +
Kennedy, D, Mass. (NA)
Kennelly, D, Conn. +
Kildee, D, Mich. +
Kolbe, R, Az. -
Kolter, D, Pa. -
Kostmayer, D, Pa. +
Kye, R, Az. (NA)
Lantos, D, Calif. +
Leach, R, Iowa +
Lehman, D, Calif. +
Lehman, D, Fla. +
Lent, R, N.Y. -
Levin, D, Miss. +
Levine, D, Calif. +
Lewis, D, Ga. +
Lightfoot, R, Iowa +
Livingston, R, La. +
Lowey, D, N.Y. (NA)
Machtley, R, R.I. (NA)
Madigan, R, Ill. -
Manton, D, N.Y. +
Markey, D, Mass. +
Martin, R, N.Y. -
Martinez, D, Calif. -
Matsui, D, Calif. +
Mavroules, D, Me. +
Mazzoli, D, Ken. +
McCloskey, D, Ind. +
McCollum, R, Fla. +
McCrory, R, La. (NA)
McDade, R, Pa. +
McDermott, D, Wash. (NA)
McEwen, R, Ohio -
McHugh, D, N.Y. +
McMillan, R, N.C. +
McMillan, D, Md. (NA)
McNulty, D, N.Y. (NA)
Mfume, D, Md. (NA)
Michel, R, Ill. +
Miller, C, Calif. +
Miller, R, Wash. +
Mineta, D, Calif. -
Mink, D, Hawaii (NA)
Moakley, D, Mass. +
Molinari, R, N.Y. -
Mollohan, D, W.V. +
Moody, D, Wis. +
Morella, R, Md. (NA)
Morrison, D, Conn. +
Morrison, R, Wash. +
Mrazek, D, N.Y. +
Murtha, D, Pa. +
Nagle, D, Iowa (NA)
Neal, D, Mass. (NA)
Nielson, R, Utah +
Oakar, D, Ohio -
Oberstar, D, Minn. +
Obey, D, Wis. +
Ortiz, D, Tex. +
Owens, D, N.Y. +
Owens, D, Utah (NA)
Oxley, R, Ohio +
Pallone, D, N.J. (NA)
Panetta, D, Calif. +
Pashayan, R, Calif. +
Paxon, R, N.Y. (NA)
Payne, D, N.J. (NA)
Pease, D, Ohio +
Pelosi, D, Calif. (NA)

Voted for 1990 Act

Penny, D, Minn. +
Pickett, D, Va. (NA)
Pickle, D, Tex. +
Porter, R, Ill. -
Poshard, D, Ill. (NA)
Price, D, N.C. (NA)
Rahall, D, W.V. +
Rangel, D, N.Y. -
Ravenel, R, S.C. (NA)
Rhodes, R, Az. (NA)
Richardson, D, N.M. +
Rinaldo, R, N.J. -
Ritter, R, Pa. -
Roe, D, N.J. +
Rohrabacher, R, Calif. (NA)
Ros-Lehtinen, R, Fla. (NA)
Roybal, D, Calif. -
Sabo, D, Minn. +
Sawyer, D, Ohio (NA)
Saxton, R, N.J. -
Scheuer, D, N.Y. +
Schiff, R, N.M. (NA)
Schroeder, D, Col. -
Schulze, R, Pa. +
Schumer, D, N.Y. +
Shays, R, Conn. (NA)
Shumway, R, Calif. +
Sisisky, D, Va. +
Skaggs, D, Col. (NA)
Skeen, D, Mo. (NA)
Slattery, D, Kan. +
Slaughter, D, N.Y. (NA)
Smith, D, Fla. +
Smith, D, Iowa (NA)
Smith, R, N.J. +
Smith, R, Tex. (NA)
Snowe, R, Me. +
Solarz, D, N.Y. +
Solomon, R, N.Y. -
Spratt, D, S.C. +
Strangeland, R, Minn. +
Stark, D, Calif. +
Stokes, D, Ohio +
Studds, R, Mass. +
Swift, D, Wash. +
Synar, D, Okla. +
Tallon, D, S.C. -
Tauke, D, Iowa +
Thomas, R, Wyo. (NA)
Torres, D, Calif. +
Torricelli, D, N.J. +
Towns, D, N.Y. -
Udall, D, Az. +
Unsoeld, D, Wash. (NA)
Upton, R, Miss. (NA)
Vento, D, Minn. +
Visclosky, D, Ind. -
Vucanovich, R, Nev. +
Walker, R, Pa. +
Washington, D, Tex. (NA)
Waxman, D, Calif. +
Weiss, D, N.Y. -
Weldon, R, Pa. (NA)
Wheat, D, Mo. +
Whittaker, R, Kan. -
Whitten, D, Miss. (NA)
Williams, D, Mont. +
Wilson, D, Tex. +
Wolf, R, Va. +
Wolpe, D, Mich. +
Wyden, R, Oreg. +
Wylie, R, Ohio +
Yates, D, Ill. +

Voted against the 1990 Act

Andrews, D, Tex. +
Applegate, D, Ohio +
Archer, R, Tex. +
Barnard, D, Ga. +
Beilenson, D, Calif. -
Bennett, D, Fla. -
Bentley, R, Md. +
Bevill, D, Alab. +
Belrakis, R, Fla. +
Browder, D, Alab. (NA)
Brown, R, Col. +
Bryant, D, Tex. (NA)
Bunning, R, Kent. (NA)
Byron, D, Md. (NA)
Campbell, R, Calif. (NA)
Chapman, D, Tex. +
Clement, D, Tenn. (NA)
Combest, R, Tex. +
Cooper, D, Tenn. -
Cox, R, Calif. (NA)
Craig, R, Idaho +
Crane, R, Ill. +
Dannemeyer, R, Calif. -
Davis, R, Mich. -
Dorman, R, Calif. (NA)
Dreier, R, Calif. (NA)
Duncan, R, Tenn. +
Dyson, D, Md. +
Eckart, D, Ohio -
Edwards, R, Okla. +
Emerson, R, Mo. +
English, D, Okla. +
Erdreich, D, Alab. +
Fields, R, Tex. +
Gallegly, R, Calif. (NA)
Geren, D, Tex. (NA)
Goodling, R, Pa. -
Gordon, D, Tenn. +
Goss, R, Fla. (NA)
Hall, D, Tex. +

Voted against 1990 Act

Hammerschmidt, R, Ark. +
Hancock, R, Mo. (NA)
Hansen, R, Utah -
Harris, D, Alab. (NA)
Hastert, R, Ill. (NA)
Hayes, D, La. (NA)
Hefley, R, Col. (NA)
Herger, R, Calif. (NA)
Hertel, D, Mich. +
Hoagland, D, Nebr. (NA)
Hopkins, R, Kent. +
Hubbard, D, Kent. +
Huckaby, D, La. -
Hutto, D, Fla. -
Inhofe, R, Okla. (NA)
James, R, Fla. (NA)
Lagomarsino, R, Calif. -
Lancaster, D, N.C. (NA)
Laughlin, D, Tex. (NA)
Lewis, D, Calif. -
Lloyd, D, Tenn. +
Long, D, Ind. -
Lowery, R, Calif. -
Marlenee, R, Mont. +
McCandless, R, Calif. -
McCurdy, D, Okla. -
Meyers, R, Kan. +
Miller, R, Ohio (NA)
Montgomery, D, Miss. -
Moorhead, R, Calif. -
Myers, R, Ind. +
Natcher, D, Kent. -
Neal, D, N.C. +
Olin, D, Va. +
Packard, R, Calif. -
Parker, D, Miss. (NA)
Parris, R, Va. +
Patterson, D, S.C. (NA)
Payne, D, Va. (NA)
Perkins, D, Ken. -
Petri, R, Wis. +
Ray, D, Ga. +
Regula, R, Ohio +
Ridge, R, Pa. +
Roberts, R, Kan. +
Rogers, R, Ken. -
Roth, R, Wis. -
Rowland, D, Ga. +
Sarpalius, D, Ga. +
Savage, D, Ill. +
Schaefer, R, Col. -
Sensenbrenner, R, Wis. +
Shaw, R, Fla. -
Shuster, R, Pa. +
Slaughter, D, Va. +
Smith, R, Nebr. (NA)
Smith, R, N.H. +
Smith, R, Oreg. (NA)
Spence, R, S.C. (NA)
Staggers, D, W.V. +
Stalkings, D, Idaho -
Stearns, R, Fla. (NA)
Stenholm, D, Tex. +
Stump, R, Az. +
Sundquist, R, Tenn. +
Tanner, D, Tenn. (NA)
Tanzin, D, La. +
Taylor, R, Miss. +
Thomas, R, Calif. -
Traficant, D, Ohio +
Valentine, D, N.C. +
VanderJagt, R, Mich. +
Volkemer, D, Mo. -
Wise, D, W.V. (NA)
Yatron, D, Pa. +
Young, R, Ark. (NA)
Young, R, Fla. +

Not Voting on the 1990 Act

Aspin, D, Wis. -
Bates, D, Calif. -
Boucher, D, Va. -
Boxer, D, Calif. -
Brennan, D, Me. (NA)
Burton, D, Calif. -
Callahan, R, Alab. -
Crockett, D, Mich. -
Derrick, D, S.C. -
Dingell, D, Mich. -
Flippo, D, Alab. -
Gingrich, R, Ga. -
Hawkins, D, CA -
Holloway, R, La. (NA)
Jenkins, D, Ga. -
Johnston, D, Fla. (NA)
Klerczka, D, Wis. -
LaFalce, D, N.Y. -
Leath, D, Tex. -
Lipinski, D, Ill. -
Luken, D, Ohio -
Martin, R, Ill. -
McGrath, R, N.Y. -
Murphy, D, Pa. -
Nelson, D, Fla. -
Nowak, D, N.Y. -
Pursell, R, Mich. -
Quillen, R, Tenn. -
Robinson, D, Ark. -
Rose, D, N.C. -
Rostenkowski, D, Ill. -
Russo, D, Ill. -
Saiki, R, Hawaii (NA)
Sangmeister, D, Ill. (NA)
Schuette, R, Miss. (NA)
Sharp, D, Ind. -
Sikorski, D, Minn. -
Skelton, D, Mo. (NA)

Not Voting on the 1990 Act

Smith, R, Vt. (NA)
Smith, R, Oreg. (NA)
Thomas, D, Ga. -
Traxler, D, Mich. -
Walgren, D, Pa. -
Walsh, R, N.Y. (NA)
Watkins, D, Okla. -
Weber, R, Minn. -

Among House Vote:
Democrats = 168 Yes, 55 No, 34 NV
Republican = 92 Yes, 63 No, 16 NV

197 Voted same as for IRCA
127 Voted differently from IRCA
102 IRCA vote not applicable

Senate Vote on the 1990 Immigration Act

Roll Call Vote #323, Yeas = 89, Nays = 8, Not Voting = 3

Voted For Immigration Act of 1990

Adams, D, Wash. (NA)
Akaka, D, Hawaii (NA)
Baucus, D, Mont. +
Bentsen, D, Tex. +
Biden, D, Del. +
Bingham, D, N.M. +
Bond, R, Mo. (NA)
Boren, D, Okla. -
Bradley, D, N.J. +
Breaux, D, Calif. (NA)
Byran, D, N.V. (NA)
Burdick, D, N.D. +
Burns, R, Mont. (NA)
Chafee, R, R.I. +
Coats, R, Ind. (NA)
Cochran, R, Miss. -
Cohen, R, Me. -
Conrad, D, N.D. (NA)
Cranston, D, Calif. +
D'Amato, R, N.Y. +
Danforth, R, Mo. +
Daschle, D, S.D. (NA)
DeConcini, D, Az. (NA)
Dixon, D, Ill. +
Dodd, D, Conn. +
Dole, R, Kan. +
Domenici, R, N.M. -
Durenberger, R, Minn. +
Ford, D, Kent. +
Fowler, D, Ga. (NA)
Garn, R, Vt. -
Glenn, D, Ohio -
Gore, D, Tenn. +
Gorton, R, Wash. -
Graham, D, Fla. (NA)
Gramm, R, Tex. -
Grassley, R, Iowa +
Harkin, D, Iowa +
Hatch, R, Vt. -
Heflin, D, Alab. -
Heinz, R, Pa. +
Hollings, D, S.C. +
Humphrey, R, N.H. -
Inouye, R, Hawaii -
Jeffords, R, Vt. (NA)
Johnston, D, La. +
Kassebaum, R, Kan. +
Kasten, R, Wis. +
Kennedy, R, Mass. -
Kerrey, D, Nebr. (NA)
Kerry, D, Mass. +
Kohl, D, Wis. (NA)
Lautenberg, D, N.J. +
Leahy, D, Vt. -
Levin, D, Miss. +
Lieberman, D, Conn. (NA)
Lugar, R, Ind. +
Mack, R, Fla. (NA)
McCain, R, Az. (NA)
McClure, R, Idaho -
Metzenbaum, D, Ohio +
Mikulski, D, Md. (NA)
Mitchell, D, Me. -
Moynihan, D, N.Y. +
Murkowski, R, Ark. -
Nickles, R, Okla. -
Nunn, D, Ga. +
Packwood, R, Oreg. +
Pell, D, R.I. +
Pressler, R, S.D. -
Reid, D, Nev. (NA)
Riegle, D, Mich. -
Robb, D, Va. (NA)
Rockefeller, D, W.V. +
Sanford, D, N.C. (NA)
Sarbanes, D, Md. +
Sasser, D, Tenn. +
Shelby, D, Alab. (NA)
Simon, D, Ill. +
Simpson, R, Wyo. +
Specter, R, Pa. +
Stevens, R, Ark. +
Symms, R, Idaho -
Thurmond, R, S.C. +
Wallop, R, Wyo. +
Warner, R, Va. +
Wilson, R, Calif. +
Wirth, D, Col. (NA)

<u>Voted Nay on 1990 Act</u>

Armstrong, R, Col. +	Helms, R, N.C. +
Bumpers, D, Ark. +	Lott, R, Miss. +
Byrd, D, W.V. -	Roth, R, Del. -
Exon, D, Nebr. -	Rudman, R, N.H. +

<u>Not Voting on 1990 Act</u>

Boschwitz, R, Minn. -	Democrats = 51 for, 3 against, 1 NV
Hatfield, R, Oreg. -	Republicans = 38 for, 5 against, 2 NV
Pryor, D, Ark. -	

Key: +, Voted same as IRCA vote; −, Voted differently from IRCA vote; (NA) IRCA vote not applicable.

APPENDIX E

IRCA Questionnaires

IRCA Questionnaires for INS Offices

1. To what extent has the passage and implementation of IRCA necessitated a shift in the allocation of your resources (budget and personnel resources)? For example, to what extent have you had to shift personnel from Border Patrol apprehension work to employer-sanctions enforcement? Or shifting personnel from other duties to process the legalization applications.
2. If personnel were shifted, how much training were such individuals provided before such shift in duties?
3. Has your office noted an increase in the use of phony documents by illegal aliens since passage of IRCA?
4. To what extent has your office noted a <u>decline</u> in the number of illegal aliens in your geographic area since passage and implementation of IRCA?
5. Now that IRCA's employer-sanctions phase has shifted from education to actual enforcement, to what degree have you targeted resources for emforcement of employer sanctions to firms or industries known to you to be egregious offenders versus the degree to which such resources are devoted to violations for failing to complete an I-9 form or to verify employment documents?
6. From your examination of I-9 forms and the like, to what degree would you characterize employer compliance with the employer sanctions provisions in your geographic area (e.g., 60%)?
7. What <u>intergovernmental</u> <u>relations</u> (either federal to state, or state agency to state agency) arrangements have you noted developed in your area as a result of IRCA?
8. What particular problems in implementing IRCA has your office experienced?
9. To what degree of successful processing of applicants for the legalization program has your office experienced in the main legalization program and among SAW applicants?
10. Which nongovernmental agencies or organizations has your office worked with in implementing IRCA (e.g., local QDEs, etc.)?

IRCA Questionnaire for QDE Agency

1. Have you experienced an actual decline in the number of illegal aliens in your area since passage of IRCA? If so, could you roughly estimate that decline (.e.g., 20%, 30%, etc.)?

2. Has your office noted any increase in the use of phony documents since passage of IRCA?

3. To what degree would you characterize the success of IRCA's <u>legalization program</u> in actually reaching qualified illegal aliens in your area?
   -The main legalization program?
   -The SAW program?

4. What <u>problems</u> in the implementation of IRCA has your office experienced?
   -With respect to the legalization program?
   -With respect to the employer sanctions program?
   -Other problems?

5. What governmental agencies or offices do you work with as a result of IRCA? (I.e., list federal, state, and local governmental agencies you regularly deal with in some manner as a result of IRCA.)

6. Has your office experienced an <u>improvement</u> in the INS as a result of the increased funding and/or staffing levels brought about by IRCA (e.g., changes in efficiency, attitudes, etc.)?

7. To what extent do you feel employers in your area are in fact complying with IRCA's employer sanctions provisions (e.g., 50%, 60%, 80%, etc.)?

8. In dealing with your clients, have you noted any increase in the discrimination they report experiencing in employment as a result of IRCA's employer sanctions provisions?

9. Have you noted any differences between or among local INS offices in the manner in which IRCA is being implemented?

10. Are there differences in the way the INS treats your clients (e.g., among the various racial, ethnic groups, etc.)?

IRCA-Related Questionnaire for State Agencies

1. I am interested in the <u>intergovernmental</u> <u>relations</u> aspects of IRCA. What are the various state/local agencies you deal regularly in connection with IRCA?
   -With respect to SLIAG?
   -With respect to employer sanctions?

2. What federal agencies do you routinely deal with in connection with IRCA?

3. Have there been changes in the relations you have with other agencies as a result of IRCA?

4. From the perspective of <u>your</u> <u>office</u>, has passage of IRCA led to a decrease in the number of illegal aliens in your geographic area?

5. Have you noted an increase in the use/availability of phony documents since IRCA's passage?

6. From your perspective, to what extent has IRCA's employer sanctions provisions been successful?

7. In dealings with clients your agency serves, have you noted an increase in employer discrimination they report or allude to since the implementation of IRCA?

8. In your dealings with the INS, have you noted an improvement (e.g., in their efficiency, attitude, etc.) as a result of the increased funding/staffing levels brought about by IRCA?

9. Have you experienced differences in the implementation of IRCA (either the legalization or employer sanctions programs) among local INS offices in the manner in which IRCA is being implemented? In the manner in which the INS treats people (e.g., among the clients your agency serves as regards the various racial, ethnic groups, etc.)?

10. What are some particular problems you have experienced with the implementation of IRCA?

IRCA-Related Questions for Congressional Members/Staff

1. To the extent that it can be rather simply stated, why did Congressman ________ vote for passage of IRCA on the October 15, 1986 roll call vote that approved the Conference Committee report thereby enacting IRCA?

2. Which lobbying groups had contact with your congressional office about IRCA? Which of those were most persuasive in your view, and why?

3. To what extent would you characterize your vote on IRCA's final passage as being influenced by the following?
   -My assessment of the law's impact on my constituency's needs:
   -My personal view or assessment of IRCA:
   -Input I received from lobby groups with their arguments pro or con IRCA:
   -The need to simply revise U.S. immigration law to better cope with the illegal alien problem, to rationalize U.S. immigration law, etc.:
   -The influence of my congressional colleagues (specify which ones):
   -Other reasons (specify):

4. Now that IRCA is being implemented, to what extent do you feel it is being successfully implemented? If so, why so? If not, why not?

5. Who do you feel were the most important players in enabling the passage of IRCA?

References

Abuse of Immigration Law Feared by Some Hispanic Groups. *New York Times,* 1 March 1987: 22–31.

AIDS Test Required for Immigrants Here. *Cumberland Times/News,* 29 August 1987: 2.

Alien Legalization Project Seeks Volunteer Helpers. *Maryland Church News,* June 1987: sec. 1, p. 8.

Alien Smuggling Ring Cracked in San Diego. *Washington Post,* 28 September 1987: A18.

Aliens Become More Diverse Over Decades. *Washington Post,* 10 June 1984: A1, 16.

Aliens Facing $185 Fee on Amnesty. *New York Times,* 16 March 1987: B15.

America: Still A Melting Pot? *Newsweek,* 9 August 1993: 16–25.

American Public Welfare Association. 1988. *Report.* Washington, D.C.: APWA, June, pp. 4–5.

America's Unwelcome Mat. *Washington Post,* 17 May 1992: C1, 4.

The Amnesty Program. *Washington Post,* 1 May 1988: C6.

Amnesty Program Means Phony Document Business Will Flourish. *Cumberland Sunday Times,* 2 November 1986: A16.

Amnesty Sending Fearful Aliens for Help, Only Some of It Useful. *New York Times,* 15 January 1987: B1, 7.

Anderson, Jack. 1988a. Meese Transfers of Officers Weakens Mexican Borders. *Cumberland Times/News,* 25 February: A15.

——. 1988b. Bogus Birth Certificates, Easy to Come By, Aid to Illegals. *Cumberland Times/News,* 5 April: A15.

Anderson, James. 1979. *Public Policy Making.* New York: Holt, Rinehart and Winston.

Arizona Civil Rights Advisory Board. 1989. *A Review of the Discriminatory Impact of the Employers Sanctions of the Immigration Reform and Control Act.* Phoenix: ACRAB, 4 October.

Arocha, Zita. 1987a. Illegals Fill Day Care Jobs. *Washington Post,* 16 August: A1, 16.

——. 1987b. Immigration Law Backer Declares Success Amid Others' Doubts. *Washington Post,* 6 November: A12.

——. 1988. INS Reaches Out to Grab Attention on Amnesty. *Washington Post,* 27 March: B3.

Art of Negotiation as Applied to Immigration. *Congressional Weekly Report,* 10 May 1986: 1037.

Asayesh, Gelareh. 1989. As Refugees Flood In, Localities Must Foot the Bill for the American Dream. *Governing* 2 (May): 23–31.

Asch, B., and K. Crane. 1988. The Effects of IRCA on the Flow of Undocumented Immigrants to the United States. Paper prepared for the Rand Corporation/ Urban Institute Conference on Illegal Immigration before and after IRCA, July 21, Washington, D.C.

Asian-Americans Top Growth Pace. *San Bernardino Sun,* 19 February 1993: A3.

Ayuda Inc. v. Meese, 687 F. Supp. 650 (D.D.C. 1988).

Baby Boomlet, Immigrants Splitting State's Seams. *San Bernardino Sun,* 10 February 1993: A1.

Back to the Melting Pot. *Governing* 5 (June 1992): 31–35.

Baker, Susan Gonzalez. 1990. *The Cautious Welcome: The Legalization Program of the Immigration Reform and Control Act.* Santa Monica, Calif.: The Rand Corporation and the Urban Institute Press.

Bean, Frank, Barry Edmonston, and Jeffrey S. Passel. 1990. *Undocumented Migration to the United States.* Santa Monica, Calif.: The Rand Corporation and the Urban Institute Press.

Bean, Frank, Allan G. King, and Jeffrey Passel. 1985. Estimates of the Size of the Illegal Migrant Population of Mexican Origin in the United States: An Assessment, Review and Proposal. In *Mexican Immigrants and Mexican-Americans: An Evolving Relationship,* ed. H. Browning and R. de la Garza, pp. 13–16. Austin, Tex.: Center for Mexican-American Studies.

Bean, Frank, and Teresa A. Sullivan. 1985. Immigration and Its Consequences: Confronting the Problem. *Society* 22 (May/June): 67–73.

Bean, Frank, Georges Vernez, and Charles B. Keely. 1989. *Opening and Closing the Doors.* Santa Monica, Calif., and Washington, D.C.: The Rand Corporation and the Urban Institute.

Bennett, Douglas C. 1985. The Enforcement of Immigration Policy and the Meaning of Citizenship. Paper delivered at the 1985 Annual Meeting of the American Political Science Association, August 29, New Orleans, La.

Bernsen, Sam. 1987. Updating the Immigration Law. In *In Defense of the Alien, Vol. 9,* ed. Lydio Tomasi, pp. 203–208. New York: Center for Migration Studies.

Beyond the Melting Pot. *Time,* 9 April 1990: 28–35.

Bilingual Education's Dilemmas Persist. *Washington Post,* 7 July 1985: A1, 12–13.

Bilingual Education Makes Sense. *San Bernardino Sun,* 10 June 1993: A11.

Bill Aiding Chinese Becomes Law. *San Bernardino Sun,* 1 July 1993: A8.

Bill on Aliens a Divisive Issue for Democrats. *New York Times,* 22 April 1990: sec. 1, p. 1.

Biskupic, Joan. 1990. Immigration Legislation. *Congressional Quarterly Weekly Report,* December 8, 4105–4107.

Bonacich, Edna. 1976. Advanced Capitalism and Black/White Relations, A Split-Labor Market Interpretation. *American Sociological Review* 41 (February): 34–41.

Border Attacks Worry INS Agents. *Washington Post,* 16 October 1988: A18.

Border Patrol Buildup Urged. *Los Angeles Times,* 7 October 1983: A1, 15.

Border Patrol Goes on Alert. *Washington Post,* 26 July 1987: A21.

Brewster, Lawrence. 1987. *The Public Agenda: Issues in American Politics.* 2nd ed. New York: St. Martin's Press.

Briggs, Vernon, Jr. 1991. Immigration Policy: Political or Economic? *Challenge* (September/October): 12–19.

Broad Immigration Changes Approved. *Washington Post,* 28 October 1990: A1, 16.

Brubaker, William Roger, ed. 1989. *Immigration and the Politics of Citizenship in Europe and North America.* New York: University Press of America and the German Marshall Fund of the United States.

Bryce-LaPorte, R. S., ed. 1981. *A Scrapbook on the New Immigration.* New Brunswick, N.J.: Transaction Books.

Brye, David L., ed. 1983. *European Immigration and Ethnicity in the United States and Canada: A Historical Bibliography.* Santa Barbara, Calif.: Clio Press.

Bureau of the Census, U. S. Department of Commerce. 1989. *The Hispanic Population in the United States: March, 1988.* Washington, D.C.: U.S. Government Printing Office.

Bustamente, Antonio Rios, ed. 1981. *Mexican Immigrant Workers in the United States.* Los Angeles: UCLA, Chicano Studies Research Center.

Canada Moves to Stem Increasing Flow of Aliens Seeking Refuge. *New York Times,* 21 February 1987: 30.

Canlen, Brae. 1993. San Diego Burning. *California Lawyer* (August): 44–49.

Carroll, Vincent. 1989. U.S. Has Become Churlish Over Its Immigration Policies. *Cumberland Times/News,* 17 October: A8.

Catholic Social Services v. Meese, 685 F. Supp. 1149 (C.D. Cal. 1988).

Central Americans Willing to Risk Illegal Entry. *Cumberland Sunday Times/News,* 26 February 1989: A1.

Ceremony Used Wrong Language. *San Bernardino Sun,* 14 July 1993: A7.

Chavez, Leo R. 1992. *Shadowed Lives: Undocumented Immigrants in American Society.* New York: Harcourt Brace Jovanovich.

Cheng, Chih-Yu, and Lawrence H. Nitz. 1989. Demand-Side Legislation in a Supply-Side World: The Muddle Over Illegal Immigration Policy. Paper presented at the American Political Science Association Meeting, September 3, Atlanta, Ga.

Chief Sponsor Moves to Rescue Immigration Bill. *New York Times,* 4 August 1984: 24.

Chinese Emigrants Land in Mexico Only to Board Flights Back Home. *San Bernardino Sun,* 18 July 1993: A11.

Chiswick, Barry. 1988. *Illegal Aliens: Their Employment and Employers.* Kalamazoo, Mich.: W. E. Upjohn Institute for Employment Research.

Chiswick, Barry, ed. 1982. *The Gateway: U.S. Immigration Issues and Policies.* Washington, D.C.: American Enterprise Institute.

Church World Service. 1987. *Fulfilling the Promise: Church Orientation Guide to the New Immigration Law.* New York: CWS.

Closing the Golden Door. *Time,* 18 May 1981, 24.

Cockroft, James D. 1986. *Outlaws in the Promised Land: Mexican Immigrant Workers and America's Future.* New York: Grove Press.

Cohodas, Nadine. 1987. Immigration Law Brings Anxiety, Ambiguity. *Congressional Quarterly,* 2 May, 838–841.

Colleges Fear Plan to Tighten Immigration Rules Would Curb Financial Aid to Foreign Students. *Chronicle of Higher Education,* 6 August 1986, 15.

Coming to America. *U.S. News and World Report,* 21 June 1993, 26–30.

Conferees Agree on Vast Revisions in Laws on Aliens. *New York Times,* 15 October 1986: A1, B11.

Congressional Quarterly Weekly Report, 18 October 1986, 2595–2598, 2612–2613.

Congressional Quarterly Weekly Report, 3 November 1990, 3753.

Congressional Record—House, 16 December 1982, H-10069.

Congressional Record—House, 18 December 1982, H-10319, H-10336.

Congressional Record—House, 10 October 1986, H-9800–H-9801.

Congressional Record—House, 15 October 1986, H-10586.

Congressional Record—House, 26 October 1990, H-13203–H-13240.

Congressional Record—House, 27 October 1990, H-12359–H-12369.

Congressional Record—Senate, 12 August 1982, S-10337.

Congressional Record—Senate, 13 August 1982, S-10461.

Congressional Record—Senate, 26 October 1990, S-17105–S-17118.

Congressional Research Service. 1981. The Immigration and Nationality Act—Questions and Answers. 81-65EPW. Washington, D.C.: Library of Congress.

——. 1981. Immigration and Refugee Policy. MB81244. Washington, D.C.: Library of Congress.

——. 1982a. Refugees in the United States: The Cuban Emigration Crisis. IB80063. Washington, D.C.: Library of Congress.

——. 1982b. U.S. Immigration and Refugee Policy: A Guide to Sources of Information. Research Guide JV6201. Washington, D.C.: Library of Congress.

——. 1986. Immigration Issues and Legislation in the 99th Congress. Update 12/16/86. Washington, D.C.: Library of Congress.

Congressional Staff Directory, 1990–1991. 1990. Mt. Vernon, Va.: Staff Directory.

Conover, Ted. 1987. *Coyotes: A Journey through the Secret World of America's Illegal Aliens.* New York: Vintage Books.

Contested Immigration Bill Ready on Immigration Legislation. *Congressional Quarterly Weekly Report,* 9 June 1984, 1354.

Cooper, Davalene. 1988. Promised Land or Land of Broken Promises? Political Asylum in the United States. *Kentucky Law Journal* 76: 923–947.

Cornelius, W. A., et al. 1989. *The Role of Mexican Labor in California's Immigrant-Dependent Firms and Industries: A Longitudinal Study.* San Diego: Center for U.S./Mexican Studies, Univ. of California.

Cornelius, W. A., and Ricardo A. Montoya. 1983. *America's New Immigration Law: Origins, Rationales and Potential Consequences.* San Diego: Center for U.S./Mexican Studies, Univ. of California.

Corruption in Consulates on Rise as More Aliens Seek U.S. Visas. *New York Times,* 16 January 1980: 1A.

Costs of Illegal Immigration. *San Bernardino Sun,* 22 August 1993: D4.

CQ Votes—204-216, 220-226. *Congressional Quarterly Weekly Report,* 16 June 1984, 1456–1459; 1462–1463; 1514–1515, 1518–1519.

Crane, Keith, et al. 1990. *The Effect of Employer Sanctions on the Flow of Undocumented Immigrants to the United States.* Santa Monica, Calif.: The Rand Corporation and the Urban Institute Press.

Creppy, Michael. 1988. Overview of the INS Enforcement Philosophy and Strategy in Implementing IRCA. *Georgetown Immigration Law Journal* 2 (Fall): 507–516.

Crewdson, John. 1983. *The Tarnished Door.* New York: Times Books.

Cross, Harry E., and James Sandes. 1981. *Across the Border*. Berkeley, Calif.: Institute of Government Studies.

Developments in Law—Immigration Policy and the Rights of Aliens. *Harvard Law Review* 96 (1983): 1268–1465.

Dinnerstein, Leonard, Roger Nichols, and David Reimers. 1989. *Natives and Strangers*. 2nd ed. New York: Oxford University Press.

Don't Blame Congress for Refugee Problem. Letter to the Editor, Congressman William Lipinski (D., Ill.). *Washington Post,* 6 October 1989: A30.

A Door of Opportunity Closed. *Washington Post,* 18 February 1990: D1, 6.

Dye, Thomas. 1987. *Understanding Public Policy*. Englewood Cliffs, N.J.: Prentice-Hall.

Eight Maryland Companies Cited for Illegal Alien Violations. *Cumberland Times/News,* 30 November 1987: 3.

Electing to Vote. *Atlanta Journal and Constitution,* 3 November 1980: A1, 15.

Ellis Island Open, Again. *USA Weekend,* 31 August 1990: 15.

Embassy Setting New Immigration Procedures. *Cumberland Times/News,* 27 September 1989: 22.

English Only Movement Is Xenophobic. *San Bernardino Sun,* 4 June 1993: A11.

Ethier, Wilfred. 1986. Illegal Immigration: The Host-Country Problem. *American Economic Review* 76 (1): 56–71.

Europe's Migrants Swell Refugee Wave. *Washington Post,* 6 October 1989: A41, 48.

Ex-INS Official and Lawyer Indicted. *Atlanta Journal and Constitution,* 3 November 1988: A1, 19.

Farm Work Applications Scrutinized. *Cumberland Times/News,* 27 September 1988: 3.

Ferris, Elizabeth, ed. 1985. *Refugees and World Politics*. New York: Praeger.

Fitting In: The New Californians. *San Bernardino Sun,* 7 March 1993: A1, 4.

Fix, Michael, and Paul Hill. 1990. Enforcing Employer Sanctions: Challenges and Strategies. Santa Monica, Calif.: The Rand Corporation/Urban Institute.

A Flood to a Trickle. *The Economist,* 21 March 1987, 22–27.

Foster, Charles. 1988. Constitutional and Procedural Issues in INS Enforcement of the Employer Verification and Sanctions Provisions of the Immigration Reform and Control Act of 1986. *Georgetown Immigration Law Journal,* 2 (Fall): 461–472.

Fragomen, Austin T., Jr. 1975. Permanent Resident Status Redefined. *International Migration Review* 9 (1): 63–68.

Fritz, Sara. 1988. New Activists Dilute Power in Congress. *Los Angeles Times,* 25 January: A1.

Fuchs, Lawrence. 1983. Immigration, Pluralism, and Public Policy: The Challenge of the *Pluribus* to *Unam*. In *U.S. Immigration and Refugee Policy,* ed. Mary Kritz. Lexington, Mass.: D. C. Heath.

——. 1989. Beyond IRCA: Legal Immigration and National Interest. In *In Defense of the Alien, Vol. 11,* ed. Lydio Tomasi, pp. 55–62. New York: Center for Migration Studies.

Game Traces Undocumented Immigrants' Trek. *Daily News/Sun,* Sun City, Ariz., 31 October 1989: EE10.

The Gatekeepers. *Wall Street Journal,* 9 May 1985: 1–2, 7.

General Accounting Office. 1982. Information on the Enforcement of Laws Regarding Employment of Aliens in Selected Countries. Washington, D.C.: U.S. Government Printing Office.

——. 1987a. Immigration Reform: Status of Implementing Employer Sanctions after One Year. GAO/GGD-88-14. Washington, D.C.: U.S. Government Printing Office.

——. 1987b. Survey of Employer Views of the 1986 Immigration Reform and Control Act. GGD/WBH/11-87. Washington, D.C.: U.S. Government Printing Office.

——. 1988a. Immigration Control: A New Role for the Social Security Card. GAO-HRD-88-4. Report by the General Accounting Office. Washington, D.C.: U.S. Government Printing Office.

——. 1988b. Immigration Reform: Status of Implementing Employer Sanctions after Second Year. GAO/GGD-89-16. Washington, D.C.: U.S. Government Printing Office.

——. 1990. Immigration Reform: Employer Sanctions and the Question of Discrimination: Report to Congress. GAO/GGD-90-62. Washington, D.C.: U.S. Government Printing Office.

Germany's Refugee Plan Slams Doors on Asylum-Seekers. *San Bernardino Sun,* 8 December 1991: 1.

Glazer, Nathan, ed. 1985. *Clamor at the Gates: The New American Immigration.* San Francisco: ICS Press.

Gordon, Charles. 1988. An Overall View of the Implementation of the Legalization Program by INS. *Georgetown Immigration Law Journal* 2 (Fall): 517–525.

Governor Denounces Commercial. *San Bernardino Sun,* 19 August 1993: A4.

Governor's Immigration Coordination Committee. 1989. *Immigration Reform and Control Act of 1986: The Oregon Experience.* Salem, Oreg.: GICC, February.

Green, Stephen. 1984. Immigration Politics. *Cumberland Times/News,* 1 November: 13.

Groups Lash Out at Wilson's Plan to Curb Immigration. *San Bernardino Sun,* 18 August 1993: B3.

Guitierrez v. Ilchert, 682 F. Supp. 467, 473-75 (N.D. Cal. 1988).

Haitian Refugee Center Inc. et al. v. Nelson et al., Case No. 88-1066-Civ-Atkins (S.D. Fla. 22 August 1988).

Hammar, Thomas. 1985. *European Immigration Policy: A Comparative Study.* Cambridge, U.K.: Cambridge University Press.

Hampe, Carl. 1988. Intent of Congress Behind Certain Provisions of the Immigration Reform and Control Act. *Georgetown Immigration Law Journal* 2 (Fall): 499–505.

Hart, Jeffrey. 1985. Illegal Immigration. *Cumberland Times/News,* 22 July: 8.

Harwood, Edwin. 1983. Can Immigration Laws Be Enforced? *The Public Interest* 17 (Summer): 105–123.

Helton, Arthur. 1988. The Alien Legalization Program in New York: A Review. *Georgetown Immigration Law Journal* 2 (Fall): 447–460.

Hernandez, Roger. 1993. America Shouldn't Slam Door Shut Yet. *San Bernardino Sun,* 18 August 1993: A7.

Hewlitt, S. 1981. Coping With Illegal Aliens. *Foreign Affairs* 60: 358–378.

Hill Revises Immigration Law. *Washington Post,* 18 October 1986: A1, 7–8.

Hispanic Americans Haven't Found Their Pot of Gold. *Washington Post National Weekly Edition,* 28 May 1984: 9–10.

Hispanic Population of U.S. Growing Fastest. *Washington Post,* 12 October 1989: A3.

Hoefer, Michael. 1986. An Interim Report on Illegal Aliens. *New York Times,* 16 October: B15.

——. 1988. An Interim Report on Aliens Legalizing Under IRCA. Paper presented at the Population Association of America Annual Meeting, April 23, New Orleans, La.

Hollifield, James. 1989. Migrants into Citizens: The Politics of Immigration in France and the United States. Paper presented at the Annual Meeting of the American Political Science Association, August 31–September 3, Atlanta, Ga.

House Approves Compromise Bill on Illegal Aliens. *New York Times,* 16 October 1986: B15.

House Passes Compromise Immigration Bill. *Washington Post,* 16 October 1986: A5.

House Passes Immigration Bill by Five Votes. *Congressional Quarterly Weekly Report,* 23 June 1984, 1493–1500.

House Rules Near Action on Immigration. *Congressional Quarterly Weekly Report,* 14 April 1984, 847.

Idelson, Holly. 1993. Baird's Wrenching Withdrawal Mars Inaugural Week. *Congressional Quarterly Weekly Report,* 23 January, 179–181.

Illegal Alien Curbs: House Action Stalled. *Congressional Quarterly Weekly Report,* 30 March 1976, 637.

Illegal Alien Influx: Illusion v. Reality. *Washington Post,* 24 April 1988: A4.

Illegal Aliens: Invasion Out of Control. *U.S. News and World Report,* 29 January 1979, 38–43.

Illegal Child Labor Recurring in U.S. *Washington Post,* 14 April 1991: A1, 8–9.

Illegal Farm Workers Apply for Residency. *Cumberland Times/News,* 1 December 1988: A3.

An Illegal Immigrant's Cruel Journey to an Uncertain End. *Washington Post,* 27 November 1989: B1, 10.

Illegal Immigrants Must Take 2nd Step to Amnesty. *Washington Post,* 6 August 1989: D9.

Illegal Immigration. *Cumberland Evening Times,* 22 July 1985: 8.

Illegal Migration's Fact of Life, Study Concludes. *Washington Post,* 15 November 1987: 18.

Illegal Workers Fear Seeking Quake Aid. *Sacramento Bee,* 24 October 1989: A1.

Immigrants: The Changing Face of America. *Time* (Special Edition Issue), 8 July 1985, 24–101.

Immigration and Naturalization Service. 1988a. Immigration Statistics: Fiscal Year 1987, Advance Report. Washington, D.C.: U.S. Government Printing Office.

——. 1988b. Provisional Legalization Applications Statistics. Washington, D.C.: INS.

——. 1992. *1991 Statistical Yearbook of the Immigration and Naturalization Service.* Washington, D.C.: U.S. Government Printing Office.

Immigration Backlash. *Newsweek,* 9 August 1991, 18–29.

Immigration Begs for Responsible Approach. *San Bernardino Sun,* 22 August 1993: D2.

Immigration Bill: A Blow. *New York Times,* 9 October 1983: sec. 4, p. 19.

Immigration Bill Approved, Bars Hiring Illegal Aliens, But Gives Millions Amnesty. *New York Times,* 15 October 1986: A1, 8.

Immigration Bill: How "Corpse" Came Back to Life. *New York Times,* 13 October 1986: A16.
Immigration Bill Mixed Blessing for Aliens. *Washington Post,* 24 June 1984: C1, 7.
Immigration Commissioner Would Disband Policy Unit. *Cumberland Times/News,* 21 December 1988: A2.
Immigration: Has Our Melting Pot Boiled Over? *Washington Post,* 18 October 1987: D1, 4.
Immigration in Washington. *Washington Post Magazine,* 10 April 1983, 8–21.
Immigration Is Getting Out of Hand. *San Bernardino Sun,* 21 April 1993: A7.
Immigration Issue Heats Up Again. *Washington Post,* 28 July 1985: A15.
Immigration Law Alone Can't Work. *Chicago Sun-Times,* 10 April 1987: A42.
Immigration Legislation Voted Down. *Cumberland Times/News,* 14 September 1985: A1.
Immigration Measure Is Put in Doubt. *New York Times,* 26 July 1984: A14.
Immigration Measure Produces Sharp Division in House Hispanic Caucus. *Washington Post,* 18 March 1984: A2.
Immigration Myopia Threatens Basic Rights. *Cumberland Times/News,* 19 September 1989: A9.
Immigration Reform: A Mess on the Border. *Newsweek,* 22 December 1986, 27.
Immigration Reform and Control Act. HR1510, 98th Congress, First Session. Washington, D.C.: U.S. Government Printing Office, 1983.
Immigration Reform Bill Dies as Compromise Efforts Fail. *Congressional Quarterly Weekly Report,* 13 October 1984, 2623.
Immigration Reform Elusive Goal. *Minneapolis Star and Tribune,* 24 June 1985: A10.
Immigration Reform Measure Nearing Final Vote. *Congressional Quarterly Weekly Report,* 16 June 1984, 1407–1411.
Immigration Rules Called Hard on Poor. *Washington Post,* 9 April 1987: A22.
Immigration Stops More Illegal Aliens. *Cumberland Times/News,* 2 March 1989: A1.
Immigration: What We Promised, Where to Draw the Line. *National Issues Forum.* Dubuque, Iowa: Kendall/Hunt, 1987.
Ingraham, Patricia W. 1987. Towards More Systematic Consideration of Policy Design. *Policy Studies Journal* 15 (4): 610–628.
INS Breaking Up Smuggling Rings at Airports. *Washington Post,* 12 March 1989: A24.
INS Finds False Filings Pervasive. *Austin American Statesmen,* October 1989: A1, 12.
INS Policy of Confining Suspect Children Backed. *Washington Post,* 24 March 1993: A14.
INS Ready to Crack Down on Firms That Hire Illegal Aliens. *Milwaukee Journal,* 31 May 1988: 3A.
INS Tries New Approach. *Washington Post,* 23 August 1987: A1, 18–19.
INS Violates Pact, Right Group Says. *San Bernardino Sun,* 18 July 1993: A1.
Is Hatred of Japanese Making A Comeback? *Washington Post,* 7 July 1985: B1, 4.
Is Immigration Good for Our Culture? *San Bernardino Sun,* 29 July 1993: A11.
Isgro, Francesco. 1988. Administrative and Judicial Review of Denials of Temporary Resident Status. *Georgetown Immigration Law Journal* 2 (Fall): 473–490.
Keely, Charles. 1982. Illegal Migration. *Scientific American* 246 (March): 31–37.
Kemp Quashes Denial of Aid to Illegal Aliens. *Washington Post,* 24 June 1990: A24.
Kirstein, Peter N. 1977. *Anglo Over Bracero: A History of the Mexican Worker in*

the United States from Roosevelt to Nixon. San Francisco: R & E Research Associates.

Kiser, George C., and Martha W. Kiser. 1979. *Mexican Workers in the United States.* Albuquerque, N.M.: University of New Mexico Press.

Knickrehm, Kay. 1985. Congress, the Executive, and Immigration Policy. Paper delivered at the Annual American Political Science Association Meeting, August 29, New Orleans, La.

Koehn, Peter H. 1991. *Refugees from Revolution: U.S. Policy and Third World Migration.* Boulder, Colo.: Westview Press.

Kritz, Mary M. *U.S. Immigration and Refugee Policy: Global and Domestic Issues.* Lexington, Mass.: Lexington Books, 1983.

Kurzban, Ira. 1989. Amnesty: Can We Learn a Simple and More Generous Approach? In *In Defense of the Alien, Vol. 11,* ed. Lydio Tomasi, pp. 19–26. New York: Center for Migration Studies.

Lamm, Richard D., and Gary Imhoff. 1985. *The Immigration Time Bomb: The Fragmenting of America.* New York: Truman Talley Books, E. P. Dutton.

Last Chance on Immigration. *Washington Post,* 9 October 1984: A18.

Last Tribe Out of Bondage. *Washington Post,* 11 March 1990: B5.

Lawmakers Want Moratorium to Review Political Asylum Policies. *San Bernardino Sun,* 13 July 1993: B4.

LeMay, Michael. 1985. *The Struggle for Influence.* Lanham, Md.: University Press of America.

——. 1986. U.S. Immigration Policy: Entering a Revolving-Door Era? Paper presented at the Annual Meeting of the Midwest Political Science Association, April 8–11, Chicago, Ill.

——. 1987. *From Open Door to Dutch Door: An Analysis of U.S. Immigration Policy since 1820.* New York: Praeger Press.

——. 1988. The Impact of the Immigration Reform and Control Act of 1986 on Minority Groups in the U.S. Paper delivered at the Annual Meeting of the Southern Political Science Association, November 3–5, Atlanta, Ga.

——. 1989. Is IRCA Working?: An Initial Assessment. Paper delivered at the Annual Meeting of the American Political Science Association, September 2, Atlanta, Ga.

——. 1992. The Flying Dutchman Dilemma: The Right of Racial and Ethnic Groups to Emigrate versus the Sovereign Right to Exclude. Paper presented at the Annual Meeting of the Southern Political Science Association, November, Atlanta, Ga.

LeMay, Michael, ed. 1989. *The Gatekeepers: Comparative Immigration Policy.* New York: Praeger Publishers.

Living with the New Law. *Cumberland Times/News,* 10 September 1987: A14.

Lundberg, Shelly J. 1987. Equality and Efficiency: Anti-Discrimination Policies in the Labor Market. Nelson A. Rockefeller Center for the Social Sciences, Working Paper Series, 27 June.

Mamut, Patricia. 1974. *Foreign Medical Graduates in America.* Springfield, Ill.: Charles Thomas.

Maraniss, David. 1988. Illegal Alien Influx: Illusion vs. Reality. *Washington Post,* 24 April: A4.

Marcos Filipinos Flock to America. *Cumberland Times/News,* 17 July 1985: A7.

Marriages of Convenience. *Washington Post,* 21 October 1984: A1, 18–19.

Maryland Growers Assisting with New Immigration Laws. *Cumberland Sunday Times,* 19 July 1987: C12.

Massey, Douglas S. 1987a. Do Undocumented Migrants Earn Lower Wages Than Legal Immigrants?: New Evidence from Mexico. *International Migration Review* 21: 236–274.

——. 1987b. Understanding Mexican Migration to the United States. *American Journal of Sociology* 92 (May): 1372–1403.

Massey, D. S., K. M. Donato, and Z. Liang. 1989. *Effects of the Immigration Reform and Control Act of 1986: Preliminary Data from Mexico.* Chicago: Population Research Center, National Opinion Research Center, University of Chicago.

Matthews, Jay. 1988. Successful Refugee Program Faces Cutoff As Many Newcomers Find Alternatives to Welfare. *Washington Post,* 20 March 1988: A3.

McCarran–Walter Act Reborn? *Washington Post,* 18 November 1990: C7.

McCarthy, Kevin, and R. Burciaga Valdez. 1986. *Current and Future Effects of Mexican Immigration in California.* R-3365-CR. Santa Monica, Calif.: The Rand Corporation.

McClellan, Grant S., ed. 1981. *Immigrants, Refugees, and U.S. Policy.* New York: H. W. Wilson.

McDonnell, Lorraine M., and Paul T. Hill. 1989. First Steps in Applying a Policy Design Framework: The Case of Immigration Reform. Paper delivered at the 1989 Annual Meeting of the American Political Science Association, September 2, Atlanta, Ga.

McKenna, George. 1981. *That Delicate Balance: A Guide to the Constitution.* New York: Random House.

Meissner, Doris M., and Demetrios G. Papademetriou. 1988. *The Legalization Countdown: A Third Quarter Assessment.* Washington, D.C.: Carnegie Endowment for International Peace.

Melting Pot Boiling from Racial Tension. *Cumberland Evening Times,* 10 January 1984: A5.

Mexican Hearts, California Dreams. *Los Angeles Times Magazine,* 7 September 1987, 7–28.

Mexicans Reacting Angrily to U.S. Border Patrol Ditch Plans. *Cumberland Times/News,* 28 January 1989: A3.

Mexico's People Boom. *Cumberland Evening Times,* 4 October 1985: A10.

Miles, Jack. 1992. Immigration and the New American Dilemma. *The Atlantic* 270 (4): 41–68.

Miller, Harris M. 1985. The Right Thing to Do: A History of Simpson-Mazzoli. In *Clamor at the Gates: The New American Immigration,* ed. Nathan Glazer. San Francisco: Institute for Contemporary Studies.

Miller, Mark, and Philip L. Martin. 1982. *Administering Guest Worker Programs: Lessons from Europe.* Lexington, Mass.: Lexington Books.

Montero, Darell. 1979. *Vietnamese Americans.* Boulder, Colo.: Westview Press.

More than 3 Million Bet on Visa Lottery. *Cumberland Times/News,* 10 May 1989: 1.

Morris, Milton. 1985. *Immigration: The Beleagured Bureaucracy.* Washington, D.C.: The Brookings Institution.

Most Immigrants Help, Not Hurt, U.S. Economy. *San Bernardino Sun,* 16 February 1993: A1.

Muller, Thomas, and Thomas Espanshade. 1985. *The Fourth Wave.* Washington, D.C.: The Urban Institute.

Murphy, Caryle. 1984. Sanctuary: How Churches Defy Immigration Law. *Washington Post National Weekly Edition,* 17 September 1984: 8–9.

National Research Council. 1985. *Immigration Statistics: A Story of Neglect.* Washington, D.C.: National Academy Press.

Nelson, Candace, and Marta Tienda. 1988. Structuring of Hispanic Ethnicity. In *Ethnicity and Race in the USA: Toward the 21st Century,* ed. Richard Alba, pp. 49–74. New York: Routledge.

The New Immigrants. *Newsweek,* 7 July 1980, 26–31.

New Law Leaves Immigrants Confused and Fearful. *New York Times,* 21 February 1987: 1–29.

New Mosaic of Race: Age, Income and Immigration Replace Black–White Conflict. *Washington Post,* 19 November 1989: D1, 4.

New Rules for a Human Tide. *The Economist,* 17 January 1987: 29.

The New Slave Trade. *Newsweek,* 21 June 1993, 34–41.

New York State, Department of Social Services. 1988. Workplace Discrimination Under the Immigration Reform and Control Act of 1986: A Study of Impacts on New Yorkers. New York: Department of Social Services.

Newcomers' Impact on a Small Town. *Washington Post,* 11 August 1991: A18–20.

North, David S. 1978. *Seven Years Later: The Experiences of the 1970 Cohort of Immigrants in the U.S. Labor Market.* Washington, D.C.: New Transcentury Foundation.

——. 1980. *Immigration and Income Transfer Policies in the United States: An Analysis of a Nonrelationship.* Washington, D.C.: New Transcentury Foundation.

Officials Can Do Little to Stop Immigrants. *San Bernardino Sun,* 6 June 1993: A1.

O'Neill Pulls Immigration Reform Measure. *Congressional Quarterly Weekly Report,* 8 October 1983, 2088.

Palmer, Ransford W., ed. 1990. *In Search of a Better Life: Perspectives on Migration from the Caribbean.* New York: Praeger.

Panel on Immigration Statistics. 1985. *Immigration Statistics: A Story of Neglect.* Washington, D.C.: National Academy Press.

Papademetriou, Demetrious G., and Mark J. Miller, eds. 1984. *The Unavoidable Issue.* Philadelphia: Institute for the Study of Human Issues.

Paper Provides Homeland News to Indian Immigrants. *Cumberland Times/News,* 17 July 1985: A7.

Parlin, Bradley W. 1977. Immigrants, Employers, and Exclusion. *Society* 14 (6): 23–26.

Passel, Jeffrey, and Karen A. Woodrow. 1984. Geographic Distribution of Undocumented Immigrants: Estimates of Undocumented Aliens Counted in the 1980 Census by State. *International Migration Review* 18: 642–671.

Pear, Robert. 1984a. Reagan Raises New Obstacles to House Bill on Immigration. *New York Times,* 9 August: D23.

——. 1984b. Conferees Agree on Sanctions in Immigration Bill. *New York Times,* 14 September: B4.

Perotti, Rosanna. 1989a. Beyond Logrolling: Integrative Bargaining in Congressional Policymaking. Paper presented at the American Political Science Association

Meeting, August 31-September 3, Atlanta, Ga.
——. 1989b. Resolving Policy Conflict: Congress and Immigration Reform. Dissertation, University of Pennsylvania.
Pessar, Patricia, ed. 1988. *When Borders Don't Divide: Labor Migration and Refugee Movements in the Americas.* New York: Center for Migration Studies.
Peter Rodino Turns Judiciary into a Legislative Graveyard. *Congressional Quarterly Weekly Report,* 12 May 1984, 1097–1102.
Peters, Ronald M., Jr., and Arturo Vega. 1986. The Role of House Democratic Party Leaders on Non-Party Position Legislation with Partisan Consequences: The Immigration Bill. Paper presented at the 1986 meetings of the American Political Science Association, August 28–31, Washington, D.C.
Piore, Michael J. 1979. *The Birds of Passage.* Cambridge, Mass.: Cambridge University Press.
Playing Politics With Immigration. *Time,* 17 October 1983, 19.
Poll: Illegal Immigration Draws Fire. *San Bernardino Sun,* 19 August 1993: A1.
Pozzetta, George, ed. 1991. *Contemporary Immigration and American Society.* New York: Garland Publishing.
President Endorses Immigration Proposal. *Washington Post,* 17 October 1986: A4.
"Productive" Congress Wraps Up. *Washington Post,* 19 October 1986: A1, 16–17.
A Push to Delay Deportation of Aliens. *Washington Post,* 26 July 1987: 4.
Quirk, Paul. 1989. The Cooperative Resolution of Policy Conflict. *American Political Science Review* 83 (3): 905–921.
Quiz Traps Fraudulent Immigrants. *Cumberland Sunday Times,* 3 November 1985: A3.
Raids Nab Hi-Pay Aliens, Make Jobs, Outrage Clergy. *Washington Post,* 2 May 1982: A10.
Rare Genetic Blood Disorder Strikes Asian Immigrants. *San Bernardino Sun,* 16 February 1993: A5.
Reaction to Immigration Bill Is Sharply Split. *New York Times,* 16 October 1986: B15.
Reagan Said to Favor Signing New Aliens Bill. *New York Times,* 17 October 1986: A2.
Reagan's Plan for Illegal Aliens. *U.S. News and World Report,* 3 August 1981, 42–43.
Redrawing Political Maps: An America of Groups? *Washington Post,* 24 March 1991: C1, 4.
Refugee Policy Group. 1988. Serving the Newly Legalized: Their Character and Current Needs. Washington, D.C.: Center for Policy Analysis and Research on Refugee Issues.
A Refugee's Despair. *Newsweek,* 17 November 1986, 12.
Reimers, David. 1982. Recent Immigration Policy: An Analysis. In *The Gateway: U.S. Immigration Issues and Policies,* ed. Barry Chiswick. Washington, D.C.: American Enterprise Institute.
——. 1985. *Still the Golden Door: The Third World Comes to America.* New York: Columbia University.
Report: Mexican General Part of Smuggling Plot. *San Bernardino Sun,* 16 July 1993: A5.
Reprieve Sought for Haitian Refugees. *Washington Post,* 2 February 1992: A3.
Research Institute on Immigration and Ethnic Studies. 1981. Female Immigrants to the U.S. RIIES Occasional Papers, No. 2. Washington, D.C.: Smithsonian Institute Press.
——. 1983. Caribbean Immigration to the United States. RIIES Occasional Papers, No. 1. Washington, D.C.: Smithsonian Institution Press.

Ringer, Benjamin, and Elinor R. Lawles. 1989. Blacks and the White Immigrants. In *Race, Ethnicity and Society,* pp. 201–223. New York: Routledge.

Ronfeldt, David, and Monica Ortize de Oppermann. 1990. *Mexican Immigration, U.S. Investment, and U.S.-Mexican Relations.* Santa Monica, Calif.: The Rand Corporation and the Urban Institute Press.

Rowan, Carl. 1983. Tip O'Neill Goofs on Immigration. *Washington Post,* 13 October: A23.

Salvation by Immigration. *Cumberland Times/News,* 20 October 1988: A8.

Scanlon, Joseph, and Gilburt D. Loescher. 1982. Mass Asylum and Human Rights in American Foreign Policy. *Political Science Quarterly* 97: 39–56.

Schmidt, Ronald. 1989. The Political Incorporation of Recent Immigrants: A Framework for Research and Analysis. Paper presented at the Annual Meeting of the American Political Science Association, August 31-September 3, Atlanta, Ga.

Schneider, A., and Patricia Ingraham. 1988. Behavioral Theories in Policy Designs. Paper presented at the Midwest Political Science Association meeting, April, Chicago, Ill.

Schrag, Peter. 1993. Immigration Getting Out of Hand. *San Bernardino Sun,* 21 April 1993: A7.

Schroeder, John R. 1987. The Immigration Reform and Control Act. In *In Defense of the Alien, Vol. 10,* ed. Lydio Tomasi, pp. 3–9. New York: Center for Migration Studies.

Schuck, Peter H. 1984. The Transformation of Immigration Law. *Columbia Law Review* 84 (1): 39–56.

Select Commission on Immigration and Refugee Policy. 1981. *Final Report.* Washington, D.C.: U.S. Government Printing Office.

Senate Spending Bill Targets Immigrants. *San Bernardino Sun,* 30 July 1993: A2.

Senate Votes to Ban Immigration of AIDS-Infected People. *San Bernardino Sun,* 19 February 1993: A1.

Should Congress Adopt the Impending Reform and Control Act? *Congressional Digest* 62 (August/September 1983): 195–224.

Should United States Open Doors to Foreigners Waiting to Come In? *National Journal,* 7 March 1981: 390–393.

Siegel, Jacob, Jeffrey Passel, and J. Gregory Robinson. 1980. Preliminary Review of Existing Studies of the Number of Illegal Residents in the U.S. In *U.S. Immigration Policy and the National Interest: The Staff Report of the Select Commission on Immigration and Refugee Policy, Appendix E: Papers on Illegal Immigration to the U.S.* Washington, D.C.: U.S. Government Printing Office.

Sieghart, Mary Ann. 1984. Border Patrol: A Revolving Door Policy. *Washington Post National Weekly Edition,* 17 September: 7.

Simcox, David E. 1985. *U.S. Immigration in the 1980s: Reappraisal and Reform.* Boulder, Colo., and Washington, D.C.: Westview Press and the Center for Immigration Studies.

Simpson Tackles Immigration Reform Again. *Minneapolis Star and Tribune,* 24 June 1985: A10.

Simpson: The "Anglo" Behind the Immigration Bill. *Washington Post,* 19 October 1986: A8–9.

659 Chinese Found Off Coast. *San Bernardino Sun,* 8 July 1993: A3.

Sklar, Helen. 1991. *The Immigration Act of 1990 Handbook.* New York: Clark Boardman.

Soviet Immigrants Flood Israel. *Washington Post,* 21 January 1990: A29, 34.
The Speaker and the Big Wink. *New York Times,* 5 October 1983: 26A.
Speaker O'Neill Opens Door to Immigration Reform. *Christian Science Monitor,* 5 December 1983: 3–4.
Sponsor Says Alien Bill Is Not Dead. *Washington Post,* 26 July 1984: A3.
Spotlight on Immigration Bill's Cost. *Washington Post,* 12 October 1986: A4.
Stalemate on Immigration? *Washington Post,* 14 October 1990: C6.
Staley, Joseph. 1981. Law Enforcement and the Border. In *United States Relations with Mexico,* ed. Richard D. Erb and Stanley R. Ross, pp. 106–120. Washington, D.C.: American Enterprise Institute.
State Panel Faults Enforcement of New Federal Immigration Law. *New York Times,* 16 March 1987: A15.
Stevens, Rosemary. 1978. *The Alien Doctors.* New York: Wiley.
Stolzenberg, Ross M. 1982. Occupational Differences Between Hispanics and Non-Hispanics. N-1889-NCEP. Santa Monica, Calif.: The Rand Corporation.
Stowers, Genie. 1989. Cuban Political Incorporation into Miami Politics: A Model for the "New Immigrants." Paper presented at the Annual Meeting of the American Political Science Association, August 31–September 3, Atlanta, Ga.
Striving for the American Dream. *Washington Post,* 24 June 1990: D1, 5.
Study Shows Indochina Refugees Doing Well. *Cumberland Times/News,* 24 July 1985: A5.
Success Outweigh Failures in First Year of Amnesty Program. *Washington Post,* 6 November 1987: A12.
Suit Alleges Amnesty Law Puts Many Aliens in Limbo. *New York Times,* 7 February 1987: 6.
Suits, Daniel B. 1985. U.S. Farm Migration: An Application of the Harris–Todaro Model. *Economic Development and Cultural Change* 33: 815–828.
Surge in Bogus Papers Predicted in Wake of Change in Alien Law. *New York Times,* 20 October 1986: A1, 24.
Sweeping Reforms Announced. *San Bernardino Sun,* 28 July 1993: A1, 3.
Tanton, John. 1980. *Rethinking Immigration Policy.* FAIR Immigration Paper I. Washington, D.C.: Federation for American Immigration Reform.
Teitelbaum, Michael S. 1985. *Latin Migration North: The Problem for U.S. Foreign Policy.* New York: Council on Foreign Relations.
Tepon, William. 1988. Immigration Reform and Control Act of 1986 (IRCA), Hearings Before Administrative Law Judges As Part of the Enforcement Process. *Georgetown Immigration Law Journal* 2 (Fall): 491–498.
Thornburgh, Dick. 1989. More Refugees?: It's Up to Congress. Letters to the Editor. *Washington Post,* 1 October: D6.
Thousands Eligible for Alien Amnesty Across Maryland. *Cumberland Times/News,* 11 November 1986: A10.
Thousands More East Germans Flock to West. *Washington Post,* 5 November 1989: A1, 41.
Tomasi, Lydio, ed. 1987. *In Defense of the Alien, Vol. 9.* New York: Center for Migration Studies.
——. 1988. *In Defense of the Alien, Vol. 10.* New York: Center for Migration Studies.
——. 1989. *In Defense of the Alien, Vol. 11.* New York: Center for Migration Studies.

——. 1990. *In Defense of the Alien, Vol. 12*. New York: Center for Migration Studies.

——. 1991. *In Defense of the Alien, Vol. 13*. New York: Center for Migration Studies.

Tortilla Curtain Fails to Stem Tide of Illegal Aliens. *Washington Post,* 13 May 1985: A8.

Tragedy Spotlights Immigration Rise. *Milwaukee Journal,* 12 July 1987: A1.

Truman, David. 1951. *The Governmental Process*. New York: Knopf.

Trying to Reform the Border. *Newsweek,* 27 October 1986, 32, 35.

2,800 Illegal Aliens Arrested in a Week-Long Border Sweep. *New York Times,* 20 October 1986: A20.

U.S. Becomes Silent on Chinese Workers. *San Bernardino Sun,* 14 July 1993: A3.

U.S. Border Patrol Going "High Tech." *Cumberland Times/News,* 17 October 1985: 23.

United States Congress, House, Committee on the Judiciary, Subcommittee on Immigration. Illegal Aliens: Hearings, February 4–March 19, 1975 on HR 982 and Related Bills. 94th Congress, First Session, Series No. 8.

——. Illegal Aliens: Hearings, Parts 1 to 5. 92nd Congress, Series No. 13.

United States Congress, House of Representatives. 1983. Immigration Reform and Control Act of 1983. (The Mazzoli Bill), HR-1510, 98th Congress, First Session, 17 February, 1–163.

United States Congress, Senate, Committee on the Judiciary. 1985. Immigration Reform and Control Act of 1985. 99th Congress, First Session, Report 99-132. Washington, D.C.: U.S. Government Printing Office.

United States Congress, Senate, Committee on the Judiciary, Subcommittee on Immigration and Refugee Policy. *Temporary Workers Hearings*. 97th Congress, First Session, Serial J-97-77, 22 October 1981, 33.

United States, Department of Commerce, Bureau of the Census. 1987. *Statistical Abstract of the United States, 1988*. Washington, D.C.: U.S. Government Printing Office.

——. 1989. *The Hispanic Population in the United States: March 1988*. P-20, No. 438. Washington, D.C.: U.S. Government Printing Office.

U.S. Department of Health and Human Services. 1988. State Legalization Impact Assistance Grant: Eligible Legalized Alien Fact Sheet. Provisional Data, 1989 Projections. Texas Department of Health, Bureau of State Health Data and Policy Analysis, Austin, Tex. 78756.

U.S. Department of Justice. 1988. Immigration and Naturalization Service, *INS Reporter*. Washington, D.C.: U.S. Government Printing Office.

——. 1989. Special Counsel for Immigration Related Unfair Employment Practices. Statement of the Special Counsel before the Subcommittee on Immigration, Refugees, and International Law, Committee of the Judiciary, U.S. House of Representatives, May 10.

U.S. Department of Labor. 1989. The Effects of Immigration on the U.S. Economy and Labor Market, Immigration Policy and Research Report 1. Washington, D.C.: U.S. Department of Labor, Bureau of International Labor Affairs.

U.S. Has to Control Its Borders. *San Bernardino Sun,* 12 July 1993: A7.

U.S. Hispanics "Melting" But Not Prospering. *Washington Post,* 13 May 1984: A1, 8.

United States Immigration and Naturalization Service. 1989. Provisional Legalization Application Statistics. Statistical Division, Office of Plans and Analysis. Washington, D.C.: Immigration and Naturalization Service.

U.S. Immigration Bill Assailed. *New York Times,* 19 October 1986: A12.

U.S. President's Select Commission on Immigration and Refugee Policy (SCIRP). 1981a. *U.S. Immigration Policy and the National Interest: Final Report.* Washington, D.C.: U.S. Government Printing Office.

——. 1981b. *U.S. Immigration Policy and the National Interest: Staff Report.* Washington, D.C.: U.S. Government Printing Office.

U.S. Recession Export That Could Cripple Mexico's Economy. *Cumberland Times/News,* 26 November 1987: A5.

Vega, Arturo. 1985. Extrinsic Representation and Informal Groups in Congress: The Case of the Congressional Hispanic Caucus. Paper delivered at the 1985 Southwestern Political Science Association Annual Meeting, March, Houston, Tex.

Vernez, Georges. 1989. Immigration Reform and Control Act of 1986: Status Report. Santa Monica, Calif.: The Rand Corporation.

Vernez, Georges, ed. 1990. *Immigration and International Relations.* Santa Monica, Calif.: The Rand Corporation/Urban Institute Press.

Vialet, Joyce. 1980. A Brief History of U.S. Immigration Policy. *Report 80-223 EPW.* Education and Public Welfare Division. Washington, D.C.: Immigration and Naturalization Service.

Waiting Anxiously: Amnesty Seekers Hope to Prevent Family Separation. *Dallas Morning News,* 4 January 1988: A13, 15.

Walters, Robert. 1985. Immigration and Jobs. *Cumberland Times/News,* 25 October: A8.

Warren, Robert, and Jeffrey Passel. 1987. A Count of the Uncountable: Estimates of Undocumented Aliens Counted in the 1980 United States Census. Paper presented at the 1983 Meeting of the Population Association of America, Pittsburgh, Pa. Revised and published in *Demography* 24 (3): 375–393.

Wave of Irish Immigrants Hidden "Underground." *Washington Post,* 12 March 1989: A1, 25.

Weda, Reed. 1984. Naturalization and Citizenship. In *Dimensions in Ethnicity,* ed. Stephen Thernstrom. Cambridge, Mass.: Cambridge University Press.

Weisman, Alan. 1987. Mexican Hearts, California Dreams. *Los Angeles Times Magazine,* 7 September 1987, 7–28.

Weissbrodt, David. 1984. *Immigration Law and Procedure.* St. Paul, Minn.: West Publishing.

Wendy's Pleads Guilty to Hiring Illegal Aliens. *USA Today,* 3 November 1988: 1.

White, M. J., F. D. Bean, and T. J. Espanshade. 1989. *The U.S. Immigration Reform Act and Undocumented Migration to the U.S.* Washington, D.C.: The Urban Institute.

Whitman, Dave. 1987. Asian Un-Success Stories—Many Refugees Are on Welfare, Not Honor Rolls. *Washington Post,* 27 December: C1, 4.

Why They Excel. *Washington Post, Parade Magazine,* 21 January 1990: 4–5.

Will Immigration Law Hurt the West? *Washington Post,* 15 January 1989: H4.

Wilson Backs Plan, Denies Ulterior Motive. *San Bernardino Sun,* 22 August 1993: B6.

Wilson: Cut Immigration Incentives. *San Bernardino Sun,* 10 August 1993: A1.

Wilson, Pete. 1993. Has America Reached Its Quota? *San Bernardino Sun,* 22 August: D1, 4.

Wilson Resorts to Scare Tactics in Fight Against Immigration. *San Bernardino Sun,* 22 August 1993: D1, 4.

Wolchok, Carol, and Leslie Wolchock. 1987. What Kind of Refugees Are These? *Washington Post,* 3 August: B7.

Woodrow, K. A., and J. S. Passel. 1989. *Post-IRCA Undocumented Immigration to the United States: An Assessment Based on June, 1988 CPA*. Washington, D.C.: Bureau of the Census, Population Division.

Yances, Matt. 1988. Illegal Immigrants Lower Pay of Legal Workers, GAO Says. *Washington Post,* 20 March: H20.

Yearn to Be Free. *Arizona Republic,* 29 January 1989: C1, 3.

Yzaquirre, Raul. 1983. What's Wrong with the Immigration Bill. *Washington Post National Weekly Edition,* 12 December: 29.

Zucker, Norman L., and Naomi Flink Zucker. 1987. *The Guarded Gate: The Reality of American Refugee Policy*. New York: Harcourt Brace Jovanovich.

Index

ABOUT THE AUTHOR

MICHAEL C. LeMAY is Professor and Chairman, Department of Political Science, and Director, National Security Studies Program, California State University, San Bernardino. Among his earlier publications are *From Open Door to Dutch Door* and *The Gatekeepers* (Praeger, 1987 and 1989, respectively).

ISBN 0-275-94902-8

90000>

EAN

9 780275 949020

HARDCOVER BAR CODE